English Language Education

Volume 40

Series Editor
Xuesong Gao, School of Education, The University of New South Wales, Sydney, Australia

Editorial Board
Stephen Andrews, Faculty of Education, University of Hong Kong, Hong Kong, Hong Kong

Anne Burns, University of New South Wales, Ryde, Australia

Yuko Goto Butler, Penn Graduate School of Education, University of Pennsylvania, Philadelphia, USA

Suresh Canagarajah, Department of Applied Linguistics and English, Pennsylvania State University, University Park, USA

Jim Cummins, OISE, University of Toronto, Toronto, Canada

Christine C. M. Goh, Nanyang Technological University, National Institute of Education, Singapore, Singapore

Margaret Hawkins, Department of Curriculum and Instruction, University of Wisconsin, Madison, USA

Ouyang Huhua, Faculty of English Language and Culture, Guangdong University of Foreign Studies, Guangzhou, Guangdong, China

Andy Kirkpatrick, School of Humanities, Languages and Social Science, Griffith University, Nathan, Australia

Michael K. Legutke, Institut für Anglistik, Justus Liebig University Giessen, Gießen, Germany

Constant Leung, Department of Education and Professional Studies, King's College London, University of London, London, UK

Bonny Norton, Department of Language and Literacy Education, University of British Columbia, Vancouver, Canada

Elana Shohamy, School of Education, Tel Aviv University, Tel Aviv, Israel

Qiufang Wen, Beijing Foreign Studies University, Beijing, China

Lawrence Jun Zhang, Faculty of Education and Social Work, University of Auckland, Auckland, New Zealand

This series publishes research on the development, implementation and evaluation of educational programs for school-aged and adult learners for whom English is a second or additional language, including those who are learning academic content through the medium of English. The series has a dual focus on learners' language development and broader societal and policy-related issues, including the implications for teachers' professional development and policy support at the institutional and system level. The series seeks to engage with current issues in English language teaching (ELT) in educational institutions from a highly situated standpoint, examining theories, practices and policies with a conscious regard for historical lineages of development and local (re)contextualisation. By focusing on multiple educational contexts and adopting a comparative perspective, the series will transcend traditional geographical boundaries, thus will be relevant to both English-speaking countries and countries where English is a very much an additional, but important language for learning other content. This series will also cross disciplinary and methodological boundaries by integrating sociocultural and critical approaches with second language acquisition perspectives and drawing on both applied linguistics and educational research. In drawing together basic and applied policy-related research concerns, the series will contribute towards developing a more comprehensive, innovative and contextualized view of English language education internationally. Authors are invited to approach the Series Editor with ideas and plans for books.

Feng Geng · Shulin Yu

Understanding the Emotions of Second Language Writing Teachers

A Chinese Tertiary Educational Context

Feng Geng
School of Foreign Languages
Civil Aviation University of China
Tianjin, China

Shulin Yu
Faculty of Education
University of Macau
Macao, China

ISSN 2213-6967　　　　　　　ISSN 2213-6975　(electronic)
English Language Education
ISBN 978-981-97-4483-1　　　ISBN 978-981-97-4484-8　(eBook)
https://doi.org/10.1007/978-981-97-4484-8

© The Editor(s) (if applicable) and The Author(s), under exclusive license to Springer Nature Singapore Pte Ltd. 2024

This work is subject to copyright. All rights are solely and exclusively licensed by the Publisher, whether the whole or part of the material is concerned, specifically the rights of translation, reprinting, reuse of illustrations, recitation, broadcasting, reproduction on microfilms or in any other physical way, and transmission or information storage and retrieval, electronic adaptation, computer software, or by similar or dissimilar methodology now known or hereafter developed.
The use of general descriptive names, registered names, trademarks, service marks, etc. in this publication does not imply, even in the absence of a specific statement, that such names are exempt from the relevant protective laws and regulations and therefore free for general use.
The publisher, the authors and the editors are safe to assume that the advice and information in this book are believed to be true and accurate at the date of publication. Neither the publisher nor the authors or the editors give a warranty, expressed or implied, with respect to the material contained herein or for any errors or omissions that may have been made. The publisher remains neutral with regard to jurisdictional claims in published maps and institutional affiliations.

This Springer imprint is published by the registered company Springer Nature Singapore Pte Ltd.
The registered company address is: 152 Beach Road, #21-01/04 Gateway East, Singapore 189721, Singapore

If disposing of this product, please recycle the paper.

Preface

Teacher emotions are part and parcel of both the learning and the teaching of L2 writing. Initiated by the "affective turn" in teacher education research since the 1990s, a substantial amount of literature has addressed the centrality and multidimensional role of emotions in teachers' day-to-day professional lives in and outside the classroom. From a sociocultural perspective, teacher emotions could be defined as "socially constructed, personally enacted ways of being that emerge from conscious and/or unconscious judgments regarding perceived successes at attaining goals or maintaining standards or beliefs during transactions as part of social-historical contexts" (Schutz et al., 2006, p. 344). While previous research has examined student emotional experiences in the process of learning to write, little attention has been directed to L2 writing teachers' emotional experiences in the teaching of writing. Regarded as an "emotional practice", teacher emotions are at the epicenter of L2 classroom teaching. Therefore, addressing the impact of teacher emotions in L2 writing classrooms is deemed essential to understanding how L2 writing teachers conduct teaching in emotionally challenging contexts, and offers a complex and broad range of research possibilities.

This book aims to contribute to our understanding of L2 writing teachers' emotional experiences in the Chinese tertiary educational context. In Chap. 1, the book presents the background and rationales against which the study has been situated. In specific, this chapter presents (1) the status quo of research on teacher emotions; (2) who are L2 writing teachers; (3) how do L2 writing teachers teach and assess student writing; and (4) why and how emotions are important to L2 writing teachers by drawing on the extant literature on teacher emotions and L2 writing education research. Chapter 2 reveals how the research on teacher emotions is theoretically supported and what issues are recommended to be considered in the research. This chapter starts with an introduction to the definitions of teacher emotions. Afterwards, it proceeds to review the multidimensional theoretical perspectives on teacher emotions and relevant empirical research that has contributed to our understanding of teacher emotions. In specific, this chapter presents (1) an appraisal theoretical perspective of teacher emotions; (2) a sociocultural theoretical perspective of teacher emotions; and (3) a positive psychological perspective of teacher emotions. Chapter 3 frames teacher emotions in the L2 writing classroom context. This chapter develops a model of the causes and effects of teacher emotions in teaching L2 writing by illustrating (1) contextual and personal antecedents of L2 writing teacher emotions; (2) the appraisal and regulation process of L2 writing teacher emotions; and (3) the consequences of L2 writing teacher emotions. This chapter ends with the specific research questions that the study aimed to address. Chapter 4 presents the methodology, including research context and participants, data collection and analysis, and ethical issues.

Chapters 5, 6, and 7 further explore the teachers' emotional experiences and the impact on instructional practices in L2 writing classrooms. The three chapters draw insights from a qualitative case study of three Chinese university L2 writing teachers' emotional experiences in their writing classrooms. Multiple qualitative data were collected from three rounds of teacher interviews and classroom observations, teaching materials, reflection journals, and students' multiple drafts. The findings reveal that the three teachers experienced diverse emotions. Their emotions were triggered by the inconsistency between the goals and norms set for specific stages of classroom instruction in the L2 writing classroom. The study further reveals that teacher emotions could directly shape student emotions and the teacher-student relationship, and the utilization of emotion-regulation strategies could mediate teachers' pedagogical behaviors, including feedback-giving practice and writing assessment practice.

Chapter 8 summarizes the book by drawing on the qualitative findings. It first summarizes the major findings and addresses the research questions. This chapter then presents the contribution that indicates the research significance. Afterwards, this chapter presents the theoretical and pedagogical implications for future research. This chapter finally offers suggestions for future research in consideration of the findings and limitations of the study.

Tianjin, China Feng Geng
Macao, China Shulin Yu

Acknowledgements

We would like to thank all of the teacher participants with whom we have worked over the years for providing us with invaluable insight into teacher emotions in teaching L2 writing in Chinese mainland university classrooms. They have attended rounds of interviews and informal talks, invited us to observe their teaching activities in classrooms, and partnered with us on other forms of data collection. Special thanks also go to the anonymous reviewers, editors, and my supervisor Prof. Shulin Yu and co-supervisor Prof. Rui Yuan for their scholarly feedback and guidance, without which this book would not have been possible.

On a personal level, I'd like to express great appreciation to my families, who have given me unwavering love and support, and offered their continuous and unyielding encouragement. Words alone cannot describe how much I love them and appreciate their support leading up to this book.

Feng Geng

We started working on this book when Feng was completing his Ph.D. dissertation at the Faculty of Education, University of Macau, in January 2021. I would like to thank Feng for his great efforts and hard work in writing this book with me. I would also like to extend our deepest gratitude to those who have read and reviewed the earlier versions of this book. We appreciate the reviewers' informative and constructive comments and suggestions.

Shulin Yu

Contents

1 **Teacher Emotions in L2 Writing Instruction** 1
   1.1 Research Background 1
      1.1.1 Teacher Emotions Research 2
      1.1.2 Teacher Emotions in L2 Teaching Research 3
      1.1.3 The Under-Research of Teacher Emotions in L2
            Writing 4
   1.2 Aims and Purposes of This Book 6
      1.2.1 Research Gaps 6
      1.2.2 Research Objectives 7
      1.2.3 Research Significance 8
      1.2.4 Main Research Questions 9
   1.3 Definitions of Major Terms in This Book 10
   1.4 Structure of the Book 13
   References 13

2 **Multidimensional Theoretical Perspectives of Teacher Emotions** 17
   2.1 Introduction 17
   2.2 Appraisal Theoretical Perspective of Teacher Emotions 17
      2.2.1 Emotional Appraisal Theory 18
      2.2.2 Subjective Experience of Emotions 19
      2.2.3 Physiological Changes and Emotional Expression 20
      2.2.4 Action Tendency Emotions 20
   2.3 Sociocultural Theoretical Perspective of Teacher Emotions ... 22
   2.4 Positive Psychological Perspective of Teacher Emotions 25
   2.5 Summary 27
   References 27

3	**Framing Teacher Emotions in the L2 Writing Classroom Context**		**31**
	3.1	Introduction	31
	3.2	Contextual Antecedents of L2 Writing Teacher Emotions	32
		3.2.1 Macro-contextual Antecedents	33
		3.2.2 Meso-contextual Antecedents	35
		3.2.3 Micro-contextual Issues	39
	3.3	Personal Antecedents of L2 Writing Teacher Emotions	42
		3.3.1 Teachers' Emotional Intelligence	43
		3.3.2 L2 Writing Teachers' Knowledge, Values, and Skills	45
		3.3.3 L2 Writing Teachers' Self-efficacy and Professional Identity	47
		3.3.4 L2 Writing Teachers' Adaptive Expertise in L2 Writing Instruction	48
	3.4	L2 Writing Teachers' Emotional Labor and Emotional Labor Strategies	49
		3.4.1 Teachers' Emotional Labor	50
		3.4.2 Teachers' Emotional Labor Strategies	50
		3.4.3 Mediated Effect of Teachers' Emotional Labor Strategies on Their Well-Being in L2 Writing	53
		3.4.4 Mediated Effects of Emotional Labor Strategies on Teaching Behaviors in L2 Writing	56
	3.5	Consequences of L2 Writing Teacher Emotions	58
		3.5.1 Consequences of L2 Writing Teacher Emotions on Their Well-Being	58
		3.5.2 Consequences of L2 Writing Teacher Emotions on Teacher-Student Relationships	60
		3.5.3 Consequences of L2 Writing Teacher Emotions on Teaching Behaviors	61
		3.5.4 Recursive Effect of Teachers' Well-Being, Teaching Behavior, and Student Outcomes on Teacher Emotions	63
		3.5.5 A Conceptual Framework on the Reciprocal Model of Causes and Effects of Teacher Emotions in L2 Writing Context	63
	3.6	Summary	66
	References		66
4	**Understanding L2 Writing Teachers' Emotions in Chinese Tertiary Context: A Qualitative Inquiry**		**73**
	4.1	L2 Writing Teachers in Chinese Tertiary Context	73
	4.2	A Qualitative Inquiry	77
	4.3	Research Methodology and Ethical Issues	86
	4.4	Summary	87
	References		88

5	**Teacher Emotions and Instructional Practices: Evidence from a Genre Based L2 Writing Classroom**		91
	5.1	Introduction	91
	5.2	Alex's Emotional Experiences: A Genre based L2 Writing Pedagogical Approach	92
	5.3	Goals and Norms Supporting Alex's Appraisal of Emotional Situations	95
	5.4	Influence of Alex's Emotion-Regulation Strategies on L2 Writing Instruction and His Psychological Well-Being	95
		5.4.1 Alex's Use of Emotion Regulation Strategies and Impact: Macro-Level	96
		5.4.2 Alex's Use of Emotion Regulation Strategies and Impact: Meso-Level	97
		5.4.3 Alex's Use of Emotion Regulation Strategies and Impact: Micro-Level	98
	5.5	Summary	104
	References		106
6	**Teacher Emotions and Instructional Practices: Evidence from a Process based L2 Writing Classroom**		109
	6.1	Introduction	109
	6.2	Lina's Emotional Experiences: A Process based L2 Writing Pedagogical Approach	110
	6.3	Types of Triggering Situations of Lina's Emotional Experiences	112
	6.4	Goals and Norms Supporting Lina's Appraisal of Emotional Situations	113
	6.5	Influences of Lina's Emotion-Regulation Strategies on L2 Writing Instruction and Her Psychological Well-Being	114
		6.5.1 Lina's Use of Emotion-Regulation Strategies and Impact: Macro Level	115
		6.5.2 Lina's Use of Emotion-Regulation Strategies and Impact: Meso-Level	117
		6.5.3 Lina's Use of Emotion-Regulation Strategies and Impact: Micro-Level	118
	6.6	Summary	131
	References		133

7 Teacher Emotions and Instructional Practices: Evidence from a Process-Genre L2 Writing Classroom 135
- 7.1 Introduction 135
- 7.2 Olivia's Emotional Experiences: A Process-Genre L2 Writing Pedagogical Approach 137
- 7.3 Goals and Norms Supporting Olivia's Appraisal of Emotional Situations 143
- 7.4 Influence of Olivia's Emotion-Regulation Strategies on L2 Writing Instruction and His Psychological Well-Being 147
  - 7.4.1 Olivia's Use of Emotion-Regulation Strategies and Impact: Macro-Level 147
  - 7.4.2 Olivia's Use of Emotion-Regulation Strategies and Impact: Meso-Level 148
  - 7.4.3 Olivia's Use of Emotion-Regulation Strategies and Impact: Micro-Level 152
- 7.5 Summary 156
- References 158

8 Concluding Thoughts 161
- 8.1 A Reciprocal Model of L2 Writing Teacher Emotions and Pedagogical Behaviors 161
  - 8.1.1 Teacher Emotions Could Directly Transmit from Teachers to Students 162
  - 8.1.2 Teacher Emotions Could Shape the Quality of Teacher-Student Relationships 163
  - 8.1.3 The Use of Emotion-Regulation Strategies Could Mediate L2 Writing Teachers' Commitment and Well-Being 164
  - 8.1.4 The Use of Emotion-Regulation Strategies Could Mediate L2 Writing Teachers' Feedback-Giving Practice 165
  - 8.1.5 The Use of Emotion-Regulation Strategies Could Mediate the L2 Writing Pedagogical Practices 168
- 8.2 How Does This Book Contribute to Theory, Research and Practice? 169
  - 8.2.1 Contribution to Theory 170
  - 8.2.2 Contribution to Research 171
  - 8.2.3 Contribution to Practice 174
- 8.3 How Does This Book Bridge the Gap Between Research and Practice in L2 Writing? 175
  - 8.3.1 Implications for Research 175
  - 8.3.2 Implications for Pedagogical Practice 176
  - 8.3.3 Implications for L2 Writing Teachers 177

		8.3.4 Implications for L2 Writing Teacher Educators	178
		8.3.5 Implications for University Administration	179
	8.4	Concluding Remarks	180
	References		182

Appendix A: Interview Guides for the Main Study 185

Appendix B: Lesson Plan of Alex 189

Appendix C: Lesson Plan of Lina 193

Appendix D: Lesson Plan of Olivia 197

References 201

Chapter 1
Teacher Emotions in L2 Writing Instruction

This book delves into the critical yet often overlooked subject of L2 writing teachers' emotions, a domain that is essential to both L2 writing research and teacher education (Chen, 2016; Hargreaves, 2001; Isenbarger & Zembylas, 2006; Yin et al., 2013). The primary objective is to dissect the precursors, mechanisms, and outcomes of teacher emotions, with a particular emphasis on the emotional landscape experienced by L2 writing teachers within their classrooms. The exposition begins in this chapter with an exploration of the research backdrop, encompassing the role of emotions in teacher education and their impact on L2 writing instruction. This foundational discussion is followed by an articulation of the research's rationale, where gaps in the current literature, the books objectives, and its broader significance are elucidated. Subsequently, the chapter outlines the key research questions that this book seeks to answer, thereby mapping out the study's intellectual position and direction. The chapter concludes with a concise overview of the book's organizational framework, providing readers with a roadmap for the journey ahead.

1.1 Research Background

This section establishes the context for the study, providing an overview of the current state of research on teacher emotions. It examines the pivotal role that teacher emotions occupy in the field of L2 writing research and delves into the existing body of literature that pertains to the emotional experiences of L2 writing teachers within the Chinese tertiary educational landscape. This background sets the stage for a deeper exploration of the subject matter and underscores the relevance of the study's focus.

1.1.1 Teacher Emotions Research

Initiated by the "affective turn" in teacher education research since the 1990s, a wealth of literature has illuminated the profound and multifaceted influence of emotions on teachers' professional lives, both within and beyond the classroom (Hargreaves, 1998, 2001; Nias, 1996; Sutton & Wheatley, 2003). It is now widely acknowledged that emotions are the very essence of the teaching profession; hence, teaching can aptly be described as "an emotional practice" (Hargreaves, 1998), with the classroom being recognized as "an emotional place" (Pekrun & Linnenbrink-García, 2014). Consequently, understanding the role of teacher emotions is crucial for comprehending the dynamics of teaching in environments that are inherently emotionally charged. Several factors have historically contributed to the relative scarcity of research on teacher emotions. Initially, emotions were often dismissed in earlier studies as being overly subjective, irrational, and stereotypically associated with femininity, making them difficult to quantify and analyze (Benesch, 2012). As a result, emotions were commonly perceived as antithetical to the esteemed qualities of "reason" and "morality." This perspective led to the marginalization of teacher emotions in research until the late 1990s, when a growing body of work began to shed light on their significance (e.g., Hargreaves, 1998; Lasky, 2000; Nias, 1996). A second prevailing viewpoint posits that emotions serve as influential determinants of cognitive processes (Swain, 2013). Despite this recognition, rationality continues to take precedence, and emotional dimensions are often sidelined, with insufficient consideration given to the contextual factors that shape emotional experiences. These underlying issues may account for the persistent underrepresentation of teacher emotions as a focal point in academic research.

Over the past few decades, there has been a paradigm shift in understanding the role of emotions in teaching. It is now widely acknowledged that emotions are not merely intertwined with cognition but are central to the very essence of the teaching profession (Geng et al., 2023; Hargreaves, 2001; Yin et al., 2017; Yu et al., 2021). This realization emerged within the field of teacher education research, where the humanistic approach to education, developed in the latter half of the twentieth century, brought a new focus on the inner lives of individuals, including their thoughts, feelings, and emotions (Lei, 2007). This shift paved the way for a more nuanced examination of teacher emotions as a distinct area of study. A multitude of research has since explored the complex interplay among the various components of teacher emotions. Chen's (2019, p. 17) comprehensive review of literature and models from 1985 to 2019, for example, led to the refinement of the Teacher Emotion Model (TEM). This model identifies three interconnected themes: antecedents, teacher emotions, and consequences. Within TEM, two types of antecedents are underscored—personal and contextual—and it is recognized that teachers' emotional competencies, such as emotional intelligence, emotional labor, and strategies for managing emotional labor, are shaped by the interplay of these antecedents. Moreover, these competencies significantly influence the outcomes associated with teacher emotions, further underscoring the importance of considering emotions as a foundational aspect of teaching.

A substantial body of research has converged on the significant influence of teacher emotions on various professional dimensions, including their beliefs (such as self-efficacy, identity, commitment, and sense of responsibility), motivation and engagement, well-being (including job satisfaction and burnout), and teaching effectiveness. Among these, the negative repercussions of teacher emotions have been particularly emphasized, with studies documenting issues such as emotional burnout, diminished job satisfaction, and teacher attrition (Brown & Roloff, 2011; Hakanen et al., 2006). These studies predominantly focus on the detrimental effects of negative emotions, which can constrict teachers' cognitive and behavioral capacities by distracting them from their instructional objectives (Derryberry & Tucker, 1994) and diminishing their intrinsic motivation, as negative emotions are typically at odds with the enjoyment and engagement associated with intrinsic motivation (Pekrun, 2006). However, this research has largely overlooked the cultivation of positive emotions among teachers and their role in shaping teacher psychology. It is important to recognize that positive emotions, such as joy, interest, contentment, and love, coexist with negative ones and that moments of positive emotional experience are not necessarily overshadowed by negative emotions like anxiety, sadness, or anger (Fredrickson, 2001, p. 218). Furthermore, positive emotions extend beyond fleeting moments of pleasure; they have a lasting impact, influencing teachers' long-term well-being (Diener, 2009). This suggests that a more holistic and balanced theoretical framework is required to fully capture the spectrum of teacher emotions.

Seligman's (2002, 2011) well-being theory, a cornerstone of positive psychology, emerged from a paradigm that focuses on the study of positive human attributes, behaviors, and mental constructs, rather than dwelling on deficits and negative traits (Seligman & Csikszentmihalyi, 2000). This influential theory posits that positive emotions, though transient, are instrumental in fostering enduring, beneficial outcomes. It suggests that by nurturing positive emotions, educators can accumulate personal and social capital, leading to profound personal growth and an enhanced future. This conceptualization has significantly broadened our perspective on teacher emotions. It redirects research focus from the negative to the positive dimensions of emotional experience, emphasizing the cultivation of teachers' overall well-being. This includes fostering positive emotions, engagement, a sense of meaning, positive relationships, and a feeling of accomplishment (Cherkowski, 2018; Dollansky, 2014; Gross & John, 2003; Weiland, 2021). By doing so, it offers a more comprehensive approach to understanding and supporting the emotional lives of educators.

1.1.2 Teacher Emotions in L2 Teaching Research

Emotions are recognized as a cornerstone of language teacher professional development (Golombek & Doran, 2014) and are indispensable in the discourse of L2 teaching research. Teacher emotions profoundly influence not only their professional knowledge, values, beliefs, identities, and well-being but also their decision-making and interactions with students, classroom management strategies, and the academic success of their learners. Despite their significance, emotions are frequently overlooked or undervalued in the learning-to-teach journey and within teacher education programs. The prevailing focus on L2 teachers' subject matter expertise and pedagogical content knowledge often fails to equip them with the necessary skills to navigate the intense and complex emotional landscape of classroom teaching. Addressing how L2 teachers effectively manage emotionally charged classroom experiences is therefore central to the conversation. As Chen (2016) aptly points out, one of the most formidable challenges for L2 teachers is to gain insight into their own emotions, understand their role in the teaching and classroom context, and develop the competencies to manage these emotions effectively. This challenge underscores the need for a more comprehensive approach to teacher education that encompasses emotional intelligence and regulation as integral components of a teacher's professional toolkit.

There is a growing recognition of the importance of exploring the emotional terrain of L2 teaching, driven by the need for robust teacher education and professional development. The significance of teacher emotions as a pivotal factor that mediates classroom instructional practices and significantly impacts students' academic outcomes is increasingly acknowledged. Given the substantial emotional demands inherent in the process of learning to teach an L2 and the journey to becoming an effective L2 teacher, a profound comprehension of the emotional aspects of teaching is not just beneficial but essential. This understanding is crucial for fostering a supportive educational environment that nurtures both teacher well-being and student success.

1.1.3 The Under-Research of Teacher Emotions in L2 Writing

The significance of L2 writing research in the field of second language education is well-established, with a wealth of literature highlighting the crucial elements that contribute to L2 writing teachers' professional growth. These elements include their conceptualizations of writing, curriculum development, and pedagogical strategies (Cumming, 2003). L2 writing educators are expected to facilitate students' acquisition of language, content, and rhetorical skills essential for effective writing (Lo & Hyland, 2007). They should employ teaching methodologies that draw from process, product, and genre perspectives (Badger & White, 2000), foster students' interest and autonomy in the writing process (Hyland, 2003), and provide focused, constructive, and adaptable feedback on student writing (Ferris et al., 2013; Yu et al., 2020). Additionally, they must utilize appropriate assessment tools to identify and address writing challenges (e.g., Lee, 2017; William, 2011) and enhance students' feedback literacy (Han & Xu, 2021; Yu & Liu, 2021). While there is an abundance of research on L2 writing teachers' knowledge, beliefs, practices, expertise, and professional development, there remains a gap in understanding their emotional experiences and

1.1 Research Background

the strategies they employ to manage emotions within the complex interplay of individual differences and sociocultural contexts. This emotional landscape and its regulation are critical yet underexplored areas that warrant further investigation to support the holistic development of L2 writing educators.

Despite extensive research on L2 writing teachers' beliefs, knowledge, and pedagogical practices, a notable gap often exists between their theoretical perspectives and the actual implementation of writing instruction (e.g., Diab, 2005). One factor that may impede the effectiveness of L2 writing teachers in the classroom is the challenges they encounter when dealing with negative emotions. These can range from managing student misconduct to navigating strained student relationships and coping with insufficient support from the school environment and colleagues. Another significant hurdle for L2 writing teachers is the lack of understanding regarding their own emotional responses, the function of emotions in the teaching process, and the strategies for managing emotions that arise from specific teaching tasks. For instance, they may grapple with providing constructive feedback, assessing student writing, and orchestrating classroom dynamics. These challenges underscore the need for a more comprehensive approach to L2 writing teacher education that addresses not only pedagogical skills but also emotional intelligence and regulation. By doing so, teacher education programs can better prepare educators to navigate the emotional complexities of the teaching profession, ultimately enhancing their overall effectiveness and well-being.

In the realm of L2 writing teacher emotion research, the focus has predominantly been on the emotional experiences of L2 teachers in general, rather than those specifically involved in writing instruction. This oversight neglects the unique demands and expertise required in L2 writing contexts. L2 writing instruction, by its nature, is an emotionally charged endeavor. Research has revealed a complex interplay between L2 writing teachers' emotions and the feedback process (Yu et al., 2021). The act of providing detailed and targeted feedback on student writing demands significant cognitive and emotional investment from L2 writing teachers, potentially leading to a spectrum of emotions, both negative (such as burnout, anger, anxiety, and disappointment) and positive (like joy, pleasure, satisfaction, and contentment). These emotional responses, in turn, influence the strategies L2 writing teachers employ when giving feedback. However, the majority of existing studies have concentrated on students' emotional reactions to teacher feedback (e.g., Mahfoodh, 2017; Pekrun et al., 2014; Ryan & Henderson, 2018), often sidelining the vital role of teachers' emotional experiences and their responses to student writing. Consequently, research into the emotional landscape of university L2 writing teachers is of equal, if not greater, importance than that concerning student emotions. To address the "teacher expertise gap" in L2 writing research, Lee and Yuan (2021) introduce the concept of "adaptive expertise" as a framework for understanding the expertise of writing teachers. Their review identifies six components of L2 writing teacher expertise: an integrated knowledge base on writing and teaching writing; a student-centered pedagogy that fosters learner motivation and confidence; professional visions, self-agency, and reflectivity; leadership in writing innovations; passions as both teachers of writing and writers; and a commitment to ongoing learning and progressive problem-solving. While emotional capacity is acknowledged as part of this expertise, further empirical research is necessary to delve into the development and operational mechanisms of teacher emotions and their impact on the cultivation of L2 writing teacher expertise.

Another obvious limitation in the current conceptualization of L2 writing teacher emotions is its primary focus on educators in primary and secondary school settings, which differ markedly from university contexts. Despite the widespread inclusion of L2 writing instruction in college curricula and its recognized significance for L2 learners' academic success and socio-affective growth, the literature provides scant insight into the emotional experiences of L2 writing teachers in their professional and personal spheres. Furthermore, the literature inadequately addresses how these emotions intrinsically influence their cognitive processes and actions. To bridge this gap, there is a pressing need for research that delves into the emotional landscape of L2 university writing teachers. Such research should examine the intricate interplay between their emotional dimensions and their cognitive and behavioral involvement in the teaching of writing. By doing so, we can better understand the nuanced dynamics at play and develop more targeted strategies to support the emotional well-being and pedagogical effectiveness of L2 writing educators in higher education settings.

In essence, this book provides a foundation for understanding the complex process by which L2 writing teachers develop their emotional frameworks. It explores how they interpret and manage their emotions, influenced by a tapestry of personal and contextual factors, and examines the potential repercussions these emotions may have on both the teachers' well-being and their effectiveness in L2 writing instruction.

1.2 Aims and Purposes of This Book

This book aims to offer a comprehensive exploration of the emotional landscape of L2 university writing teachers within the context of naturalistic L2 writing instruction. The subsequent sections will elucidate the rationale, objectives, and importance of the research presented herein.

1.2.1 Research Gaps

This book endeavors to address a significant theoretical void by focusing on the emotional experiences of L2 writing teachers within the university educational setting. It seeks to highlight and rectify the underexplored area of teacher emotions in L2 writing, with a particular emphasis on the EFL environment in mainland China, where such research is notably sparse. In the domain of L2 writing teacher research, a modest number of studies have concentrated on the practices and expertise of teachers in delivering writing instruction (e.g., Lee & Yuan, 2021; Lee et al., 2016;

Mak & Lee, 2014). However, the majority of these studies target L2 writing educators in primary and secondary settings, whose cognitive and emotional experiences are shaped by a distinct set of factors compared to those encountered by university-based instructors.

In the context of university education, L2 writing teachers are characterized by several distinctive attributes. Firstly, they must possess an extensive knowledge base encompassing both writing and teaching writing, equipping them to employ pedagogical strategies effectively. Secondly, they require a solid foundation in writing assessment literacy, which includes the ability to utilize and develop assessment tools, offer and interpret feedback, and foster students' ability to engage in peer and self-review. Thirdly, L2 writing teachers must exhibit strong self-agency and reflective skills to ensure their teaching practices are in harmony with their educational beliefs. Fourthly, they play a pivotal role in spearheading writing program innovations and educational reforms, which invariably present novel challenges and complexities to their teaching and professional growth. Lastly, as L2 writing and instruction are lifelong endeavors of progressive problem-solving (Casanave, 2017), L2 writing teachers must maintain a persistent commitment and invest cognitive and emotional resources into continuous learning and professional development. Given these unique characteristics and the particularities of the university educational setting, it is both pertinent and valuable to delve into the emotional experiences of L2 writing teachers. Such investigation can provide insights crucial for enhancing their teaching effectiveness and overall well-being.

Previous studies on L2 writing teacher emotions have largely examined the broader educational context, emphasizing the adverse effects of these emotions on teachers' physical health, job satisfaction, and commitment to the teaching profession (Weiland, 2021). Yet, there is a conspicuous absence of detailed exploration into the nuanced construction of L2 writing teacher emotions within their specific educational settings. Moreover, a burgeoning body of literature on teacher emotions advocates for a reorientation of focus from the negative—such as stress, burnout, and attrition—to the positive aspects of emotions (Cherkowski, 2018; Dollansky, 2014). Consequently, there is a significant gap in our understanding of the regulatory mechanisms L2 writing teachers employ to navigate their emotional responses amidst personal and contextual factors, as well as the elements that may foster or obstruct their journey towards enhanced well-being and professional development.

1.2.2 Research Objectives

Based on the premise that teacher emotions lie at the heart of their pedagogical activities and well-being, a longitudinal study was conducted in L2 writing classrooms in mainland Chinese universities with the overarching purpose of exploring L2 writing teacher emotions by capturing the changing processes in more temporally and spatially precise ways (Fried et al., 2015). To achieve this purpose, the following objectives have been set. Underpinned by the notion that teacher emotions are central to pedagogical practices and educators' well-being, a longitudinal study was undertaken in L2 writing classrooms across Chinese mainland universities. The primary goal of this book was to delve into the emotional landscape of L2 writing teachers, aiming to document the dynamic evolution of their emotions in a manner that is both temporally and spatially nuanced (Fried et al., 2015). To realize this objective, this book established the following specific aims.

First, this book sets out to provide a holistic understanding of the emotional experiences of L2 university writing teachers in mainland China. By examining their teaching practices in detail, the aim is to capture not only the distinct emotions they experience but also the underlying causes, the cognitive appraisals, and the emotional regulation strategies they employ in response to particular situations. This comprehensive approach seeks to reveal the antecedents that trigger these emotions and the subsequent emotional outcomes, offering a more nuanced depiction of the emotional landscape within this educational context.

Second, this book aims to advance the field by proposing a theoretical framework that elucidates the interplay among L2 writing teacher emotions, the strategies they employ for emotional labor, their pedagogical actions, and their overall sense of well-being. By mapping out this intricate relationship, this book seeks to provide a coherent perspective on how teacher emotions intersect with the teaching process in L2 writing environments. This exploration is designed to guide future research, offering a well-defined lens through which to examine the dynamic interplay between teacher emotions and instructional practices in the L2 writing context.

The third objective of this book is to uncover the distinct characteristics of emotional labor as experienced by L2 writing teachers and the strategies they utilize to manage and navigate the emotional tensions that surface both within and beyond the writing classroom. By shedding light on these aspects, the book aspires to pinpoint the specific challenges L2 writing teachers face in emotional regulation. Such insights are invaluable for the enhancement of teacher education programs, as they can inform the development of targeted interventions and support systems aimed at fostering more effective emotional management skills among educators.

1.2.3 Research Significance

In recent years, the role of emotions in teaching has emerged as a compelling area of focus within educational research. This growing interest is fueled by the prevalence of emotional burnout, high attrition rates, and diminished commitment—key challenges within the teaching profession. Consequently, there is a mounting demand to unravel the determinants that foster a more positive emotional climate and enhance the well-being of educators (Weiland, 2021; Yin et al., 2013). Research into the emotional experiences of L2 university writing teachers, particularly within the realm of their pedagogical practices, is of paramount importance. It holds significant implications for theoretical, methodological, and pedagogical advancements in the field (Lee & Yuan, 2021; Yin et al., 2013, 2015).

Theoretically, this book responds to the call for a more profound investigation into the emotional facets of teachers' professional lives (Sutton & Wheatley, 2003) by elucidating the interplay between L2 writing teachers' emotional intelligence, emotional labor strategies, and their well-being. This study is anchored in a synthesis of quantitative and qualitative insights, derived from the authentic professional environments of L2 writing teachers. The study leverages established theories on teacher emotions, particularly the widely acknowledged significance of emotional intelligence and emotional labor in the teaching profession (Yin et al., 2013; Zembylas, 2003), to underpin the initial inquiry. Furthermore, the well-being theory proposed by Seligman (2002) serves as a conceptual framework, allowing the exploration of how L2 writing teachers manage their emotions and cultivate well-being through their pedagogical approaches. The findings of this research aim to fill a theoretical void and pave the way for subsequent studies in the field.

Pedagogically, this book offers insights into enhancing L2 writing teachers' ability to perceive, understand, and manage their emotions effectively by employing suitable regulatory strategies within the writing classroom. It emphasizes the importance of teachers' self-regulation in fostering more effective decision-making and maintaining a positive demeanor in the intricate and dynamic settings of teaching. By bridging the gap between L2 writing teacher emotions, emotional labor strategies, and their impact on pedagogical actions and well-being, the book contributes to the development of targeted teacher training programs. For instance, it suggests methods to motivate teachers to adopt adaptable approaches that mitigate stress and anxiety in the classroom. Additionally, it explores strategies for fostering positive emotions, enhancing self-efficacy, boosting motivation, and strengthening commitment, which in turn can improve teaching satisfaction and engagement in both professional and personal spheres. These insights are instrumental in crafting training modules that support L2 writing teachers in achieving a balanced and fulfilling teaching experience.

1.2.4 Main Research Questions

Two main research questions are raised to fulfill the research objectives of the book:

(1) What are L2 writing teachers' emotional experiences in the Chinese tertiary educational context?
(2) How do L2 writing teachers appraise and regulate their emotions elicited by situations in a discrete context, and how can their pedagogical behaviors be affected?

Specific research questions are operationalized and presented in Sect. 1.2.3 after a systematic review of the theoretical framework of the study.

1.3 Definitions of Major Terms in This Book

Since the book attempts to investigate university L2 writing teachers' emotions, it is crucial to explain how the important terms, namely, university L2 context, L2 writing, and L2 writing teachers, are defined. The definitions of the key terms are explained in the following sections to demonstrate the study's stance in exploring those issues in their authentic context. Operational definitions of other terms, such as emotional intelligence, emotional labor strategy, and well-being, are listed in the following chapters when they are brought up.

Given the book's focus on exploring the emotional experiences of university L2 writing teachers, it is imperative to clarify the pivotal terms that underpin the study. The subsequent sections will delineate the operational definitions of "tertiary L2 context," "L2 writing," and "L2 writing teachers," thereby establishing the study's framework for examining these elements within their genuine settings. Additionally, operational definitions for other critical terms, including "emotional intelligence," "emotional labor strategy," and "well-being," will be presented in the chapters where they are introduced, ensuring a coherent and contextually grounded exploration of the subject matter.

Tertiary L2 context

In this book, the term "second language (L2)" encompasses both second and foreign languages, with a particular emphasis on English as a subject of study in both ESL (English as a Second Language) and EFL (English as a Foreign Language) contexts (Lee, 2017). In mainland China, English is taught as an EFL across various educational levels, including primary schools, universities, and beyond. The focus of this book is on the tertiary L2 context within China. By adopting this definition, the book aims to provide researchers with a more precise lens through which to direct their inquiries and to yield findings that are deeply relevant to this particular educational milieu.

L2 writing

The increasing significance of written communication, which spans from casual social media interactions to the structured demands of academic scholarship, has rendered the development of writing proficiency a critical goal for university students learning English as a second language (L2). Despite the widespread integration of L2 writing into the curricula of numerous university settings, the existing body of L2 writing literature remains underrepresented. By concentrating on the university L2 writing context, this book seeks to rectify this imbalance and contribute to a more comprehensive understanding of the subject.

L2 writing teachers

In this book, the term "university L2 writing teachers" denotes educators who are dedicated to instructing L2 writing as a distinct academic discipline. This classification extends to instructors who teach writing skills to students pursuing English as a major, as well as those whose primary field of study is not English. This inclusive definition aims to encompass the broad spectrum of educators within this often overlooked community. For university L2 writing teachers, this book offers a trove of practical strategies designed to enhance the teaching and learning of L2 writing. For researchers and teacher educators in the field of L2 writing, the book serves as a resource, proposing potential avenues for future research into the emotional dimensions of L2 writing instruction. Such explorations are pertinent to the broader discourse on L2 writing and are essential for advancing the pedagogical practices and professional development of L2 writing teachers.

Teacher emotions

Teacher emotions, as a multi-component construct, emotions could be conceptualized from physiological, psychological, sociocultural, and positive psychological perspectives (Sutton & Wheatley, 2003). In recent decades, scholars have been calling for a shift in studying the complexity of teacher emotions situated within their sociocultural context. In other words, language teacher emotions should not just be viewed as psychological phenomena nor as discrete affective states but rather as feelings experienced and performed in relation to other people and particular situations. This book grounded L2 writing teacher emotions primarily from a sociocultural approach that highlights the relational nature between teachers and their social environment (Golombek & Doran, 2014; Gkonou & Miller, 2021). Teacher emotions, in this regard, could be defined as "socially constructed, personally enacted ways of being that emerge from conscious and/or unconscious judgments regarding perceived successes at attaining goals or maintaining standards or beliefs during transactions as part of social–historical contexts" (Schutz et al., 2006, p. 344). Central to this approach is the idea that all emotions may act as valuable guides in the interpretation of teachers' decision-making and pedagogical practices. Equally important is the inclusion of both positive and negative emotions as potential sources of teacher agency based on the assumption that emotions may act as useful signals to teachers and their colleagues about whether the current conditions are favorable or not (Benesch, 2017). Along these lines, three theoretical constructs could act as useful tools to probe into L2 teachers' emotions: feeling rules, emotional labor, and regulation strategies.

Teacher emotions are usually a result of "emotional rules" or "feeling rules", which are the implicit or explicit guidelines teachers adopt in assessing and managing their feelings in a given situation (Benesch, 2017; Hochschild, 1983). Zembylas (2007, p. 447) writes that feeling rules in school contexts "delineate a zone within which certain emotions are permitted and others are not permitted and can be obeyed or broken, at varying costs". Yin and Lee (2012) further pronounce that the feeling rules "reflect the cultural expectations, social standards, or professional norms that lead and direct teachers' emotional labor either in the form of internalized self-regulation or external control" (p. 58). The feeling rules of schools and classrooms, though usually implicit and often subconsciously recognized, nevertheless shape what language teachers believe they should feel in their professional roles and how they should perform emotions.

Related to the feeling rules in language teaching is the notion of emotional clash that might occur when teachers are asked to display certain emotions but are in violation of how they authentically feel, and this clash is termed "emotional labor" by Hochschild (1983). As a multicomponent construct, teachers' emotional labor could be conceptualized as the process, applied in the context of teaching, in which teachers are expected to inhibit, generate, and manage their feelings and expression of emotions according to the normative beliefs and expectations held about the teaching profession (Hochschild, 1983; Wharton, 2009; Winograd, 2003). Despite the intense emotional labor involved in teaching languages, the ethical standard for the teaching profession encourages teachers to make efforts to manage their displays and experiences of emotions in order to become better, more professional teachers, and teachers' emotional labor has long been considered a standard procedure in L2 writing classrooms and as a "natural aspect of teaching". Given the intrinsically rewarding but discretionary nature of teachers' emotional labor, it could act as a robust tool for examining teachers' emotional clashes triggered by the inconsistency between the feeling rules and their internal feelings in the teaching of L2 writing. Several clashes account for the distinctive features of L2 writing teachers' emotional labor.

In the light of Hochschild's (1983) concept of emotional regulation, teachers' emotional regulation could be defined as the ability and process of using strategies to manage and regulate the expression of emotions and the experiences of emotional labor (Gross, 2002; Yin, 2016). Hochschild (1983) proposed the first approach to emotional regulation: surface acting and deep acting. Surface acting refers to the strategy by which teachers express unfelt emotions or modify their emotional displays to comply with the emotional rules of teaching (Yin & Lee, 2012). Whereas deep acting is the process by which teachers, following the emotional rules of teaching, change their feelings using cognitive techniques (e.g., attention deployment or self-persuasion) to display the required emotional expressions (Yin, 2016). In addition, some researchers (e.g., Ashforth & Humphrey, 1993; Diefendorff et al., 2005) suggest that the expression of naturally felt emotions be the third strategy for emotion regulation, which refers to teachers' spontaneous displays of care and love towards their students. The second approach was proposed by Gross (1998) who put forward antecedent-focused and response-focused strategies to distinguish the emotional regulation before and after the initiation of the emotional arousal stages. Given the close interconnection between teachers' emotional labor and regulation strategies, Grandey (2003) argued that emotional labor could be conceptualized as emotional regulation, in that surface acting and deep acting could well correspond with Gross' (1998) classification of antecedent-focused and response-focused regulation strategies.

1.4 Structure of the Book

The book is structured into five parts, with the first part consisting of a single chapter. Part I, this chapter, sets the stage by presenting the study's background and underscoring the significance of teacher emotions within the realm of L2 writing research. This inaugural chapter offers a comprehensive overview of the research rationale, highlighting the existing gaps in the literature, delineating the study's objectives, and discussing the broader implications of the research for L2 writing contexts.

Part II of the book, comprising Chaps. 2 and 3, delves into a thorough examination of theoretical frameworks and models pertaining to teacher emotions. It also reviews the latest research from psychodynamic, sociocultural, and positive psychological standpoints to provide a comprehensive understanding of teacher emotions. Chapter 3, titled "Framing Teacher Emotions in L2 Writing Classroom Context," offers a detailed analysis of the emotional landscape within L2 writing classrooms. This chapter constructs a sophisticated theoretical model of L2 writing teacher emotions, which is articulated through three interconnected themes: emotional antecedents, emotional appraisal and regulation processes, and emotional consequences. The section culminates with the formulation of targeted research questions that guide the study. Part III, represented by Chap. 4, outlines the methodological approach employed in the book, detailing the research design and procedures that underpin the investigation.

Part IV of the book, encompassing Chaps. 5–7, provides an in-depth exploration of the antecedents, mechanisms of appraisal and regulation, and consequences of teacher emotions. This segment offers a detailed examination of the emotional journeys of three L2 writing teachers, focusing on the specific situations that elicit their emotions, the strategies they employ for emotional labor, and the impact of these emotions on their instructional practices, feedback to students, writing assessments, teacher-student interactions, and overall psychological well-being. These analyses are grounded in the real-world educational contexts in which these teachers operate, offering a rich tapestry of insights into the complex interplay of emotions in L2 writing instruction.

Concluding the book, Part V is encapsulated in Chap. 8. This final xchapter synthesizes the key findings from Part IV, offering a comprehensive summary of the study's essential discoveries. It further delves into the theoretical, practical, and pedagogical implications that arise from the research. Additionally, the chapter provides thoughtful recommendations for future research endeavors, aiming to inspire continued exploration and development in the field of L2 writing teacher emotions.

References

Ashforth, B. E., & Humphrey, R. H. (1993). Emotional Labour in Service Roles: The Influence of Identity. *Academy of Management Review, 18*, 88-115.

Badger, R., & White, G. (2000). A process genre approach to teaching writing. *ELT Journal, 54*(2), 153–160.

Benesch, S. (2012). *Considering emotions in critical English teaching*. Routledge. https://doi.org/10.4324/9780203848135

Brown, L., & Roloff, M. (2011). Extra-role time, burnout, and commitment: The power of promises kept. *Business Communication Quarterly, 74*(4), 450–474.

Casanave, C. P. (2017). *Controversies in second language writing: Dilemmas and decisions in research and instructions* (2nd ed.). The University of Michigan Press.

Chen, J. (2016). Understanding teacher emotions: The development of a teacher emotion inventory. *Teaching and Teacher Education, 55*, 68–69.

Chen, J. (2019). Exploring the impact of teacher emotions on their approaches to teaching: A structural equation modeling approach. *British Journal of Educational Psychology, 89*(1), 57–74.

Cherkowski, S. (2018). Positive teacher leadership: Building mindsets and capacities to grow well-being. *International Journal of Teacher Leadership, 9*, 63–78.

Cumming, A. (2003). Experienced ESL/EFL writing instructors' conceptualizations of their teaching: Curriculum options and implications. In *Exploring the dynamics of second language writing* (pp. 71–92). Cambridge University Press.

Derryberry, D., & Tucker, D. M. (1994). Motivating the focus of attention. In P. M. Niedenthal & S. Kitayama (Eds.), *The hearts eye: Emotional influence in perception and attention* (pp. 167–196). Academic Press.

Diab, R. L. (2005). Teachers' and students' beliefs about responding to ESL writing: A case study. *TESL Canada Journal, 23*(1), 28–43.

Diefendorff, J. M., Croyle, M. H. & Gosserand, R. H. (2005). The dimensionality and antecedents of emotional labor strategies. *Journal of Vocational Behavior, 66*, 339–357.

Diener, E. (2009). Subjective well-being. In E. Diener (Eds.), *The science of well-being* (Vol. 37, pp. 11–58). Springer. https://doi.org/10.1007/978-90-481-2350-6_2

Dollansky, T. (2014). The importance of the beginning teachers' psychological contract: A pathway toward flourishing in schools. *International Journal of Leadership in Education, 17*(4), 442–461.

Ferris, D., Liu, H., Sinha, A., & Senna, M. (2013). Written corrective feedback for individual L2 writers. *Journal of Second Language Writing, 22*, 307–329.

Fredrickson, B. L. (2001). The role of positive emotions in positive psychology: The broaden and build theory of positive emotions. *American Psychologist, 56*(3), 218–226. https://doi.org/10.1037/0003-066X.56.3.218

Fried, L., Mansfield, C., & Dobozy, E. (2015). Teacher emotion research: Introducing a conceptual model to guide future research. *Issues in Educational Research, 25*(4), 415–441.

Geng, F., Yu, S., & Yuan, R. E. (2023). Exploring L2 writing teachers' feeling rules, emotional labor and regulation strategies. *System, 119*, 103160.

Golombek, P., & Doran, M. (2014). Unifying cognition, emotion, and activity in language teacher professional development. *Teaching and Teacher Education, 39*, 102–111.

Grandey, A. A. (2003). When "The show must go on": surface acting and deep acting as determinants of emotional exhaustion and peer-rated service delivery. *Academy of Management Journal, 46*(1), 86–96.

Gross, J. J. (2002). Emotion Regulation: Affective, Cognitive, and Social Consequences. *Psychophysiology, 39*, 281–291.

Gross, J., & John, O. (2003). Individual differences in two emotion regulation processes: Implications for affect, relationships, and well-being. *Journal of Personality and Social Psychology, 85*(2), 348–362.

Hakanen, J. J., Bakker, A. B., & Schaufeli, W. B. (2006). Burnout and work engagement among teachers. *Journal of School Psychology, 43*(6), 495–513.

Han, Y., & Xu, Y. (2021). Student feedback literacy and engagement with feedback: A case study of Chinese undergraduate students. *Teaching in Higher Education, 26*(2), 181–196. https://doi.org/10.1080/13562517.2019.1648410

Hargreaves, A. (1998). The emotional practice of teaching. *Teaching and Teacher Education, 14*(8), 835–854.

References

Hargreaves, A. (2001). The emotional geographies of teaching. *Teachers College Record, 103*(3), 1056–1080.

Hochschild, A. R. (1983). *The managed heart: The commercialization of human feeling.* Berkeley, CA: Univ. Calif. Press.

Hyland, K. (2003). Genre-based pedagogies: A social response to process. *Journal of Second Language Writing, 12*(1), 17–29.

Isenbarger, L., & Zembylas, M. (2006). The emotional labor of caring in teaching. *Teaching and Teacher Education, 22*(1), 120–134.

Lasky, S. (2000). The cultural and emotional politics of teacher-parent interactions. *Teaching and Teacher Education, 16*, 843–860.

Lee, I. (2017). *Classroom writing assessment and feedback in L2 school contexts.* Springer.

Lee, I., & Yuan, R. (2021). Understanding L2 writing teacher expertise. *Journal of Second Language Writing*, 100755.

Lee, I., Mak, P., & Burns, A. (2016). EFL teachers' attempts at feedback innovation in the writing classroom. *Language Teaching Research, 20*(2), 248–269.

Lei, Q. (2007). EFL teachers' factors and students' affect. *US-China Education Review, 4*(3), 60–67.

Lo, J., & Hyland, F. (2007). Enhancing students' engagement and motivation in writing: The case of primary students in Hong Kong. *Journal of Second Language Writing, 16*(4), 219–237.

Mahfoodh, O. H. A. (2017). "I feel disappointed": EFL university students' emotional responses toward teacher written feedback. *Assessing Writing, 31*, 53–72.

Mak, P., & Lee, I. (2014). Implementing assessment for learning in L2 writing: An activity theory perspective. *System (Linköping), 47*, 73–87.

Pekrun, R. (2006). The control-value theory of achievement emotions: Assumptions, corollaries, and implications for educational research and practice. *Educational Psychology Review, 18*(4), 315–341.

Pekrun, R., Cusack, A., Murayama, K., Elliot, A. J., & Thomas, K. (2014). The power of anticipated feedback: Effects on students' achievement goals and achievement emotions. *Learning and Instruction, 29*, 115–124.

Pekrun, R., & Linnenbrink-García, L. (Eds.). (2014). *International handbook of emotions in education.* Routledge.

Nias, J. (1996). Thinking about feeling: The emotions in teaching. *Cambridge Journal of Education, 26*(3), 293–306.

Ryan, T., & Henderson, M. (2018). Feeling feedback: Students' emotional responses to educator feedback. *Assessment & Evaluation in Higher Education, 43*(6), 880–892. https://doi.org/10.1080/02602938.2017.1416456

Schutz, P. A., Hong, J. Y., Cross, D. I., & Osbon, J. N. (2006). Reflections on investigating emotion in educational activity settings. *Educational Psychology Review, 18*(4), 343–360.

Seligman, M. E. P. (2002). Positive psychology, positive prevention, and positive therapy. In C. R. Snyder & S. Lopez (Eds.), *Handbook of positive psychology* (pp. 3–13). Oxford University Press.

Seligman, M. E. P. (2011). *Flourish: A visionary new understanding of happiness and well-being.* Simon & Schuster.

Seligman, M., & Csikszentmihalyi, M. (2000). Positive psychology: An introduction. *American Psychologist, 55*, 5–14.

Sutton, R. E., & Wheatley, K. F. (2003). Teachers' emotions and teaching: A review of the literature and directions for future research. *Educational Psychology Review, 15*(4), 327–358.

Swain, M. (2013). The inseparability of cognition and emotion in second language learning. *Language Teaching, 46*(2), 195–207.

Weiland, A. (2021). Teacher well-being: Voices in the field. *Teaching and Teacher Education, 99*, 103250.

Wharton, A. S. (2009). The Sociology of Emotional Labor. *Annual Review of Sociology, 35*, 147–165.

Wiliam, D. (2011). *Embedded formative assessment*. Solution Tree Press. https://doi.org/10.1017/CBO9780511794537

Winograd, K. (2003). The functions of teacher emotions: The good, the bad, and the ugly. *Teachers College Record, 105*(9), 1641–1673.

Yin, H. (2015). The effect of teachers' emotional labour on teaching satisfaction: moderation of emotional intelligence. *Teachers and Teaching, 21*(7), 789–810.

Yin, H. (2016). Knife-like mouth and tofu-like heart: Emotion regulation by Chinese teachers in classroom teaching. *Social Psychology of Education, 19*(1), 1–22.

Yin, H. B., & Lee, J. C. K. (2012). Be passionate, but be rational as well: Emotional rules for Chinese teachers' work. *Teaching and Teacher Education, 28*, 56–65.

Yin, H., Lee, J. C. K., Zhang, Z., & Jin, Y. (2013). Exploring the relationship among teachers' emotional intelligence, emotional labor strategies and teaching satisfaction. *Teaching and Teacher Education, 35*, 137–145.

Yin, H., Han, J., & Lu, G. (2017). Chinese university teachers' goal orientations for teaching and teaching approaches: The mediation of teacher engagement. *Teaching in Higher Education, 22*(7), 766–784.

Yu, S., & Liu, C. (2021). Improving student feedback literacy in academic writing: An evidence-based framework. *Assessing Writing, 48*, 100525.

Yu, S., Jiang, L., & Zhou, N. (2020). *The impact of L2 writing instructional approaches on student writing motivation and engagement*. Language Teaching Research.

Yu, S., Zheng, Y., Jiang, L., Liu, C., & Xu, Y. (2021). "I even feel annoyed and angry": Teacher emotional experiences in giving feedback on student writing. *Assessing Writing, 48*, 100528.

Zembylas, M. (2003). Interrogating "teacher identity": Emotion, resistance, and self-formation. *Educational Theory, 53*(1), 107–127.

Zembylas, M. (2007). Emotional capital and education: Theoretical insights from Bourdieu.*British Journal of Educational Studies,55*, 443–463.

Suggested Readings

Benesch, S. (2017). *Emotions and English language teaching: Exploring teacher's emotion labor*. Routledge.

Chen, J. (2016). Understanding teacher emotions: The development of a teacher emotion inventory. *Teaching and Teacher Education, 55*, 68–69.

De Costa, P., Li, W., & Rawal, H. (2020). 12. Should I stay or leave? Exploring L2 teachers' profession from an emotionally inflected framework. In C. Gkonou, J. Dewaele, & J. King (Eds.), *The emotional rollercoaster of Language Teaching* (pp. 211–227). Multilingual Matters.

Gkonou, C., & Miller, E. R. (2021). An exploration of language teacher reflection, emotion labor, and emotional capital. *Tesol Quarterly, 55*(1), 134–155.

Golombek, P., & Doran, M. (2014). Unifying cognition, emotion, and activity in language teacher professional development. *Teaching and Teacher Education, 39*, 102–111.

Hargreaves, A. (1998). The emotional politics of teaching and teacher development. *International Journal of Leadership in Education, 1*, 315–336.

Sutton, R. E., & Wheatley, K. F. (2003). Teachers' emotions and teaching: A review of the literature and directions for future research. *Educational Psychology Review, 15*(4), 327–358.

Yu, S., Zheng, Y., Jiang, L., Liu, C., & Xu, Y. (2021). "I even feel annoyed and angry": Teacher emotional experiences in giving feedback on student writing. *Assessing Writing, 48*, Article 100528.

Zembylas, M. (2004). The emotional characteristics of teaching: An ethnographic study of one teacher. *Teaching and Teacher Education, 20*(2), 185–201.

Chapter 2
Multidimensional Theoretical Perspectives of Teacher Emotions

2.1 Introduction

This chapter begins by elucidating the definitions and core components of teacher emotions, highlighting the theoretical underpinnings that support the study of these emotions and the considerations that should be taken into account in research. It then delves into a comprehensive review of the multifaceted theoretical perspectives on teacher emotions, along with the empirical research that has enriched our comprehension of the factors that precede, regulate, and result from these emotions. As Dewaele et al. (2019) remarked, "emotions are at the heart of language learning and teaching, and yet they have largely remained in the shadows in the past decades of applied linguistic research." This statement underscores the importance of shedding light on the nature of teacher emotions and the various theoretical lenses through which they have been examined. Understanding the theoretical foundations and the empirical evidence surrounding teacher emotions is crucial for advancing the field and for informing educational practices that support the emotional well-being and effectiveness of teachers.

2.2 Appraisal Theoretical Perspective of Teacher Emotions

The initial wave of research on teacher emotions, which emerged in the 1980s, was deeply rooted in the theoretical principles of psychological studies. This research strand predominantly regarded emotions as manifestations of the teachers' internal experiences. The prevailing approach to investigating teacher emotions involved the use of standardized psychological assessment tools, such as questionnaires, which positioned emotions as a psychological construct inherent to individuals. This perspective emphasized the subjective and personal nature of emotional experiences, focusing on how teachers internalize and process their emotions within the context of their professional roles.

Within the framework of the psychodynamic perspective, researchers have recognized the intricate and dynamic nature of teacher emotions. Berry et al. (2002), for instance, delineated emotions as encompassing a sequence of elements: antecedent events, situational appraisals, subjective feelings, physiological responses, readiness for action, behavioral manifestations, and regulatory mechanisms. Lewis (2005) similarly posited that emotions are composed of arousal, tendencies for action, attentional focus, and affective sensations. Schutz and Pekrun (2007, p. 344) further elaborated on the concept of emotions as "socially constructed, personally enacted ways of being that emerge from conscious and/or unconscious judgments regarding perceived successes at attaining goals or maintaining standards or beliefs during transactions as part of social–historical contexts." This perspective underscores the role of social and historical contexts in shaping emotional experiences. In essence, this line of research and emotional theory tends to view emotions as multifaceted psychological processes (Sutton & Wheatley, 2003). These processes typically involve emotional appraisal, the subjective experience of emotions, physiological changes, the expression of emotions, and the tendencies for action. This comprehensive approach to understanding emotions acknowledges the interplay of cognitive, physiological, and behavioral elements, providing a nuanced framework for examining teacher emotions.

2.2.1 Emotional Appraisal Theory

Theoretical perspectives on emotions often posit that the emotional process initiates with an evaluative judgment or appraisal, which interprets the significance or relevance of an event in relation to an individual's motives, objectives, or concerns (Roseman & Smith, 2001; Scherer et al., 2001). From an educational psychological standpoint, Lazarus (1991, 1999) differentiated between primary and secondary appraisals. Primary appraisals involve assessments of goal relevance and goal congruence. Specifically, goal relevance appraisals occur when teachers evaluate the significance of an event in relation to their goals, standards, or beliefs. Goal congruence appraisals, on the other hand, involve judgments about whether the event aligns with their expectations or desired outcomes. In essence, positive emotions emerge from perceived goal congruence, whereas negative emotions stem from perceived goal incongruence. Secondary appraisals pertain to the teachers' assessments of their capacity to manage a given situation. These appraisals are closely linked to concepts such as agency or perceived control (Lazarus, 1999; Pekrun & Schutz, 2007; Schutz & Davis, 2000) and problem efficacy (Bandura, 1997; Schutz & Davis, 2000), which Lazarus (1991) referred to as coping potential. This term encapsulates the teacher's confidence in their ability to effectively navigate and respond to the situation at hand.

Understanding these appraisal processes is crucial for grasping the emotional experiences of teachers and for developing strategies to support their emotional well-being and teaching efficacy.

In summary, "emotional appraisal theory" elucidates the variability in emotional responses among individuals exposed to the same external stimuli, accounting for the individual differences in teachers' reactions to contextual factors. This theory also highlights the cultural dimension of emotional experiences, suggesting that cultural norms and values shape how events are perceived and interpreted. Mesquita and Ellsworth (2001) posited that the cultural variations in emotional expression and experience are rooted in systematic differences in the way cultures process and understand seemingly identical events. Consequently, teachers from diverse cultural backgrounds or professional contexts may have distinct appraisals of a particular classroom occurrence. For example, language teachers in ESL (English as a Second Language) and EFL (English as a Foreign Language) settings might have divergent perspectives on their professional development and teaching practices, leading to varied emotional experiences. These emotions, whether aligned or misaligned with their goals, can significantly impact their cognitive processes and the strategies they employ to manage their emotions, ultimately shaping their teaching practices and interactions with students.

2.2.2 Subjective Experience of Emotions

Emotional appraisal theory, which is foundational to understanding the subjective experience of emotions, suggests that individuals' responses are influenced by their evaluations or judgments of events (Lazarus, 1991). This perspective considers emotions as a unique and private mental state (Oatley, 1992). In educational settings, research has indicated that students' behaviors, whether disruptive or supportive, can significantly impact teachers' goal congruence in teaching. Such classroom dynamics can, in turn, shape teachers' assessments of their relationships with students and their daily emotional experiences.

Broadly, teachers encounter a spectrum of emotions, including positive (e.g., happiness), negative (e.g., anxiety), and discrete emotions (Frenzel et al., 2009; Frenzel et al., 2016). In language teaching, studies have revealed that educators experience a variety of discrete emotions related to classroom interactions, such as enjoyment, enthusiasm, warmth, affection, caring, anger, anxiety, frustration, fatigue, relaxation, and pride (Kunter et al., 2011; Oplatka & Eizenberg, 2007; Sutton, 2007; Sutton & Wheatley, 2003; Zembylas, 2005). However, there is a relative dearth of research focusing on the broader contextual factors that trigger emotions in language teachers, such as the quality of teacher-student relationships, the processes of student assessment and evaluation, and feedback received on their own teaching performance. This gap in the literature underscores the need for further investigation into the emotional landscape of language teachers within the context of their educational environments.

2.2.3 Physiological Changes and Emotional Expression

The emotional experience is intertwined with physiological responses, such as fluctuations in body temperature, heart rate, and blood pressure. Emotional expression can manifest either concurrently with or subsequent to an individual's conscious or subconscious decisions regarding the experience and expression of emotions. This decision-making process is, in reality, an integral aspect of the emotional regulation mechanism (Yin et al., 2017). Consequently, the observable emotional expressions of teachers may not always be indicative of their true emotional states, as these expressions are subject to emotional regulation. Emotion expression encompasses both verbal and nonverbal elements. The verbal aspect refers to the use of speech or language, whereas nonverbal expression involves facial expressions, body movements, and gestures, which tend to follow predictable patterns in response to emotional experiences (Keltner & Ekman, 2000).

Empirical research has delineated four predominant patterns of teacher emotional expression: natural expression, direct staging, suppression, and faking (Gong et al., 2013; Hagenauer & Volet, 2014; Hosotani & Imai-Matsumura, 2011; Jiang et al., 2016; Taxer & Frenzel, 2015). Natural expression denotes genuine and unprompted reactions to emotionally charged situations, often occurring without conscious regulation or self-awareness (Salmela, 2005). Direct staging, on the other hand, involves the deliberate portrayal of an emotion following the conscious modulation of an undesired emotion or the amplification of a desired one (Hosotani & Imai-Matsumura, 2011; Sutton & Harper, 2009). Suppression is characterized by the conscious restraint of emotional display, such as concealing an emotion or disguising a negative one with a positive facade (Gross, 1998a, 1998b). Lastly, faking entails the intentional display of an emotion that is not genuinely felt, with emotions like happiness, affection, enthusiasm, and pride being the most commonly feigned in educational settings (Taxer & Frenzel, 2015). While these insights into teacher emotional expression have predominantly been garnered from classroom observations, where teachers engage directly with students, it is crucial to extend this focus to the extracurricular emotional landscape of educators. For instance, in the realm of L2 writing instruction, much of the pedagogical work unfolds outside the classroom, encompassing activities such as curriculum development, student assessment, and providing feedback on written assignments. By exploring the emotional experiences and regulatory strategies of teachers in these contexts, we can gain a more profound understanding of the emotional lives of educators, the management of their emotions, and the implications these emotions have on their professional practice.

2.2.4 Action Tendency Emotions

The concept of "action tendencies of emotions" describes the inherent power of specific emotions to prompt particular judgments and/or behavioral reactions

(Lazarus, 1991). These action tendencies forge a connection between distinct emotional experiences and the ensuing judgments and behavioral selections, which are shaped by alterations in cognitive, physiological, and action-related responses to the triggering event (Lerner & Keltner, 2000, 2001). It is posited that emotions exert a significant influence on the processes of persuasion and behavior, attributable to their inherent action tendencies. Certain well-defined emotions are known to consistently evoke particular patterns of judgment, intention, and behavior (Lazarus, 1991; Lerner et al., 2007).

On one hand, since negative emotions are conceptualized as goal-incongruent emotions, behaviors associated with them are considered in the effort to return to a state of congruency (Lazarus, 1991). For instance, it has been found that the emotions of anger, guilt, and a moderate amount of fear can elicit problem-solving actions to neutralize the existing obstacle (Nabi, 2002) or recover the loss (Dillard & Peck, 2001; Lazarus, 1991). Similarly, the emotion of sadness is likely to elicit either problem-solving actions to recover the loss (Dillard & Peck, 2001; Nabi, 1999) or empathetic responses. Given the emotional nature of language teaching, these action tendencies also apply to language teachers and require them to regulate their emotions appropriately, return to a state of balance, and maintain their professionalism. On the other hand, positive emotions are generally conceptualized as goal-congruent emotions, it is argued that the lack of noxious states of mind and perceived imbalance reduce teachers' cognitive activity when compared with negative emotions (Dillard & Meijnders, 2002; Nabi, 1999). Empirical evidence has proven that positive emotions, in general, would generate people's prosocial behaviors. For instance, the emotion of happiness or joy is likely to generate people's trusting and sharing behaviors (Nabi, 2002). The emotion of pride is likely to generate assisting behaviors in an effort to appear humble and not overly proud (Lazarus, 1991), and the emotion of compassion is likely to generate people's assisting behaviors (Lazarus, 1991).

Negative emotions, often perceived as being at odds with one's goals, drive behaviors aimed at restoring congruency (Lazarus, 1991). Research indicates that emotions such as anger, guilt, and a moderate level of fear can prompt problem-solving behaviors designed to overcome obstacles or rectify losses (Dillard & Peck, 2001; Lazarus, 1991; Nabi, 2002). Similarly, sadness may lead to actions aimed at resolving the loss or eliciting empathetic responses. In the context of language teaching, which is inherently emotional, these action tendencies necessitate that teachers effectively manage their emotions to maintain equilibrium and uphold professional standards. Conversely, positive emotions are typically seen as aligning with one's goals. The absence of distressing mental states and a sense of balance are thought to reduce cognitive activity in teachers compared to when they experience negative emotions (Dillard & Meijnders, 2002; Nabi, 1999). Empirical studies have shown that positive emotions generally foster prosocial behaviors. For example, happiness or joy can inspire trust and sharing (Nabi, 2002), while pride may motivate behaviors aimed at appearing modest and unassuming (Lazarus, 1991). Compassion, too, is likely to encourage helping behaviors (Lazarus, 1991). These insights underscore the importance of understanding and managing both positive and negative emotions in the teaching profession to enhance the educational environment and outcomes.

While the emotions discussed exhibit distinct action tendencies, the manifestation of these behaviors in language teaching is intricate and subject to change. The emotional landscape for language teachers is multifaceted and influenced by a myriad of contextual elements. It remains uncertain to what degree factors such as individual differences between teachers and students, the nature of teacher-student relationships, the assessment and evaluation of student learning, and other course-related evaluations might impact the emotions and professional practices of language teachers. To enhance our understanding in this area, further research is warranted to address several key questions: (a) Which of these factors might trigger specific emotional experiences in language teachers? (b) What behavioral responses are likely to emerge from these discrete emotional experiences? (c) Which emotions could be most effective in motivating language teachers to enhance their teaching practices? By exploring these questions, we can gain insights into the nuanced interplay between emotions and teaching, ultimately aiming to foster an educational environment that leverages the positive aspects of teacher emotions to improve student learning outcomes.

2.3 Sociocultural Theoretical Perspective of Teacher Emotions

Since the 1980s, disciplines such as anthropology, sociology, and communications have increasingly emphasized the situated nature of emotions, positing that emotions are cultural constructs that convey sociocultural messages. This perspective is deeply rooted in the theories of Vygotsky and other social-cultural theorists (Vygotsky, 1978; Wertsch, 1985), who advocate the sociocultural approach to understanding emotions. This approach views emotions not as mere reflections of internal states but as communicative experiences. A core tenet of this perspective is that "the experience and expression of emotions are contingent upon learned norms and rules, and to the extent that cultures vary in their discussions and conceptualizations of emotions, their experience and expression will also vary across different cultures" (Cornelius, 1996, p. 188). This sociocultural lens has been applied to the study of teacher emotions, providing valuable insights into the social and emotional dynamics within the classroom and school environment (Hargreaves, 1998, 2000, 2001; Nias, 1996; van & Lasky, 2005; Zembylas, 2005). Generally, research within this framework suggests that the nature of teacher emotions and their responses are embedded within specific social contexts. Thus, teacher emotions are shaped not only by personal attributes but also by the relationships and interactions with other participants in the educational setting. In this context, both teachers and students interpret and evaluate emotions based on their accumulated knowledge and beliefs, constructing a shared understanding that is influenced by the cultural and social milieu.

Teachers' emotional labor is one of the most popular concepts constructed in line with the sociocultural perspective. The notion of emotional labor was first proposed by Hochschild (1983) as "for getting paid, the staff manages their emotions and

2.3 Sociocultural Theoretical Perspective of Teacher Emotions

performance to meet the requirements of visible facial expressions or body language that are required by the organization". She identified three features of emotional labor: (a) there is face-to-face or voice-direct dialogue; (b) it is under the supervision and control of the others; and c) to influence others' emotions for the purpose. Hochschild's notion of emotional labor was used in the research of teacher education in the 1980s, but it was not until the 2000s that teachers' emotional labor was recognized as unique to language teachers (Cowie, 2003). Benesch (2017, pp. 37–38) viewed teachers' emotional labor as efforts by which "humans actively negotiate the relationship between how they feel in particular work situations and how they are supposed to feel according to social expectations". Benesch (2017) also incorporated teacher agency into the research on teachers' emotional experience by examining how teachers "actively negotiate" their emotions according to situated feeling rules. Different from Hoschchild's (1983) emphasis on emotional labor as leading to individuals' estrangement from their authentic or true emotional selves, Benesch (2017) viewed the selves as historically and socially constituted, not merely internal states, but contingent upon external environments in which individuals are embedded and upon the social expectations they need to abide by. However, Zembylas (2005) noted that in most cases, language teachers' emotional labor comes to be treated as routine practice, as a "natural aspect of teaching". In this sense, teachers' emotional labor is not restricted to extraordinary, highly charged situations but is folded into the everyday relational dynamics of teaching, such as when teachers manage classroom discussions, respond to student essays, or contend with tardy students (Benesch, 2017).

The concept of emotional labor, particularly as it pertains to teachers, has gained significant attention within the sociocultural framework. Initially introduced by Hochschild (1983), emotional labor is defined as the process by which individuals "for getting paid, the staff manages their emotions and performance to meet the requirements of visible facial expressions or body language that are required by the organization." Hochschild outlined three key characteristics of emotional labor: (a) it involves face-to-face or voice-directed interaction; (b) it is subject to the supervision and control of others; and (c) it aims to influence the emotions of others.

This concept was initially applied to teacher education research in the 1980s, but it wasn't until the 2000s that the unique emotional labor of language teachers was widely acknowledged (Cowie, 2003). Benesch (2017, pp. 37–38) expanded on this by describing teachers' emotional labor as the efforts through which "individuals actively negotiate the gap between their actual feelings in specific work situations and the emotions they are expected to display according to societal norms." Benesch also introduced the concept of teacher agency, examining how teachers "actively negotiate" their emotions in accordance with the emotional norms of their situation. Contrasting Hochschild's (1983) focus on emotional labor as a process that leads to estrangement from one's true emotional self, Benesch (2017) posits that the self is not merely an internal state but is historically and socially constructed, contingent upon the external environment and societal expectations. Zembylas (2005), however, points out that the emotional labor of language teachers is often normalized, treated as a routine part of teaching rather than an exceptional or emotionally charged activity.

This means that teachers' emotional labor is woven into the fabric of daily teaching interactions, such as managing classroom discussions, responding to student work, or dealing with latecomers (Benesch, 2017).

The concept of teacher emotional labor, as defined, underscores the significance of "emotional display rules" mandated by educational institutions and the "emotional labor strategies" employed by teachers themselves. Winograd (2003) identified five key emotional display rules for teachers: (a) nurturing students; (b) demonstrating enthusiasm for teaching; (c) refraining from extreme emotional expressions; (d) having a passion for the teaching profession; and (e) addressing mistakes with humor. Yin and Lee (2012a, 2012b), through their examination of teachers' emotional experiences in Hong Kong primary schools, proposed four additional rules: (a) teaching with passion; (b) concealing negative emotions; (c) sustaining a positive emotional demeanor; and (d) strategically using emotions to fulfill teaching objectives. In the context of language teaching, emotional labor is often understood as the process in which teachers regulate their internal feelings and external expressions of emotions to align with the expectations and beliefs of their profession (Yin & Lee, 2012a, 2012b). Despite the demanding nature of this emotional labor, the ethical standards of the teaching profession call for teachers to manage their emotional displays and experiences in pursuit of becoming more effective and professional educators. Yin (2016) highlighted two distinctions between the emotional labor of teachers and Hochschild's (1983) original conceptualization of emotional labor. The first distinction is rooted in the ethical commitment to care inherent in teaching, which makes teachers' emotional labor inherently rewarding. The second difference pertains to the discretionary nature of teaching work, as opposed to the more prescribed emotional labor found in other professions (Oplatka & Eizenberg, 2007). This discretionary element acknowledges the autonomy teachers have in navigating their emotional labor, which can lead to a more fulfilling and authentic teaching experience.

In summary, the sociocultural perspective provides a robust framework for understanding the construction of teacher emotions, which are shaped by a complex interplay of personal and contextual factors. This perspective is particularly relevant for L2 writing teachers as they navigate the challenges and difficulties inherent in their teaching practice. Their emotional labor strategies are not only a means to manage the demands of the classroom but also a way to cope with the specific challenges presented by L2 writing instruction. To fully grasp the functions and consequences of L2 writing teacher emotions and their emotional labor strategies, a holistic approach is necessary. This approach should consider the multifaceted nature of emotions and how teachers engage with them. It is crucial to understand the mechanisms by which teachers regulate negative emotions and foster positive ones, as these strategies can significantly impact their teaching effectiveness and overall well-being. By examining the emotional labor of L2 writing teachers, we can identify the practices that contribute to a supportive and conducive learning environment, as well as those that may lead to burnout or dissatisfaction. A comprehensive perspective also allows for the development of interventions and professional development opportunities that can enhance teacher resilience, emotional intelligence, and pedagogical strategies, ultimately leading to improved teaching outcomes and teacher satisfaction.

2.4 Positive Psychological Perspective of Teacher Emotions

The integration of Positive Psychology into the study of teacher psychology and education has significantly broadened our understanding of teacher emotions, with a particular emphasis on the role of positive emotions in fostering emotional well-being. This approach shifts the focus from a narrow view on negative emotions to a more comprehensive exploration of the elements that contribute to the prosperity of individuals, communities, and societies. Positive emotions are recognized as indicators of optimal well-being, aligning with the core objectives of Positive Psychology (Seligman & Csikszentmihalyi, 2000). From this perspective, emotions are seen as multifaceted response patterns that evolve over time, encompassing cognitive, physiological, and behavioral dimensions.

Cultivating positive emotions is valuable not only for their inherent benefits but also for their role in fostering psychological growth and enhancing well-being in the long term (Frederickson, 2001). These emotions typically encourage individuals to actively engage with their surroundings and participate in various activities. To deepen our comprehension of positive emotions, Fredrickson (1998) introduced the "broaden-and-build" theory. This model posits that specific positive emotions such as joy, interest, contentment, pride, and love, though distinct in their own right, collectively serve to expand an individual's immediate thought and action possibilities. Moreover, they contribute to the development of lasting personal resources that encompass physical, intellectual, social, and psychological assets (Fredrickson, 1998, p. 219). Unlike negative emotions, which offer immediate and direct adaptive advantages in survival-threatening scenarios, the expanded thought-action repertoires induced by positive emotions confer indirect, long-term benefits. This is because they build up personal resources that can be tapped into later to cope with future challenges (Frederickson, 1998, p. 220). In essence, the "broaden-and-build" theory characterizes positive emotions by their capacity to expand cognitive and behavioral repertoires and by their function in accumulating resources that endure over time. This framework offers a novel perspective on the evolutionary significance of positive emotions, highlighting their adaptive value in promoting resilience and well-being.

The "broaden-and-build" theory posits that positive emotions are instrumental in fostering personal growth and fostering social bonds. They enrich individuals by accumulating personal and social resources, thereby enhancing their future quality of life. This theory identifies four pivotal roles of positive emotions: (1) positive emotions expand our cognitive and behavioral horizons, while negative emotions tend to constrict them (Fredrickson et al., 2000); (2) positive emotions serve as effective remedies against the residual impact of negative emotions, potentially neutralizing their adverse effects (Frederickson & Levenson, 1998); (3) by counteracting negative emotions, positive emotions can improve psychological and possibly physical health when experienced at strategic times (Tugade & Fredrickson, 2002); (4) positive emotions contribute to psychological resilience by widening attention spans, promoting adaptive thinking, and strengthening long-term coping mechanisms, thereby initiating a positive cycle towards greater emotional well-being. In essence, positive emotions are not just feel-good states; they are transformative forces that can elevate our well-being and resilience over time.

The growing focus on teacher positive emotions and well-being within the realms of teacher emotions and positive psychology can be attributed to several compelling reasons. Firstly, the well-being of teachers is an important end in itself, deserving attention and support (Holmes, 2005). Recognizing that teachers are the cornerstone of any education system, their welfare and ongoing contributions to teaching should be a top priority for educational leaders (Maslach & Leiter, 1999, p. 303). Secondly, the contemporary educational environment is marked by continuous reforms, heightened administrative demands, and rigorous evaluations of teaching performance. Teachers face escalating workloads, the challenge of managing large classes, dealing with student behavior issues, and navigating the competitive and stressful landscape of professional advancement. These factors collectively amplify the complexities of teaching and are associated with the negative emotions that teachers frequently encounter (Day & Gu, 2010; Kyriacou, 2001; Rogers, 2012). Thirdly, the existing body of literature on teacher education predominantly emphasizes the development of instructional and pedagogical skills. However, these skills often fall short in equipping teachers to emotionally manage the stress inherent in their profession. As Day and Gu (2010, p. 36) have argued, teachers' positive emotions and well-being are crucial for their capacity to positively influence student learning and life outcomes. Given the pivotal role that positive emotions play in the field of positive psychology, there is a pressing need to explore the positive emotions of L2 writing teachers. These emotions serve as catalysts for personal growth and social connection, making them essential for the success and fulfillment of educators in their professional roles.

This book delves into the nuanced understanding of L2 writing teachers' positive emotions and well-being, providing several key insights. Firstly, it contributes to a deeper comprehension of the professional lives of L2 writing teachers. By exploring the factors that are most salient to them, we can cultivate classroom and school environments that not only enhance job commitment but also mitigate the risk of teacher attrition or even departure from the profession. This is particularly important given the challenges that L2 writing teachers face. Secondly, understanding what brings the most satisfaction and reward to L2 writing teachers offers valuable perspectives on their views regarding L2 writing instruction and educational reform policies (e.g., van Veen et al., 2005). Teachers are the driving force behind educational change, and their well-being is a critical factor in the successful implementation of reforms. Insights into their emotional and psychological state can inform the development of targeted intervention programs within educational settings. Lastly, empirical research has consistently shown that teacher well-being significantly impacts students' academic performance and sociocultural development (e.g., Lars-Erik Malmberg & Hagger, 2009). In the L2 writing context, this is particularly pertinent, as L2 writing teachers play a pivotal role in shaping students' academic trajectories. Their positive emotions and overall well-being are not only beneficial for themselves but also have a profound influence on the educational experiences and outcomes of their students.

In summary, adopting the lens of positive psychology to explore the emotions of L2 writing teachers can facilitate a more balanced examination of both negative and positive emotional experiences. This balanced approach can lead to a more accurate prediction of teachers' perceived well-being, which is essential for nurturing their psychological and physical health. By understanding and supporting the full spectrum of emotions that L2 writing teachers encounter, we can create an environment that promotes their overall well-being, thereby enhancing their effectiveness and satisfaction in the classroom.

2.5 Summary

This chapter presents a comprehensive review of the theoretical underpinnings and previous research that inform the current study. The literature review has provided a robust understanding of teacher emotions, encompassing theoretical perspectives, as well as the antecedents, appraisal and regulation processes, and consequences of these emotions. These elements are crucial for the development of the conceptual model in this study. The exploration of L2 writing teachers' emotions has been enriched by examining emotional intelligence, emotional labor, regulatory strategies, and well-being. While there is a substantial body of research on teacher emotions in general education, a gap remains in the specific understanding of L2 writing teachers' emotional experiences and their emotional regulation practices. In essence, despite advancements in the broader field of teacher emotions, there is a need for a more detailed exploration of how L2 writing teachers can leverage emotional regulation strategies to enhance their well-being in the context of writing instruction. This study aims to address this gap in the literature.

References

Bandura, A. (1997). *Self-efficacy: The exercise of control*. W.H. Freeman and Company.
Berry, J. W., Poortinga, Y. H., Segall, M. H., & Dasen, P. R. (2002). *Cross-cultural psychology: Research and applications* (2nd ed.). Cambridge University Press.
Benesch, S. (2017). *Emotions and English language teaching: Exploring teachers' emotion labor*. Routledge.
Cornelius, R. R. (1996). *The science of emotion: Research and tradition in the psychology of emotion*. Prentice Hall.
Cowie, N. (2003). The emotional lives of experienced EFL teachers. In *Proceedings of JALT 2003 Conference Shizuoka Japan* (pp. 256–259). Japan Association for Language Teaching (JALT).
Day, C., & Gu, Q. (2010). *The new lives of teachers*. Routledge.
Dewaele, J., Magdalena, A., & Saito, K. (2019). The effect of perception of teacher characteristics on Spanish EFL learners' anxiety and enjoyment. *The Modern Language Journal (Boulder, Colo.)*, (2), 412–427.

Dillard, J., & Meijnders, A. (2002). *Persuasion and the structure of affect*. In J. P. Dillard, & M. P. Pfau (Eds.), *The persuasion handbook: Developments in theory and practice* (pp. 309–328). Sage Publications, Inc.

Dillard, J., & Peck, E. (2001). Persuasion and the structure of affect: Dual systems and discrete emotions as complementary models. *Human Communication Research, 27*(1), 38–68.

Fredrickson, B. L. (1998). What good are positive emotions? *Review of General Psychology, 2*, 300–319. https://doi.org/10.1037/1089-2680.2.3.300

Fredrickson, B. L. (2001). The role of positive emotions in positive psychology: The broaden and build theory of positive emotions. *American Psychologist, 56*(3), 218–226. https://doi.org/10.1037/0003-066X.56.3.218

Fredrickson, B. L., & Levenson, R. W. (1998). Positive emotions speed recovery from the cardiovascular sequelae of negative emotions. *Cognition & Emotion, 12*, 191–220.

Fredrickson, B. L., Mancuso, R. A., Branigan, C., & Tugade, M. M. (2000). The undoing effect of positive emotions. *Motivation and Emotion, 24*, 237–258.

Frenzel, A. C., Goetz, T., Stephens, E.J., & Jacob, B. (2009). Antecedents and effects of teachers' emotional experiences: An integrative perspective and empirical test. In Advances in Teacher Emotions Research: The Impact on Teachers' Lives; Schutz, P.A., Zembylas, M., Eds.; Springer: New York, NY, USA (pp. 129–148).

Frenzel, A. C., Pekrun, R., Goetz, T., Daniels, L. M., Durksen, T. L., Becker-Kurz, B., & Klassen, R. M. (2016). Measuring teachers' enjoyment, anger, and anxiety: The teacher emotions scales (TES). *Contemporary Educational Psychology, 46*, 148–163.

Gong, S., Chai, X., Duan, T., Zhong, L., & Jiao, Y. (2013). Chinese teachers' emotion regulation goals and strategies. *Psychology, 4*, 870–877.

Gross, J. J. (1998a). Antecedent- and response-focused emotion regulation: Divergent consequences for experience, expression, and physiology. *Journal of Personality and Social Psychology, 74*, 224–237.

Hagenauer, G., & Volet, S. (2014). "I don't hide my feelings, even though I try to": Insight into teacher educator emotion display. *Australian Educational Researcher, 41*(3), 261–281.

Hargreaves, A. (1998). The emotional practice of teaching. *Teaching and Teacher Education, 14*(8), 835–854.

Hargreaves, A. (2000). Mixed emotions: Teachers' perceptions of their interactions with students. *Teaching and Teacher Education, 16*(8), 811–826.

Hargreaves, A. (2001). The emotional geographies of teaching. *Teachers College Record, 103*(3), 1056–1080.

Holmes, E. (2005). *Teacher well-being: Looking after yourself and your career in the classroom*. Taylor & Francis.

Hosotani, R., & Imai-Matsumura, K. (2011). Emotional experience, expression, and regulation of high-quality Japanese elementary school teachers. *Teaching and Teacher Education, 27*(6), 1039–1048.

Jiang, J., Vauras, M., Volet, S., & Wang, Y. (2016). Teachers' emotions and emotion regulation strategies: Self-and students' perceptions. *Teaching and Teacher Education, 54*, 22–31.

Keltner, D., & Ekman, P. (2000). Facial expression of emotion. In M. Lewis, & J. Haviland-Jones (Eds.), *Handbook of Emotions* (2nd ed., pp. 236–249). New York: Guilford Publications, Inc.

Kunter, M., Frenzel, A. C., Nagy, G., Baumert, J., & Pekrun, R. (2011). Teacher enthusiasm: Dimensionality and context specificity.*Contemporary educational psychology, 36*, 289–301.

Kyriacou, C. (2001). Teacher stress: Directions for future research. *Educational Review, 53*(1), 27–35.

Lars-Erik Malmberg, L.-E., & Hagger, H. (2009). Changes in student teachers' agency beliefs during a teacher education year, and relationships with observed classroom quality, and day-to-day experiences. *British Journal of Educational Psychology, 79*, 677–769. https://doi.org/10.1348/000709909X454814

Lazarus, R. S. (1991). *Emotion and adaptation*. Oxford University Press.

Lazarus, R. S. (1999). *Stress and emotion a new synthesis*. Springer.

References

Lerner, J., & Keltner, D. (2000). Beyond valence: Toward a model of emotion-specific influences on judgement and choice. *Cognition and Emotion, 14*(4), 473–493.
Lerner, J., & Keltner, D. (2001). Fear, anger, and risk. *Journal of Personality and Social Psychology, 81*(1), 146–159.
Lerner, J., Han, S., & Keltner, D. (2007). Feelings and consumer decision making: Extending the appraisal-tendency framework. *Journal of Consumer Psychology, 17*(3), 181–187.
Lewis, M. (2005). Bridging emotion theory and neurobiology through dynamic systems modeling. *Behavior and Brain Science, 28*(2), 169–245.
Maslach, C., & Leiter, M. P. (1999). Teacher burnout: A research agenda. In R. Vandenberghe & A. M. Huberman (Eds.), Understanding and preventing teacher burnout: A sourcebook of international research and practice (pp. 295–303). Cambridge University Press.
Mesquita, B., & Ellsworth, P. C. (2001). The role of culture in appraisal. In K. R. Sherer (Ed.), *Appraisal processes in emotion: Theory, methods, research* (pp. 233–48). Oxford University Press.
Nabi, R. L. (1999). A cognitive-functional model for the effects of discrete negative emotions on information processing, attitude change, and recall. *Communication Theory, 9*, 292–320.
Nabi, R. L. (2002). The theoretical versus the lay meaning of disgust: Implications for emotion research. *Cognition & Emotion, 16*, 695–703.
Nias, J. (1996). Thinking about feeling: The emotions in teaching. *Cambridge Journal of Education, 26*(3), 293–306.
Oatley, K. (1992). Human emotions: Function and dysfunction. *Annual Review of Psychology, 43*(1), 55–85.
Oplatka, I., & Eizenberg, M. (2007). The perceived significance of the supervisor, the assistant, and parents for career development and survival of beginning kindergarten teachers. *Teaching and Teacher Education, 23*, 339–354.
Pekrun, R., & Schutz, P. (2007). Chapter 18—Where do we go from here? implications and future directions for inquiry on emotions in education. In *Emotion in education* (pp. 313–331). Elsevier Inc.
Rogers, B. (2012). *The essential guide to managing teacher stress*. Pearson.
Roseman, I. J., & Smith, C. A. (2001). Appraisal theories. In K. R. Sherer, A. Schorr, & T. Johnstone (Eds.), *Appraisal processes in emotion: Theory, method, research* (pp. 3–19). Oxford University Press.
Salmela, M. (2005). What is emotional authenticity? *Journal for the Theory of Social Behaviour, 35*, 209–230.
Seligman, M., & Csikszentmihalyi, M. (2000). Positive psychology: An introduction. *American Psychologist, 55*, 5–14.
Scherer, K. R., Schorr, A., & Johnstone, I. T. (2001). *Appraisal processes in emotion: Theory, research, application.* Oxford University Press.
Schutz, P. A., & Davis, H. A. (2000). Emotions and self-regulation during test taking. *Educational Psychologist, 35*(4), 243–256.
Schutz, P., & Pekrun, R. (2007). *Emotion in education.* Academic Press.
Sutton, R. E. (2007). Teachers' anger, frustration, and self-regulation. In P. A. Schutz & R. Pekrun (Eds.), *Emotion in education* (pp. 251–266). Academic Press.
Sutton, R. E., & Harper, E. (2009). Teachers' emotion regulation. In L. J. Saha & A. G. Dworkin (Eds.), *International handbook of research on teachers and teaching* (pp. 389–401). Springer.
Sutton, R. E., & Wheatley, K. F. (2003). Teachers' emotions and teaching: A review of the literature and directions for future research. *Educational Psychology Review, 15*(4), 327–358.
Taxer, J. L., & Frenzel, A. C. (2015). Facets of teachers' emotional lives: A quantitative investigation of teachers' genuine, faked, and hidden emotions. *Teaching and Teacher Education, 49*, 78–88.
Tugade, M. M., & Fredrickson, B L. (2002). Positive emotions and emotional intelligence. In Barrett L. Feldman & P. Salovey (Eds.). *The Wisdom of Feelings,* (pp. 319–340). New York: Guilford.
van Veen, K., & Lasky, S. (2005). Emotions as lens to explore teacher identity and change: Different theoretical approaches. *Teaching and Teacher Education, 21*, 895–898.

van Veen, K., Sleegers, P., & van de Ven, P. H. (2005). One teacher's identity, emotions, and commitment to change: A case study into the cognitive-affective processes of a secondary school teacher in the context of reforms. *Teaching and Teacher Education, 2*, 917–934.

Vygotsky, L. S. (1978). *Mind in society: The development of higher psychological processes*. Harvard University Press.

Wertsch, J. V. (1985). *Vygotsky and the social formation of mind*. Harvard University Press.

Winograd, K. (2003). The functions of teacher emotions: The good, the bad, and the ugly. *Teachers College Record, 105*(9), 1641–1673.

Yin, H. (2016). Knife-like mouth and tofu-like heart: Emotion regulation by Chinese teachers in classroom teaching. *Social Psychology of Education, 19*(1), 1–22.

Yin, H. B., & Lee, J. C. K. (2012a). Be passionate, but be rational as well: Emotional rules for Chinese teachers' work. *Teaching and Teacher Education, 28*, 56–65.

Yin, H., Han, J., & Lu, G. (2017). Chinese university teachers' goal orientations for teaching and teaching approaches: The mediation of teacher engagement. *Teaching in Higher Education, 22*(7), 766–784.

Zembylas, M. (2005). *Teaching with emotion: A postmodern enactment*. Information Age Publishing.

Suggested Readings

Gross, J. J. (1998b). The emerging field of emotion regulation: An integrative review. *Review of General Psychology, 2*, 271–299.

Gross, J. J. (2002). Emotion regulation: Affective, cognitive and social consequences. *Psychophysiology, 39*, 281–291.

Hochschild, A. R. (1983). *The managed heart: Commercialization of human feeling*. University of California Press.

Hyland, K., & Hyland, F. (2019). *Feedback in second language writing: Contexts and issues*. Cambridge University Press.

Lee, I. (2013). Becoming a writing teacher: Using "identity" as an analytic lens to understand EFL writing teachers' development. *Journal of Second Language Writing, 22*(3), 330–345.

Pekrun, R., & Linnenbrink-García, L. (Eds.). (2014). *International handbook of emotions in education*. Routledge.

Seligman, M. E. P. (2002). Positive psychology, positive prevention, and positive therapy. In C. R. Snyder & S. Lopez (Eds.), *Handbook of positive psychology* (pp. 3–13). Oxford University Press.

Yin, H., & Lee, J. C. (2012b). Be passionate, but be rational as well: Emotional-rules for Chinese teachers' work. *Teaching and Teacher Education, 28*, 56–65.

Yu, S. (2021). Feedback-giving practice for L2 writing teachers: Friend or foe? *Journal of Second Language Writing, 52*, Article 100798.

Chapter 3
Framing Teacher Emotions in the L2 Writing Classroom Context

3.1 Introduction

This chapter delves into the intricacies of teacher emotions within L2 university writing classrooms by presenting an enhanced theoretical framework. The framework is structured around three core themes that encapsulate the emotional experiences of educators in this context: (1) Emotional Antecedents: This theme delves into the precursors that shape teacher emotions, including individual traits, classroom interactions, and broader institutional influences. Gaining insight into these factors is essential for identifying the catalysts and recurring patterns that trigger emotional reactions in the teaching process. (2) Emotional Appraisal and Regulation Processes: This theme of the model scrutinizes how teachers cognitively process and interpret emotional cues, along with the coping mechanisms they use to regulate their emotional experiences. It highlights the role of emotional intelligence in effectively managing the emotional demands of teaching. (3) Emotional Consequences: The final theme focuses on the outcomes of teacher emotions, including their impact on teaching practices, student engagement, and the overall learning environment. It underscores the ripple effect of teacher emotions on educational outcomes and the importance of fostering positive emotional climates in the classroom. The chapter concludes with a set of targeted research questions that aim to guide further inquiry into the nuanced aspects of L2 writing teacher emotions, ensuring a comprehensive understanding of the emotional dimensions of teaching in a second language context.

3.2 Contextual Antecedents of L2 Writing Teacher Emotions

Contextual antecedents of L2 writing teacher emotions mainly consist of three themes: macro-contextual antecedents, meso-contextual antecedents, and micro-contextual antecedents (Fig. 3.1).

Macro-contextual Antecedents: These encompass broader social and cultural factors that can moderate the occurrence and impact of teacher emotions, as well as how teachers manage these emotions. In the realm of L2 writing, key sociocultural antecedents include the school's culture and climate (Yin, 2016), societal power dynamics or hierarchies (Matsumoto & Nakagawa, 2008), and cultural and ethical norms (Watkins, 2000). These factors create a backdrop against which teacher emotions are experienced and expressed.

Meso-contextual Antecedents: These refer to educational and school policies that directly influence teacher emotions. In the Chinese EFL (English as a Foreign Language) context, educational reforms represent a significant meso-contextual antecedent, eliciting a range of emotions among teachers (Bahia et al., 2017; Zembylas, 2011). These reforms, often implemented in a top-down manner, demand swift and innovative adoption by teachers (Hargreaves, 1998). School policies, such as course evaluation, also play a crucial role, with student evaluations potentially conflicting with expert and peer assessments, leading to negative emotions and affecting teaching practices (Wilkerson et al., 2000).

Micro-contextual Antecedents: These pertain to interpersonal relationships within the school environment, including those with students, colleagues, and school leaders. Positive relationships are known to foster positive emotions and well-being among teachers, while negative relationships can lead to anxiety, stress, and hinder collaboration and innovation (Cherkowski, 2018; Le Cornu, 2013). The quality of teacher-student interactions, particularly in activities such as providing feedback, assessing writing, and classroom engagement, can significantly impact

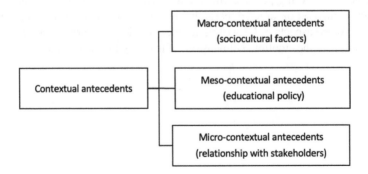

Fig. 3.1 Contextual antecedents of L2 writing teacher emotions

teacher emotions by providing internal rewards and a sense of purpose (Hargreaves, 1998; O'Connor, 2008). Similarly, teacher-colleague relationships, shaped by respect, friendship, and collegiality, also influence emotional well-being (Cowie, 2011; Schmidt et al., 2017).

In summary, teacher emotions in L2 writing classrooms are shaped by a complex interplay of macro, meso, and micro-contextual factors. Understanding these influences is crucial for fostering a supportive educational environment that promotes teacher well-being and effective teaching practices.

3.2.1 Macro-contextual Antecedents

Emotions in L2 writing teachers are indeed shaped by a complex interplay of psychological processes and sociocultural factors. As Hargreaves and Goodson (1996) articulate, teachers are not only tasked with delivering academic content but are also expected to embody the moral and social values inherent in their subject matter. This includes engaging with the curriculum and assessment practices that are deeply rooted in these values. Moreover, the collaborative culture of teaching, which involves working alongside colleagues in a supportive and cooperative environment, is another significant aspect of the profession. This collaborative spirit is essential for leveraging collective expertise to address the challenges that arise in daily educational practice. In essence, the sociocultural fabric of teaching is intricately linked to the emotional landscape of L2 writing teachers. It necessitates a keen awareness of both the emotional and cognitive aspects of teaching. Recognizing and understanding these dimensions are crucial for L2 writing teachers to effectively navigate the emotional demands of their role and to foster a conducive learning environment for their students.

On the other hand, studies suggest that cultural norms and other contextual factors could moderate the frequency and consequences of teacher emotion regulation processes (e.g., Yin, 2016). For instance, the schools in which teachers teach and the historical, social, and policy contexts that mediate these have always been important influences on their purposes and practices, their willingness, and their capacities to perform and to continue to perform to their best. Matsumoto and Nakagawa's (2008) cross-culture study found that cultures that emphasized the maintenance of social order, that is, those that were long-term oriented and valued embeddedness and hierarchy, tended to have higher scores on suppression of emotions. Reappraisal and suppression of emotions tended to be positively correlated. In contrast, cultures that minimized the maintenance of social order and valued individual affective autonomy and egalitarianism tended to have lower scores on suppression of emotions, reappraisal and suppression of emotions tended to be negatively correlated. Another important cultural value is known as power distance. Matsumoto and Nakagawa (2008) highlighted those cultures that are high on power distance or hierarchy (e.g., Asian culture) and discourage assertiveness and encourage self-regulation when interacting with people of higher status. In contrast, cultures that are low on power distance (e.g., Western culture) tend to minimize power and status differentials among individuals, encourage assertiveness, and discourage self-regulation when interacting with people of higher status.

Research indicates that cultural norms and contextual elements significantly influence the frequency and impact of teacher emotion regulation. The educational environment, including the school setting and the historical, social, and policy contexts, profoundly affects teachers' objectives, practices, and their ability to perform optimally and sustain their efforts (Yin, 2016). A cross-cultural study by Matsumoto and Nakagawa (2008) revealed that societies prioritizing social order, with a focus on long-term orientation and a respect for hierarchy, often exhibit a greater tendency towards emotional suppression. In these cultures, there is a positive correlation between the use of reappraisal and suppression strategies. Conversely, cultures that de-emphasize social order and prioritize individual emotional autonomy and equality typically score lower on emotional suppression, with a negative correlation between reappraisal and suppression. The concept of power distance is another critical cultural dimension. Cultures with high power distance, such as some Asian cultures, often discourage assertiveness and promote self-regulation, especially in interactions with those of higher status. In contrast, cultures with low power distance, like many Western societies, tend to downplay status differences, encourage assertiveness, and are less inclined to support self-regulation in interactions with authority figures. These cultural values and norms play a pivotal role in shaping the emotional regulation strategies of teachers within their professional contexts.

In addition, school climate is an influential factor on teacher emotions (Berg & Cornell, 2016; Collie et al., 2012). Berg and Cornell (2016) observed that a more supportive and structured school climate is associated with greater safety and less stress for teachers. One important factor shaping the school climate is the increasing attention paid to high-quality teaching across all educational institutions. High-quality teaching is commonly defined as teaching practices that are associated with improved student outcomes, encompassing both student attainment and harder-to-measure outcomes such as student enjoyment and well-being. In Chinese mainland, the influence of the Confucian tradition could be found in the common beliefs concerning the nature of teaching and learning held by Chinese teachers, such as "no pain, no gain", and "failure is the result of laziness" (Watkins, 2000). These cultural and ethical norms also apply to L2 writing teachers in their management of emotions. Specifically, the influence of sociocultural factors could be witnessed in the frequent teacher-student interactions in the classrooms.

In mainland China, the enduring influence of Confucianism is evident in the widely held beliefs about teaching and learning, such as the adages "no pain, no gain" and "failure is the result of laziness" (Watkins, 2000). These cultural and ethical principles extend to L2 writing teachers' emotional management, particularly in the context of teacher-student interactions within classrooms. Empirical research has demonstrated that cultural norms play a pivotal role in how emotions are managed. As Sutton and Harper (2009) noted, the prevalence and outcomes of emotion regulation can be affected by these norms. Western societies, which often value individualism and assertiveness, may foster the open expression of emotions. In contrast, Asian cultures, with their emphasis on interdependence and social harmony, might encourage the restraint of emotions to promote cooperative goals and positive social dynamics. For instance, Yin and Lee's (2012) research on Chinese teachers' emotional guidelines highlights a strong adherence to professional and ethical standards in controlling emotions. However, Ho's (2001) study suggests that despite the persistence of teacher authority, teacher-centered teaching methods, and student compliance, teacher-student interactions in Chinese classrooms are often characterized by frequent and amicable exchanges. Thus, the impact of cultural context on teachers' emotion regulation remains a subject of ongoing discussion.

3.2.2 Meso-contextual Antecedents

It is suggested that educational policies and other related policies may affect teacher emotions (Rawolle, 2013; Zembylas, 2003). In this book, meso-contextual antecedents primarily consist of, education reforms, course evaluation policies, school climate and school-level policies.

3.2.2.1 Education Reforms

Educational reforms have been identified as key contextual factors that can evoke a spectrum of emotional responses among teachers in various educational contexts (Bahia et al., 2017; Zembylas et al., 2011). Over the past twenty years, L2 education in China has seen extensive reforms, particularly at the university level. Initiatives such as the "Opinions on Deepening the Development and Reform of the Teaching Workforce in a New Era" (2018) and "China's Education Modernization 2035" have been designed to enhance university students' communicative skills, promote self-directed learning, and advocate for a student-centric educational model. In line with these goals, reforms have been introduced in the university L2 writing curriculum and instructional methods, facilitating a pedagogical transition from teacher-centric to student-centric learning. This shift emphasizes the construction of knowledge over the mere transmission of information, aligning with contemporary educational philosophies that prioritize active engagement and critical thinking in the learning process.

Current educational reforms can influence teacher emotions in several ways. Firstly, reforms often impose a standardized set of expectations for teacher performance, which can create emotional strain and challenge the professional identity of teachers who hold different educational philosophies. This one-size-fits-all approach may alienate those whose teaching styles or beliefs do not align with the mandated reforms. Secondly, the objectives of educational reforms can be overly broad, ambiguous, or ambitious, leaving teachers with the daunting task of translating abstract goals into actionable strategies within the constraints of their schools and classrooms (van & Sleegers, 1996). This disconnect between the reform's intentions and the practical realities of teaching can lead to frustration and confusion. Thirdly, teachers are frequently excluded from the early stages of reform design yet are expected to execute the changes without their input or consideration of their unique circumstances (Hargreaves et al., 2008; Van den Berg, 2002). Many reforms fail to address the individual concerns and needs of teachers, which can result in a lack of ownership and resistance to change (Hargreaves & Goodson, 1996).

In conclusion, the top-down approach of educational reforms often positions teachers as the targets of change, expecting them to embrace and effectively implement new initiatives with speed and creativity (Hargreaves, 1998; van Berg & Sleegers, 1996). However, this approach frequently overlooks the emotional responses of teachers. Teachers are expected to fully engage with and commit to the reforms, which can lead to significant emotional reactions and resistance when the reform goals conflict with their personal beliefs (Gitlin & Margonis, 1995). This dynamic may account for the disparity between the promising intentions of educational reforms and their actual implementation in specific educational settings (Fullan, 2006). For educational reforms to be successful, it is crucial that policy considerations include the emotional well-being and commitment of teachers. Neglecting these factors can lead to increased workload and potential failure in the execution of reforms. A nuanced understanding of the emotional landscape of teachers in the context of reform is essential. It provides valuable insights for teacher educators and policymakers, helping to ensure that reforms are designed and implemented in ways that are emotionally supportive and sustainable, ultimately leading to more effective educational change.

3.2.2.2 Course Evaluation Policies

Recent literature has indicated that the practice of course evaluation is widely utilized to improve the quality of teaching. Many school policies regard the course evaluation results as an important reference to evaluate teachers' teaching performance and even teachers' professional promotion. Therefore, the course evaluation policy has become an influential factor affecting teacher emotions. Four primary evaluation tools have been identified for course evaluation purposes that are in association with teacher emotions, including (1) teacher self-assessments; (2) structured observation protocols; (3) student perception surveys; and (4) career perception surveys.

Recent scholarly work has underscored the prevalence of course evaluations as a pivotal strategy for enhancing teaching quality. Numerous educational institutions use these evaluations as a critical gauge for assessing and potentially influencing teachers' professional development and promotion. Consequently, the policies surrounding course evaluations significantly impact teacher emotions. Four key assessment instruments, which are closely linked to teacher emotions, have been recognized in the course evaluation process, including (1) teacher self-Assessments: these evaluations require teachers to introspect on their instructional practices, which can foster personal growth but may also elicit self-reflective emotions. (2) Structured observation protocols: these involve systematic classroom observations that provide detailed feedback, potentially leading to both anxiety and professional insights for teachers. (3) Student perception surveys: direct feedback from students about their classroom experiences can affirm teaching methods or prompt feelings of dissatisfaction if the feedback is unfavorable. (4) Career perception surveys: these surveys assess teachers' overall job satisfaction and career outlook, influencing their emotional connection to their profession.

For L2 writing teachers, structured observations by various stakeholders, including senior staff and colleagues, play a particularly significant role in shaping their emotional responses. These high-stakes evaluations often involve assessments by teaching experts who can provide insightful commentary on the general aspects of a lesson. However, there are inherent limitations in their ability to fully comprehend and interpret the nuanced instructional decisions made by L2 writing teachers. For example, experts may lack a deep understanding of the specific content knowledge and pedagogical nuances of L2 writing courses. This knowledge gap can lead to feedback that is not only constrained by the evaluators' own teaching background but also potentially inaccurate or generic. Such feedback may fail to pinpoint the actual issues in the teaching process, leading to a misjudgment of the L2 writing teacher's performance. This situation can evoke negative emotions among L2 writing teachers, as they may feel misunderstood or undervalued. Moreover, it can create confusion and potentially lead to misguided teaching practices in the future. To mitigate these risks, it is crucial to ensure that feedback is provided by individuals who are well-versed in the complexities of L2 writing instruction and can offer tailored, constructive, and empathetic evaluations that support the teacher's growth and well-being.

In addition, the survey of student evaluation on the course is another increasingly important factor that determines the results of teacher performance and teacher emotion. Wilkerson et al. (2000) pointed out that students' own ratings of the effectiveness of their lessons are significantly more accurate in predicting student attainment on standardized tests than the ratings given by teachers or principals. In the field of L2 education, three distinct language-specific factors emerged in the measurement of effective teaching: (1) the teachers' responsiveness to the needs and interests of their students; (2) the motivation and engagement of students in language lessons; (3) the extent to which students are encouraged to adopt strategic approaches to language tasks. However, the existing literature has predominantly focused on students' measurements of teaching while largely neglecting teacher emotions that might be elicited because of the measurements. For instance, students' evaluations of the course might be inconsistent with those made by the teaching experts and collegial teachers. Such inconsistencies are likely to arouse confusion, disagreement, disappointment, and other negative emotions in teachers.

The impact of student evaluations on teacher performance and emotions is becoming increasingly recognized as a significant factor. Research by Wilkerson et al. (2000) has shown that students' own assessments of their lessons' effectiveness are more predictive of their performance on standardized tests than evaluations provided by teachers or principals. In the context of L2 education, three key language-specific factors have been identified as crucial for effective teaching: (1) teachers' responsiveness to students' needs and interests; (2) students' motivation and engagement during language lessons; (3) encouragement for students to use strategic approaches to language tasks. However, the existing body of research has primarily concentrated on student assessments of teaching effectiveness, often overlooking the emotional responses of teachers that may arise from these evaluations. Discrepancies between students' course evaluations and those of teaching experts or colleagues can lead to confusion, conflict, and feelings of disappointment among teachers. These emotional reactions underscore the importance of considering the emotional dimensions of teaching when implementing and interpreting student evaluations. It is essential to foster an environment where feedback is constructive, consistent, and supportive to minimize negative emotional outcomes and promote a positive teaching experience.

3.2.2.3 School-Level Policies

School-level policies also affect teacher emotions. School-level policies refer to the specific policies prescribed by schools that are different from the general educational policies. For example, schools usually prescribe specific policies concerning teaching effectiveness, course evaluation, teacher promotion, and a system of rewards and penalties. It has been identified that teachers' perception of what happens in school is shaped by these school-level policies. Cowie (2011) found that teachers' perceptions of the institutions that they worked for were positive when they could see improvements taking place. In contrast, teachers' emotional state was negative due to the "institutional messages" that they received being so different from their ideal. The perceived lack of trust in teachers by their administration and systems of divisive rank and hierarchy were some of the factors that contributed to the negative emotions expressed about institutions. Teachers are more likely to experience unpleasant emotions when they fail to meet the standard of school-level policies. For instance, The research conducted by Darby and colleagues in 2011 investigated the experiences of novice educators in their first year of teaching, comparing those who worked in schools with high levels of poverty to those in schools without such high poverty rates. The study revealed that new teachers in both types of schools encountered a similar frequency of negative interactions with their administrative and professional peers. However, those teaching in high poverty schools expressed more intense negative emotions regarding the pressure of high-stakes assessments. These first-year teachers often felt exhausted due to the extensive hours they dedicated to their work and were particularly upset when their relationships with students, colleagues, parents, or administrators became strained, as highlighted in studies by and Kyriacou and Kunc (2007). A lack of support was identified as a significant factor that could lead to difficulties in classroom management, which in turn could adversely affect students' outcomes on important standardized tests. This concern is a prevalent issue among educators who are just starting their teaching careers.

3.2.3 Micro-contextual Issues

The dynamics of teacher relationships with various school stakeholders, including leaders, colleagues, and students, are closely linked to teacher emotions. School leadership, in particular, plays a pivotal role in shaping the emotional climate and well-being of teachers. Leadership styles have been shown to significantly affect teacher emotions (Berkovich & Eyal, 2018; Lassila et al., 2017). School leaders are instrumental in setting standards for teacher well-being and are responsible for ensuring that teachers meet these standards and engage with school initiatives (Weiland, 2021). The quality of the relationship between school leaders and teachers can have both positive and negative implications for teacher well-being. When school leaders demonstrate a genuine concern for teacher well-being, it fosters positive relationships and enhances teacher well-being (Le Cornu, 2013). For instance, school leaders work to develop positive relationships and interactions with teachers (e.g., Cherkowski, 2018; Le Cornu, 2013), support and help teachers (e.g., Konu et al., 2010), appreciate teachers' personal commitment and investment of time (e.g., Brown & Roloff, 2011), develop an environment that promotes teachers' sense of belonging and social connectedness (Le Cornu, 2013), and show trust, respect, and caring for teachers (Cherkowski, 2018).

On the other hand, a lack of support, trust, respect, and care, along with poor communication, can negatively impact teacher well-being. School leaders may not always be fully committed or knowledgeable about how to foster positive teacher well-being. For example, school structures might promote divisiveness over inclusivity, competition over collaboration, rigid hierarchies over diverse leadership, and disrespect for students and communities. A common issue is the undervaluation of language education and L2 teachers in some university settings that prioritize science and engineering. This can lead to L2 teachers facing obstacles in developing their personal, interpersonal, and organizational skills, which may result in negative perceptions of school leadership. It is crucial for educational institutions to recognize and address these challenges to ensure a supportive environment for all teachers, including those in L2 education.

The literature found that teacher-collegial relationships affect teacher emotions (e.g., Devos et al., 2013). Cowie (2011) found that teachers' relations with colleagues are often a source of satisfaction, especially when there is emotional warmth based on friendship, respect, and collegiality. However, these relationships are viewed as negative when the teachers feel they are isolated from their colleagues or when they perceive differences in educational values. In general, positive teacher-collegial relationships enhance teacher well-being by fostering a sense of belonging and connectedness (Acton & Glasgow, 2015; Le Cornu, 2013).

Research has consistently shown that the quality of teacher-collegial relationships significantly influences teacher emotions. Studies by Devos et al. (2013) have highlighted this connection. Cowie (2011) observed that relationships with colleagues often serve as a source of professional satisfaction, particularly when they are characterized by emotional warmth, mutual respect, and a spirit of camaraderie. These positive interactions contribute to a supportive work environment that can be deeply fulfilling for teachers. Conversely, when teachers feel isolated or perceive a divergence in educational values with their colleagues, these relationships can become a source of stress and negativity. Such dynamics can undermine the sense of community and belonging that is crucial for teacher well-being. Overall, nurturing positive relationships among colleagues is essential for promoting a healthy work environment. These relationships enhance teacher well-being by creating a strong sense of belonging and connectedness, which in turn can lead to increased job satisfaction and professional growth (Acton & Glasgow, 2015; Le Cornu, 2013). It is important for schools to foster a culture that encourages collaboration, mutual support, and open communication among staff to ensure that these relationships remain a positive force in the lives of teachers. For example, the research conducted by Soini et al. (2010) investigated the factors contributing to teachers' sense of pedagogical well-being by analyzing the various scenarios that teachers perceive as either supportive and stimulating or overwhelming and stressful. The findings indicated that engaging with students in complex social and educational contexts is central to a teacher's well-being in teaching. Additionally, it was discovered that a teacher's behavior in these situations plays a crucial role in determining their level of experienced pedagogical well-being. In addition, Le Cornu's (2013) research explores the intricate and evolving interactions among personal, interpersonal, and environmental factors that contribute to the resilience of early career teachers over time. This investigation sheds light on how enduring and reciprocal relationships are instrumental in fostering the growth and resilience of novice educators. These studies highlight the importance of emotional support in teachers' personal and professional lives. In contrast, a negative school culture could damage teacher-collegial relationships, inhibit the possibility of working collaboratively, and cause anxiety and stress for teachers (e.g., Soini et al., 2010).

It is widely believed that teacher-student relationships affect teacher emotions and well-being by affording teachers internal rewards and giving meaning to their work (Hargreaves, 1998; O'Connor, 2008). It is suggested that teachers have a basic need for relatedness with their students and that they internalize interpersonal experiences with students into mental representational models (i.e., internal working model) that contain sets of beliefs and feelings regarding the self, the student, and the self-student relationship on different levels of organization. Evidence has proven that relationships with individual students, especially those involving relational conflict, influence the effects of perceptions of misbehavior on teacher well-being. On one hand, a positive teacher-student relationship contributes to the high level of personal commitment that teachers feel toward their students. Sutton and Wheatley (2003) summarized some conditions under which teachers often experience positive emotions, such as seeing students make progress, students being responsive, and spending time with students. On the other hand, the findings also suggest that experiences of high teacher-student conflict could undermine teachers' efficacy beliefs and evoke feelings of helplessness. Similarly, the percentage of teacher-student relationships in the classroom judged by the teacher has been found to be associated with teacher reports of stress and negative emotions.

3.2 Contextual Antecedents of L2 Writing Teacher Emotions

The impact of teacher-student relationships on teacher emotions and well-being is well-documented, as these relationships provide intrinsic rewards and imbue teachers' work with meaning (Hargreaves, 1998; O'Connor, 2008). Teachers have an inherent need for relatedness with their students, and they internalize their interpersonal experiences into mental models that encompass beliefs and feelings about themselves, their students, and their interactions. These internal working models operate on various levels of organization and significantly influence how teachers perceive and respond to their professional experiences.

Research has shown that the quality of relationships with individual students, particularly those marked by relational conflict, can affect teachers' well-being. For instance, positive teacher-student interactions, such as witnessing student progress, receiving student responsiveness, and engaging in meaningful interactions, can elicit positive emotions in teachers (Sutton & Wheatley, 2003). These positive relationships foster a strong sense of personal commitment and satisfaction in teaching. Conversely, high levels of teacher-student conflict can erode teachers' sense of efficacy and lead to feelings of helplessness. The proportion of teacher-student relationships that teachers perceive as challenging has also been linked to increased stress and negative emotions. In light of these findings, it is clear that fostering positive teacher-student relationships is crucial for supporting teacher well-being. Schools and educational leaders should prioritize strategies that enhance these relationships, such as professional development focused on classroom management and communication skills, as well as creating environments that encourage positive interactions between teachers and students. By doing so, educators can experience the rewarding aspects of teaching and maintain their emotional and psychological well-being.

In L2 writing classrooms, two important aspects should be highlighted in terms of teacher-student relationships. First, a great deal of teacher-student interactions and feedback on student writing is required. Therefore, the conflictual relationship with students is likely to have strong effects on teacher emotions and well-being. Second, it has been found that daily experiences of negative emotions triggered by chronic stressors (e.g., students' slow growth of writing literacy or poor engagement with writing feedback) in the L2 writing classroom are key processes in the development of teacher emotion burnout (Chang, 2009; Lazarus & Folkman, 1984). Although much research has focused on teacher stress and emotional burnout in L2 classrooms, there are limited empirical studies examining the effects of teacher-student relationships on L2 writing teacher positive emotions and well-being. The causal effects still await exploration. In short, the quality of teacher-student relationships can be one of the most rewarding aspects of the teaching profession, which contributes to L2 writing teachers positive emotions and well-being. It can also be the source of emotionally draining and discouraging experiences for L2 writing teachers. Both the positive and negative emotions have considerable implications for L2 writing teachers' performance relative to students and colleagues, and their own well-being.

In the context of L2 writing classrooms, two critical aspects of teacher-student relationships deserve special attention. First, these classrooms necessitate frequent interactions and feedback on student writing, making the quality of the teacher-student relationship particularly influential on teacher emotions and well-being.

A conflict-ridden relationship can significantly affect a teacher's emotional state. Second, ongoing stressors, such as students' slow development in writing literacy or lack of engagement with feedback, can lead to chronic negative emotions that are central to the development of teacher burnout (Chang, 2009; Lazarus & Folkman, 1984). While extensive research has addressed teacher stress and emotional burnout in L2 classrooms, there is a scarcity of empirical studies that explore the impact of teacher-student relationships on the positive emotions and well-being of L2 writing teachers. The causal relationships in this context are yet to be fully understood.

In essence, the quality of teacher-student relationships can be a double-edged sword. On one hand, it can be a source of profound satisfaction and positive emotions for L2 writing teachers, enhancing their professional experience. On the other hand, it can also lead to emotionally taxing and demotivating situations. Both positive and negative emotions have significant implications for L2 writing teachers' interactions with students and colleagues, as well as their personal well-being. It is, therefore, imperative to foster and maintain positive teacher-student relationships to support the overall emotional health and effectiveness of L2 writing teachers.

3.3 Personal Antecedents of L2 Writing Teacher Emotions

In the current study, three lines of personal antecedents of L2 writing teachers were highlighted, namely, teachers' emotional intelligence, teachers' knowledge, values, and skills, teachers' self-efficacy and professional identity, and adaptive expertise in L2 writing instruction (Fig. 3.2).

As indicated in the figure, Emotional intelligence (EI), as defined by Salovey and Mayer (1990), is a critical personal antecedent for teachers, particularly in the emotionally charged environment of L2 writing classrooms. EI encompasses the ability to appraise and express emotions, regulate emotional responses, and utilize

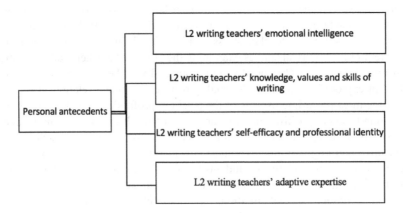

Fig. 3.2 Personal antecedents of L2 writing teacher emotions

emotions effectively to solve problems. High EI levels have been shown to enhance teachers' mental well-being and positively impact the teaching and learning process. Conversely, low EI can lead to emotional exhaustion and strained relationships within the educational community, as noted by Gallagher and Vella-Brodrick (2008) and Lopes et al. (2011).

The knowledge base of L2 writing teachers, including their understanding of writing content and pedagogical strategies, is instrumental in shaping their emotional experiences. The demanding nature of providing feedback and grading student work requires a deep understanding of writing and teaching methodologies. This process can be emotionally taxing, with teachers often facing challenges such as time constraints, stress, and the need for continuous passion and commitment, as highlighted by, Jackson and Marks (2016), Lee (2017), and others.

Self-efficacy is another key indicator of a teacher's emotional state, influencing their teaching satisfaction, commitment, and resilience to stress. Teachers with high self-efficacy are more persistent and likely to overcome obstacles, as described by Bandura (1989). Zembylas (2005) further suggests that teacher emotions and identity are interconnected, with professional identity potentially being shaped by emotional experiences. Teachers with a strong sense of identity tend to experience more positive emotions, as evidenced by Hagenauer et al. (2015). Recent studies, such as that by Lee and Yuan (2021), have demonstrated that teacher emotions play a crucial role in the development of teaching expertise. Expert L2 writing teachers' emotions contribute to their ability to teach effectively, and their expertise, in turn, is a significant personal antecedent to their emotional experiences, which are closely linked to student learning outcomes.

In summary, the emotional landscape of L2 writing teachers is multifaceted, with EI, knowledge, self-efficacy, and professional identity all playing pivotal roles in their emotional well-being and teaching effectiveness. Understanding and nurturing these aspects can lead to improved teaching practices and enhanced student learning experiences.

3.3.1 Teachers' Emotional Intelligence

Emotional intelligence (EI) is a multifaceted construct that encompasses an individual's ability to recognize, understand, and manage both their own emotions and those of others. It plays a crucial role in various aspects of personal and professional life, including interpersonal relationships, decision-making, and stress management. There are two primary types of EI: ability EI and trait EI. Ability EI, also known as cognitive-emotional EI, pertains to the cognitive abilities related to processing emotional information. This includes the skills to perceive, understand, and regulate emotions, as well as to use emotions to facilitate thinking and problem-solving. It is typically measured through performance-based tests that assess an individual's maximum potential in these areas. Trait EI, on the other hand, is a self-reported measure that reflects an individual's self-perceived abilities and dispositions related to emotions. It is considered a part of one's personality and includes traits such as self-awareness, self-control, social awareness, and relationship management. Trait EI is often assessed through self-report questionnaires and is thought to be more closely linked to personality traits and mental health outcomes. Research has shown that trait EI is more strongly associated with mental health outcomes, such as lower levels of anxiety and depression, compared to ability EI. Additionally, trait EI has been identified as a significant predictor of teacher burnout (Platsidou, 2010), suggesting that teachers with higher trait EI may be better equipped to handle the emotional demands of their profession and maintain their well-being.

Emotional intelligence (EI) is an important antecedent of teacher emotions. EI is a key factor in the educational environment, which contributes to the mental well-being of teachers and favors the teaching and learning process. The term "emotional intelligence" was initially used by Salovey and Mayer (1997), and they defined emotional intelligence as "the abilities to accurately perceive emotions, to access and generate emotions to assist thought, to understand emotions and emotional knowledge, and to reflectively regulate emotions so as to promote emotional and intellectual growth" (Salovey & Mayer, 1997, p. 10). They postulated that emotional intelligence consists of three categories of adaptive abilities: appraisal and expression of emotion, regulation of emotion, and utilization of emotion in solving problems.

Emotional intelligence (EI) plays a pivotal role as a precursor to teacher emotions and is a critical component within the educational landscape. It is instrumental in fostering the mental well-being of teachers and enhancing the overall teaching and learning experience. The concept of EI was first introduced by Salovey and Mayer (1997), who described it as "the abilities to accurately perceive emotions, to access and generate emotions to assist thought, to understand emotions and emotional knowledge, and to reflectively regulate emotions so as to promote emotional and intellectual growth" (Salovey & Mayer, 1997, p. 10). Salovey and Mayer further delineated EI into three main categories of adaptive abilities: appraisal and expression of emotion, regulation of emotion, and utilization of emotion in solving problems. EI is not only beneficial for personal growth and well-being but also for the professional development of teachers.

Recent research has increasingly focused on the importance of emotional intelligence (EI) in the daily lives of teachers, emphasizing the ability to perceive, use, understand, and regulate emotions (Bar-On & Parker, 2000; Ciarrochi et al., 2000). EI is a crucial element in the educational setting, as it supports the mental well-being of teachers and, consequently, enhances the teaching and learning process. For L2 writing teachers, developing EI is particularly beneficial as it equips them with the skills to manage their emotions effectively, leading to improved decision-making in teaching scenarios and contributing to the overall success of educational endeavors. High EI in teachers has been shown to mitigate stress and emotional exhaustion, and it correlates with increased job satisfaction and better social interactions within the educational community (Gallagher & Vella-Brodrick, 2008; Lopes et al., 2011). Molero and Ortega et al. (2019), in their review of EI and burnout syndrome in relation to teacher well-being, noted a disparity in research focus, with primary and high school teachers receiving the most attention, and university teachers, including those in L2 writing, receiving significantly less. This is noteworthy, as the emotional intelligence of L2 writing teachers is equally, if not more, vital in the field of language education.

At the university level, L2 writing teachers often face high stress and burnout, primarily due to the demanding teaching workload, which includes course preparation, providing feedback, professional development, course evaluation, and ongoing training. In this context, the ability of L2 writing teachers to recognize, understand, and regulate both their own emotions and those of their students becomes essential for achieving better emotional and personal well-being. It is imperative for educational institutions to recognize the importance of EI in teacher training and professional development, particularly for those in the demanding field of L2 writing instruction.

Another obvious limitation identified in existing studies is the excessive attention paid to the relationship between teacher EI and their negative emotions (e.g., emotional burnout, low professional commitment, and fatigue), while largely neglecting the positive aspects of teacher emotions. For instance, Platsidou (2010) pointed out that teachers with high-perceived emotional intelligence were less likely to experience emotional burnout, low levels of depersonalization, and a high sense of personal accomplishment. In this regard, it is necessary to look at L2 writing teachers' EI from the perspective of positive psychology, which enabled us to examine not only the correlation between teacher EI and negative emotions but also positive emotions, which are in close association with the flourishing of L2 writing teacher well-being.

The existing body of research on teacher emotional intelligence (EI) often focuses on its relationship with negative emotional outcomes, such as emotional burnout, depersonalization, and low professional commitment. This focus, while important, has led to a relative neglect of the positive aspects of teacher emotions and their implications for teacher well-being. Platsidou's (2010) work, for example, highlights that teachers with higher perceived EI are less prone to emotional burnout and exhibit a greater sense of personal accomplishment. To address this imbalance, it is beneficial to adopt a positive psychology lens when examining L2 writing teachers' EI. This perspective allows for a more comprehensive exploration of the interplay between EI and both negative and positive emotions. By integrating positive psychology into the study of L2 writing teachers' EI, researchers can gain insights into how EI contributes to the flourishing of these educators.

3.3.2 L2 Writing Teachers' Knowledge, Values, and Skills

Teachers' knowledge, values, and skills have been investigated as influential antecedents of their emotions (e.g., Madrid et al., 2016). In L2 writing contexts, it is found that many writing teachers are deficient in their knowledge of composition (Reichelt, 2009). For instance, many writing teachers focus on student errors and adopt a product-oriented approach to writing due to inappropriate training in giving feedback (Lee, 2008), this study delved into the mechanisms by which teachers in English as a Foreign Language (EFL) environments address their students' written work, and the motivations for their chosen methods of response. The results revealed that the feedback provided by teachers was mainly centered on correcting errors, a practice that does not align with the guidelines set forth in local educational materials. The study also uncovered through interviews that four key factors—accountability, personal and professional beliefs, the influence of exam-driven education, and inadequate training—significantly shape teachers' feedback practices. The conclusion drawn is that the manner in which teachers offer feedback is a complex interplay of various factors, including their personal convictions, values, and knowledge, all of which are influenced by broader cultural and institutional contexts, such as prevailing feedback practices and exam-oriented attitudes, as well as socio-political elements like power dynamics and teacher autonomy. In another study by Lee and Yuan (2021), they attempted to understand the notion of writing teacher expertise by using the tool of "adaptive expertise". The findings highlighted the affective dimension of expert writing teachers, namely passion and commitment as teachers of writing, which drove the teachers to put tremendous efforts in their own professional development, in helping their colleagues improve their practice, and in enhancing students' writing competence. Yu (2021) conducted a case study, which delves into the practices, knowledge sources, and challenges encountered by postgraduate students in providing genre-based peer feedback on academic writing at a research-oriented university in Macau. The findings suggest that participants found the task of offering genre-specific peer feedback to be inherently challenging. Their challenges primarily arose from a lack of detailed knowledge regarding the thesis genre, apprehensions about their own language proficiency, doubts about the efficacy and accuracy of their feedback, and concerns over the potential impact of their critiques on the emotional well-being of the writers.

Similarly, Cao (2017) noticed that most writing teachers are not well trained or provided with opportunities to be equipped with the necessary skills in teaching writing, leading to their negative emotions in their interactions with students. Furthermore, Deborah et al. (2016) emphasized the importance of teachers' writing assessment literacy (e.g., knowledge, beliefs, and practices) to the successful academic growth of students.

The TALiP framework by Xu and Brown (2016) offers a structured approach for educators to effectively conduct assessments within their teaching practices. This model becomes even more pertinent in the realm of technology-integrated learning, where a wide range of digital tools and platforms are available for educational purposes. As traditional classrooms evolve to include various forms of technology, such as video, ebooks, digital presentations, and interactive boards, the ways in which teachers can assess student learning also diversify. The concept of technology-enhanced learning environments (TELEs) extends beyond the traditional classroom, encompassing blended learning, mobile learning, and e-learning, among others. These environments provide a multitude of opportunities for integrating technology into the teaching process.

Building on this foundation, the work of Masoomeh et al. (2024) delves into the literature on teachers' assessment literacy within digital environments (TALiDE).

Their research synthesizes existing studies to identify key competencies and components that are crucial for teachers in the digital age. These elements include a robust knowledge base, cognitive skills, and an understanding of contextual factors that are essential for navigating the challenges and opportunities presented by digital assessment tools and practices.

To recap, L2 writing teachers' knowledge, values, and skills are important personal antecedents that are in close association with their emotions.

3.3.3 L2 Writing Teachers' Self-efficacy and Professional Identity

Teachers' self-efficacy is a critical precursor to their emotional well-being, influencing their ability to navigate the challenges of the teaching profession. Self-efficacy is defined as the belief in one's capacity to make a positive impact on students' lives (Darling-Hammond, 1990: 9). It serves as a strong predictor of psychological well-being, characterized by increased job satisfaction, commitment, and reduced stress and burnout (Aloe et al., 2014; Bandura, 1997; Collie et al., 2012). As Bandura (1989, p. 176) noted, a robust sense of personal efficacy is essential for sustaining the perseverance and effort required for success. Teachers with high self-efficacy are more likely to persevere through obstacles, enhancing their resilience and fostering innovative teaching practices that contribute to student learning (Goddard et al., 2004, p. 3). While self-efficacy has been extensively studied in relation to emotions, most research has focused on emotions as a consequence rather than as an antecedent. However, Locke and Latham's goal-setting theory (1990) suggests that positive emotions can inspire teachers to set more challenging goals for both their students' learning and their own teaching practices. In essence, self-efficacy is instrumental in maintaining teachers' dedication to improving the quality of their work and in fostering their resilience over time.

Understanding and enhancing teachers' self-efficacy is, therefore, a key strategy for promoting their emotional well-being and professional success. Educational leaders and policymakers should consider interventions that build and reinforce self-efficacy, such as professional development opportunities, supportive feedback, and recognition of teachers' accomplishments. By doing so, they can help create an environment where teachers are equipped to face challenges with confidence and optimism, ultimately benefiting both their own well-being and the educational outcomes of their students.

On the other hand, teacher beliefs about their professional identity serve as an antecedent to their emotions. As Zembylas (2005) argued, teacher emotion and identity are intertwined, and teacher identity could be reshaped and developed through discourses and practices of emotion. Teachers with a strong sense of professional identity are more likely to experience positive emotions (Hagenauer et al., 2015). In the L2 writing context, however, research has indicated that L2 writing teachers have a thin sense of professional identity as writing teachers (Lee & Yuan, 2021). For instance, it is reported that writing teachers primarily serve as "error hunters" or "composition slaves". They give written corrective feedback in a reflexive, mechanical, and unthinking manner (Hyland, 2009), and they prefer to view themselves as general language teachers rather than writing teachers. Given the potential of identity as an analytic tool to understand teachers' development and given the relative lack of knowledge of teachers' professional development in the field of L2 writing, particularly EFL writing, Lee (2013) investigated the identity development of four secondary teachers of English in Hong Kong as they learnt to teach writing. Using interview and classroom research report data, the findings show that teachers' identities are discursively constructed (i.e., identity-in-discourse) and reflected in the ways they talk about their work (i.e., narrated identity-in-practice). The teachers in the study developed enthusiasm and commitment to teaching writing after the WTE course and took up specific discourses about writing and writing instruction that empowered them to see their roles as writing teachers in a different light—e.g., changing from a language teacher to a writing teacher, placing a stronger emphasis on the student role in writing, and implementing new pedagogical tasks in the writing classroom. As they saw themselves taking on certain roles in the writing classroom, they acquired new language to talk about themselves and their work, constructing new identities as teachers of writing. To recap, both L2 writing teachers' self-efficacy and professional identity are malleable antecedents that are situated in relation to their emotions.

3.3.4 L2 Writing Teachers' Adaptive Expertise in L2 Writing Instruction

In L2 teacher education research and L2 writing research, it has been suggested that pivotal to L2 writing teachers' development is their expertise in teaching. Hirvela (2019) included the affective dimension of teaching in his definition of L2 writing teacher expertise as "the instructional beliefs, knowledge, and skills that may be considered essential at a certain level of proficiency in order for teachers to guide students towards the acquisition of beneficial L2 writing ability".

Since the 1980s, the study of second language writing (SLW) has emerged as a distinct academic field, leading to significant insights into the writing processes of second language learners. Despite these advancements, there has been a lack of attention given to the educators of SLW, specifically their experiences with the concept of teacher agency. In the 2018 research by Christiansen, Du, Fang, and Hirvela, they examine the experiences of three international graduate teaching assistants. They explore how these educators' sense of agency is shaped within the context of a small professional learning community and their journey towards becoming proficient SLW instructors. The results highlight the importance of linking teacher agency with the development of expertise, with a particular emphasis on the role of adaptive expertise in enhancing this understanding. Lee and Yuan (2021) also highlight the role of teacher emotions in their conceptualization of L2 writing teacher expertise, i.e., passions as teachers of writing and as writers. It should be noticed that affect is found to play an important role in contribute to the expert teaching of writing. Indeed, it is teachers' passion, enthusiasm, and commitment that prompted them to reflect, adapt, change, and contributing to their adaptive expertise. In the research, the authors considered their participants to be expert educators. They articulated their study's aim as exploring the "what" regarding the evidence of writing teacher expertise and the "why," which refers to the elements that have shaped this expertise (p. 3). This method, which could be termed a deductive approach, allowed them to concentrate on the characteristics of expertise in detail, rather than attempting to define who qualifies as an expert.

On the other hand, the study by Tardy et al. (2022), also mentioned earlier, involved the research team scrutinizing the instructional experiences of the participants. Over time, they were able to identify these individuals as "emerging experts" after gathering and analyzing evidence. This process illuminated potential categories of expertise. The approach they used could be described as inductive, aiming to discover and then categorize different types of expertise and the individuals who possess them. In this regard, writing teacher expertise, as an important personal antecedent to teacher emotions, is in close association with student learning. In other words, L2 writing teachers' "adaptive expertise" could determine their commitment to helping students develop interest, motivation, and confidence in writing and to empowering them to be assessment-capable through peer and self-review.

3.4 L2 Writing Teachers' Emotional Labor and Emotional Labor Strategies

The capacity of teachers to regulate their emotions is essential for effective teaching practices. Those skilled in emotional regulation are adept at resolving conflicts and fostering positive relationships with students, colleagues, and other educational stakeholders, thereby promoting a collaborative and empathetic learning environment (Jennings & Greenberg, 2009). Central to this ability are the concepts of emotional labor and emotional regulation strategies. Emotional labor involves the conscious effort to modulate emotional expressions to align with professional demands, while emotional regulation strategies encompass the techniques used to manage and respond to emotional experiences. Both are critical for teachers to maintain a constructive classroom atmosphere and enhance their overall teaching effectiveness.

3.4.1 Teachers' Emotional Labor

The concept of emotional labor, initially introduced by Hochschild (1983), has been further elaborated by Benesch (2017, pp. 37–38), who describes it as the active negotiation by individuals of their felt emotions in relation to the emotions deemed appropriate by societal norms within specific work contexts. In the domain of language teaching, this emotional labor is characterized by the conscious management of teachers' emotional responses, including the suppression, elicitation, and expression of emotions, in alignment with the expectations set by broader cultural and educational contexts (Yin & Lee, 2012). While language teaching demands significant emotional labor, the ethical standards of the teaching profession encourage teachers to exert control over their emotional expressions and experiences to aspire to higher levels of professionalism. This implies that teachers are expected to adhere to emotional display rules that are dictated by both the overarching societal norms and the immediate educational settings in which they work. The ability to navigate these expectations is crucial for teachers to maintain a professional demeanor and foster a conducive learning environment for their students.

In the context of L2 writing classrooms, the emotional labor of teachers is often perceived as an integral and routine part of their professional responsibilities, rather than an exception or response to particularly charged situations. This emotional labor is woven into the fabric of daily teaching activities, encompassing tasks such as course preparation, classroom management, providing feedback on student essays, and achieving teaching goals (Benesch, 2017). The discretionary and intrinsically rewarding nature of this emotional labor underscores the importance of understanding how L2 writing teachers manage their emotions within the classroom setting. Given that emotional labor is a constant and expected part of the teaching role, it becomes essential to explore the strategies and mechanisms that L2 writing teachers employ to regulate their emotions. This inquiry can provide insights into the emotional demands of the profession and inform practices that support teacher well-being and effectiveness. By examining the emotional labor of L2 writing teachers, we can better appreciate the nuanced interplay between emotional regulation and the daily practices of teaching, ultimately aiming to enhance the educational experience for both teachers and students.

3.4.2 Teachers' Emotional Labor Strategies

Emotional labor strategies refer to the ability and process of using strategies to manage and regulate the expression of emotions and the experiences of emotional labor (Gross, 2002; Yin, 2016). Teachers' emotional labor strategies have been found to impact teacher emotions (e.g., Lee & van Vlack, 2018; Wang et al., 2019) and well-being (e.g., Yin, 2015, Yin et al., 2017). Given the complex and dynamic nature of teacher emotions, it is important for teachers to regulate their emotions because

3.4 L2 Writing Teachers' Emotional Labor and Emotional Labor Strategies

inappropriate emotional labor strategies might lead to teachers' emotional burnout and exhaustion (Carson & Templin, 2007), ineffectiveness in classroom management (Olivier & Venter, 2003), and teacher attrition (Macdonald, 1999). In general, two approaches have been identified to operate emotion regulation strategies.

Emotional labor strategies are the methods and processes by which individuals manage and regulate the expression and experience of their emotions, particularly in the context of their professional roles (Gross, 2002; Yin, 2016). For teachers, these strategies are crucial as they can significantly influence their emotional well-being and job satisfaction (Lee & van Vlack, 2018; Wang et al., 2019). Given the intricate and ever-changing nature of teacher emotions, effective emotional regulation is essential. Inappropriate or inadequate emotional labor strategies can lead to negative outcomes such as emotional burnout, exhaustion (Carson & Templin, 2007), ineffective classroom management (Olivier & Venter, 2003), and even teacher attrition (Macdonald, 1999). Two primary approaches have been identified for managing emotional labor strategies.

The first approach was proposed by Hochschild (1983), who initially identified two primary regulation strategies: surface acting and deep acting. Surface acting strategies are displayed by either faking unfelt emotions or hiding felt emotions when teachers' emotions are different from those required by the organization. Deep acting strategies are displayed by teachers' constantly adjusting feelings through cognitive techniques such as distraction or self-persuasion (Yin, 2016). Ashforth and Humphrey (1993) further added the expression of genuine emotion as the third strategy of emotional regulation, which indicates that teachers' internal feelings of emotions and the organizational requirements for the performance of emotions are consistent, teachers reflect their emotions as they feel.

The second approach was proposed by Gross (1998), who put forward two types of emotional labor strategies employed by teachers: antecedent-focused and response-focused strategies. Teachers use antecedent-focused strategies before the initiation of the emotional arousal stages through cognitive change, situation selection, situation manipulation, and attention deployment. On the other hand, response-focused strategies refer to behavioral and physiological responses and emotional expression, which are activated after the initiation of the emotional arousal stages. Gross and John (2003) emphasized that the distinction between antecedent-focused and response-focused strategies is central to the theory of emotion regulation. In this regard, they proposed two specific strategies: cognitive reappraisal and expressive suppression. Specifically, cognitive reappraisal is an antecedent-focused strategy (Lazarus & Folkman, 1984). It occurs early and intervenes before the emotion response tendencies have been fully generated, which means reappraisal can efficiently alter the entire subsequent emotion trajectory. For instance, teachers could successfully reduce the experiential and behavioral components of negative emotions by using reappraisal strategies. In contrast, expressive suppression is a response-focused strategy (Gross, 1998) that comes relatively late in the emotion-generative process and primarily modifies the behavioral aspect of the emotion response tendencies. According to Gross and John (2003), suppression is effective in reducing the behavioral expression of both negative and positive emotions. John and Gross (2007) demonstrated that individuals high in reappraisal and low in suppression experienced more positive and less negative emotions, shared emotions more with others, were more well-liked, had better social support, had lower scores on depression, and higher scores on happiness, life satisfaction, self-esteem, optimism, and well-being. Essentially, reappraisal has been associated with positive outcomes, whereas suppression has been associated with negative outcomes (John & Gross, 2004).

Given the close interconnection between teachers' emotional labor and regulation strategies, Grandey (2000) argued that emotional labor can be conceptualized as emotion regulation, in that the two regulation strategies of surface and deep acting (Hochschild, 1983) have well corresponded with Gross' (1998) classification of antecedent-focused emotion regulation and response-focused emotion regulation. The former occurs before emotions are generated, while the latter occurs after response tendencies are triggered. Specifically, antecedent-focused emotion consists of (a) situation selection, which refers to approaching or avoiding certain people or situations to modify their emotional impact; (b) situation modification, which refers to directly changing a situation to regulate emotions; (c) attention deployment, where individuals focus attention on or move attention away from a situation to change the influence of the situation on individuals' emotions; and (d) cognitive change, which refers to modifying one's evaluations of a situation or one's ability to manipulate a situation in order to alter its emotional impact.

To understand language teachers' emotional labor and regulation strategies, one strand of research developed teachers' emotional labor scales with satisfying reliability and validity (Liu, 2009); another strand of research explored teachers' emotional labor in association with discrete teaching contexts (Basim et al., 2013). A review of the research results indicates that teachers generally prefer to use the strategy of expression of naturally felt emotions but are inconsistent in the use of surface and deep acting strategies. As a result, it is argued that specific characteristics of the teaching and contextual factors should be taken into consideration in future research of teachers' emotional labor strategies. Furthermore, the different combinations of teachers' emotional labor strategies would exert different influences on teachers' emotional well-being, and teachers' individual differences would make the issue even more complicated. Sutton and Harper (2009) suggested that the frequency and consequences of teacher emotional labor strategies are also moderated by cultural norms. For instance, Yin (2016) argued that the social values of independence and self-assertion held in western culture encourage the open expression of emotions, while the social values of interdependence and relationship harmony in Chinese culture are likely to cause the suppression of emotion and facilitate prosocial goals and positive social interactions. In specific, Yin and Lee (2012) claimed that Chinese teachers attach much importance to following professional and ethical norms in managing their emotions. In addition, Ho (2001) and Watkins (2000) also highlighted the influence of Confucius' values on the nature of teaching and Chinese teachers. For instance, teachers are normally compared to "silkworm or candles, which produce silk or light others until the end of life". These cultural elements, together with teacher-student relationships, pedagogical practices, and other sociocultural factors in association with teaching, determine the landscape and characteristics of Chinese L2 teachers' emotional labor and emotional labor strategies and deserve more in-depth investigation.

However, existing studies primarily focused on L2 teachers at pre-school (Yin, 2016; Zhang et al., 2020) and high school levels. Whereas little is known of L2 writing teachers in university educational institutions concerning their emotional labor and emotional labor strategies, this issue becomes particularly important given the difficulty of L2 writing teaching and the increasing accountability placed on L2 writing teachers' professional learning and teaching. Secondly, informed by the study of Bielak and Mystkowska (2022), although emotional labor strategy research has been widely conducted in the general education context, there has been little attention given to L2 writing education. Thirdly, Bielak and Mystkowska (2022) also noted a scantiness in the existing literature that has mainly focused on how individual teachers deal with negative emotions such as stress, frustration, anxiety, and burnout in the language education context (e.g., Dewaele et al., 2018), while neglecting the positive emotions such as effective interpersonal relationships, joy, and happiness. In fact, positive emotions play key roles in the L2 teachers' experience. In this regard, the regulation of both positive and negative emotions is equally important in the L2 education context, where teacher emotions contribute a lot to the quality of teacher-student relationship and communication, teaching effectiveness, and student learning achievement. More research is needed to understand the broad picture of L2 writing teachers' emotional labor, and the diversified characteristics of emotional labor strategies.

3.4.3 Mediated Effect of Teachers' Emotional Labor Strategies on Their Well-Being in L2 Writing

Teachers' emotional labor strategies reflect their awareness of the emotional demands of their profession and their efforts to regulate their emotions in the teaching context. This understanding and management of emotions are integral to their professional role and can significantly influence their overall sense of well-being.

Studies have found that surface acting is negatively related to teachers' psychological well-being, including greater occupational stress (e.g., Karim & Weisz, 2011) and lower job satisfaction (e.g., Zhang & Zhu, 2008). In addition, surface acting is found to correspond with greater emotional burnout (e.g., Akin et al., 2014; Basim et al., 2013; Yao et al., 2015) and lower perceived personal accomplishment (Yilmaz et al., 2015). Furthermore, Mahoney et al. (2011) and Taxer and Frenzel (2015) found that teachers who tended to fake positive or negative emotions or hide negative emotions reported greater emotional exhaustion. With respect to deep acting, existing findings are mixed. On one hand, studies consistently show that teachers' higher levels of deep acting are associated with greater job satisfaction (e.g., Yin,

2015; Zhang & Zhu, 2008), lower emotional burnout, and depersonalization (e.g., Akin et al., 2014; Basim et al., 2013; Zhang & Zhu, 2008). On the other hand, Wrobel (2013) found that deep acting resulted in greater emotional exhaustion. Other studies (e.g., Karim & Weisz, 2011; Noor & Zainuddin, 2011) showed nonsignificant relationships between deep acting and teachers' psychological well-being. In terms of the expression of naturally felt emotions, teachers who tend to genuinely express their emotions also report experiencing a lower level of stress and a higher level of job satisfaction (Cheung & Lun, 2015; Yin, 2015; Yin et al., 2013) and lower emotional burnout (e.g., Akin et al., 2014; Cheung & Lun, 2015; Yilmaz et al., 2015).

Research on emotional labor strategies among teachers has revealed distinct impacts on their psychological well-being. Surface acting, which involves simulating emotions that are not genuinely felt or concealing actual emotions to align with job expectations, has been linked to several negative outcomes. Studies indicate that surface acting is associated with increased occupational stress (Karim & Weisz, 2011), reduced job satisfaction (Zhang & Zhu, 2008), higher levels of emotional burnout (Akin et al., 2014; Basim et al., 2013; Yao et al., 2015), and a lower sense of personal accomplishment (Yilmaz et al., 2015). Additionally, teachers who frequently engage in surface acting may experience greater emotional exhaustion (Mahoney et al., 2011; Taxer & Frenzel, 2015). In contrast, deep acting, which involves cognitively adjusting one's internal emotional state to match the required emotional display, has yielded more varied results. On the positive side, higher levels of deep acting have been consistently linked to increased job satisfaction (Yin, 2015; Zhang & Zhu, 2008), lower emotional burnout, and reduced depersonalization (Akin et al., 2014; Basim et al., 2013; Zhang & Zhu, 2008). However, some research, such as that by Wrobel (2013), suggests that deep acting can also lead to greater emotional exhaustion. Other studies have found no significant relationship between deep acting and psychological well-being (Karim & Weisz, 2011; Noor & Zainuddin, 2011). Regarding the expression of naturally felt emotions, teachers who are able to genuinely express their emotions report lower stress levels and higher job satisfaction (Cheung & Lun, 2015; Yin, 2015; Yin et al., 2013), as well as lower emotional burnout (Akin et al., 2014; Cheung & Lun, 2015; Yilmaz et al., 2015). These findings underscore the importance of emotional authenticity in maintaining teacher well-being and suggest that allowing teachers to express their true emotions can contribute positively to their professional lives.

In specific, the study by Cheung and Lun (2015) utilized latent profile transition analysis (LPTA) and explored whether emotional labor patterns evolved over time and their impact on occupational well-being, including job satisfaction, work-life quality, psychological strain, and work-family balance. The LPTA findings depicted complex behavioral patterns over the study period and established correlations between these patterns and various well-being outcomes. It was found that employees who frequently engaged in both deep acting (modifying internal feelings) and surface acting (altering external expressions), known as display rule compliers, experienced the poorest occupational well-being among the identified groups. This suggests that the common recommendation to use deep acting as a strategy for enhancing work well-being may be too simplistic. The study implies that authentic expression of emotions might be crucial for better well-being, as those who practiced deep acting along with genuine emotion expression reported the most favorable outcomes. In another study by Yin (2015), it delves into the emotional facets of the teaching profession, particularly among Chinese teachers. By employing hierarchical regression, the study analyzes the interplay between emotional job requirements, emotional intelligence, the strategies used for emotional labor, and the overall satisfaction with teaching. It highlights the significant influence of teachers' perceptions of emotional demands and their emotional intelligence on the strategies they employ for emotional labor. The study also identifies emotional intelligence as a key factor that moderates the effects of emotional job demands on surface acting and the expression of authentic emotions, although it does not significantly moderate deep acting. The findings indicate that even when considering emotional job demands and emotional intelligence, teachers who engage in deep acting and express their genuine emotions tend to report higher levels of job satisfaction. This suggests that these emotional labor strategies are particularly beneficial for teachers. Consequently, the study suggests the implementation of teacher development programs aimed at enhancing educators' awareness of emotional demands, providing insights into various emotional labor strategies, and fostering the development of emotional intelligence.

Teachers have to manage their feelings in order to sustain a positive classroom climate. In the study by Akin et al. (2014), it focused on the emotional labor strategies employed by Turkish primary school teachers and the relationship between emotional labor and burnout. It found that these teachers commonly express genuine emotions towards their students. Female teachers were more likely to use both deep and surface acting strategies compared to their male counterparts. Additionally, teachers in private schools were observed to engage more in deep acting and expressing genuine emotions than those in public schools. The research concluded that emotional labor significantly predicts burnout among Turkish primary school teachers. The research conducted by Yilmaz et al. (2015) aimed to elucidate the relationship between the emotional labor strategies utilized by teachers and the severity of their burnout. The findings indicated that surface acting is the least commonly employed emotional labor strategy among teachers, with deep acting and the expression of genuine emotions being more frequently used. Burnout symptoms were predominantly characterized by emotional exhaustion, followed by a sense of reduced personal accomplishment and depersonalization. Regression analysis suggested that both surface acting and the expression of genuine emotions are significant predictors of emotional exhaustion and depersonalization in teachers. However, deep acting did not exert a substantial influence on these burnout dimensions. The study concludes that emotional labor is a crucial component of a teacher's professional responsibilities. Furthermore, teachers' natural expression of positive emotions is found to correspond with higher job satisfaction and lower exhaustion, while the expression of negative emotions is linked to poor job satisfaction and burnout (Taxer & Frenzel, 2015).

However, there are two apparent limitations concerning the existing findings. First, these studies have viewed teachers' positive and negative emotions as two extremely opposite emotional valences in relation to teacher well-being. In the authentic teaching context, teachers are experiencing dynamic and complex emotions that have sophisticated correlations with their well-being. On the other hand, existing studies have primarily focused on teachers in the general educational context while downplaying the characteristics and requirements of the specific subject and pedagogical knowledge of teachers. In this regard, one can expect different findings concerning L2 writing teachers' emotional labor and its correlation with their well-being.

The existing research on teachers' emotional labor and well-being has certain limitations that warrant attention. Firstly, the studies often treat positive and negative emotions as binary opposites, failing to capture the nuanced interplay between these emotional states and their impact on teacher well-being. In reality, teachers experience a spectrum of emotions that are dynamically interrelated and can have complex effects on their overall well-being. The authentic teaching context involves a rich tapestry of emotional experiences that may not be fully understood through a simple dichotomy. Secondly, much of the research has concentrated on teachers in general educational settings, overlooking the unique characteristics and pedagogical demands of specific subjects, such as L2 (second language) writing. L2 writing teachers, in particular, face distinct challenges and emotional demands that are shaped by the nature of language learning and writing instruction. Their emotional labor strategies and the resulting well-being outcomes may differ significantly from those of teachers in other subject areas.

Given these limitations, there is a need for more nuanced research that explores the intricate relationship between emotional labor and well-being in the context of L2 writing instruction. Such research should consider the specific emotional demands of teaching writing in a second language, the pedagogical knowledge required, and the unique classroom dynamics involved. By doing so, we can gain a deeper understanding of how L2 writing teachers can effectively manage their emotions to enhance their professional well-being and teaching efficacy.

3.4.4 Mediated Effects of Emotional Labor Strategies on Teaching Behaviors in L2 Writing

Existing studies have proved that teacher emotions have important effects on their teaching behaviors, specifically in terms of the quality of relationships they build with their students and their instructional behaviors (e.g., Chen, 2019; Pianta & Hamre, 2009; Praetorius et al., 2018). In general, teacher positive emotions are related to student-focused approaches to teaching. On the contrary, negative emotions are often related to teacher-focused approaches to teaching. Such relationships have been found both for primary (e.g., Chen, 2019) and higher education teachers (e.g., Trigwell, 2012). In addition, such relationships have also been found among various subjects such as mathematics (e.g., Russo et al., 2020), claiming that mathematics teachers who experienced enjoyment during teaching tend to sustain their positive attitudes when students struggled and spend more time teaching. Moreover, Frenzel et al. (2016) also found that German secondary school mathematics teachers' reported enjoyment was positively related to student-reported clarity and variety of instruction and negatively related to student-reported fast-paced instruction. In contrast, teacher-reported anger was positively related to class-reported fast-paced instruction and negatively related to variety in instruction; teacher anxiety was negatively related to the acceptance of errors. Overall, there is consistent evidence that teachers' positive emotions in teaching tend to be positively related to effective instructional strategies, while teachers' negative emotions are negatively related to unfavorable instructional strategies.

Research has consistently demonstrated that teacher emotions significantly influence teaching behaviors, particularly in the quality of teacher-student relationships and instructional practices (Chen, 2019; Pianta & Hamre, 2009; Praetorius et al., 2018). Positive emotions among teachers are generally associated with student-centered teaching approaches, which foster a supportive and engaging learning environment. Conversely, negative emotions often correlate with teacher-centered approaches, which may not be as conducive to student learning (Frenzel et al., 2021). These findings hold true across various educational levels, including primary education (Chen, 2019) and higher education (Trigwell, 2012), as well as different subject areas. For instance, mathematics teachers who experience enjoyment during teaching are more likely to maintain positive attitudes when students encounter difficulties and are more inclined to invest time in instruction (Russo et al., 2020). Frenzel's (2016) study on German secondary school mathematics teachers revealed that reported enjoyment was linked to clear and varied instruction, while teacher-reported anger was associated with fast-paced instruction and less variety. Additionally, teacher anxiety was found to be negatively correlated with the acceptance of errors. In summary, there is a robust body of evidence indicating that teachers' positive emotions contribute to effective instructional strategies, enhancing the learning experience for students. In contrast, negative emotions can lead to less favorable teaching methods. This underscores the importance of supporting teachers in managing their emotions to promote positive teaching practices and, ultimately, improve student outcomes.

In the L2 writing context, the psychological mechanisms that underpin the relationship between teacher emotions and teaching performance have not been extensively explored. If these relationships do indeed exist, further research is needed to uncover the potential non-linear associations between the emotions of L2 writing teachers and their instructional effectiveness. For instance, L2 writing teachers who experience positive emotions may be more inclined to adopt process-based approaches that emphasize students' knowledge construction and support their conceptual development. This involves a focus on the learning process itself, encouraging students to engage in critical thinking, problem-solving, and self-reflection as they write. On the other hand, teachers experiencing negative emotions might lean towards content-focused, genre-based L2 writing approaches, where the emphasis is on the technical aspects of writing, such as content, structure, organization, and presentation. While these approaches are also important, they may not foster the same level of engagement or conceptual understanding as process-based methods.

Understanding the emotional landscape of L2 writing teachers and how it influences their choice of teaching strategies is crucial. By examining these potential curvilinear links, researchers can provide insights into how emotions impact teaching practices and student outcomes. This knowledge can inform teacher training programs and professional development initiatives, helping L2 writing teachers to develop emotional awareness and regulation skills that enhance their teaching effectiveness and support student success in writing.

3.5 Consequences of L2 Writing Teacher Emotions

Teacher emotions indeed have a profound impact on various dimensions of a teacher's life, influencing both personal well-being and professional efficacy. Research by Berkovich and Eyal (2018) and others has shown that emotions can affect teachers' professional beliefs, motivation, engagement, and overall well-being (Burić et al., 2019; Seligman, 2002, 2011). Chen's (2020) review of the Teacher Emotion Model further delineates these effects, highlighting the significant role of emotions in shaping teachers' professional identities and their effectiveness in the classroom. In the context of L2 writing, the study of teacher emotions becomes particularly crucial. L2 writing teachers' emotions can significantly influence their perceived well-being, their interactions with students, and their teaching practices. The emotional demands of teaching writing in a second language are unique and can lead to specific emotional responses and coping strategies.

3.5.1 Consequences of L2 Writing Teacher Emotions on Their Well-Being

Well-being is a complex and multifaceted concept that encompasses various dimensions of an individual's life. It is commonly examined in two main forms: subjective well-being and psychological well-being. Subjective well-being, as described by Diener (2009), is composed of three interconnected elements: life satisfaction, positive affect (pleasant emotions), and negative affect (unpleasant emotions). This form of well-being focuses on an individual's cognitive evaluations of their life and the emotions they experience. Psychological well-being, on the other hand, pertains to an individual's assessment of their mental and physical health, life satisfaction, work, and overall happiness. It is a broader concept that includes not only emotional states but also personal growth, self-acceptance, and the ability to cope with life's challenges. Chen's (2020) review of the Teacher Emotion Model highlights the impact of teacher emotions on three key aspects of well-being: emotional burnout, teaching satisfaction, and personal life. These aspects align with Seligman's (2002, 2011) framework of well-being within the context of positive psychology, which emphasizes the importance of positive emotions, engagement, relationships, meaning, and accomplishment in achieving a fulfilling life.

Emotional burnout is a prevalent and concerning consequence of teacher emotions, with a direct correlation to the emotional experiences of educators. Burnout is typically described as a state of chronic emotional, mental, and physical exhaustion, often accompanied by feelings of cynicism and a diminished sense of personal accomplishment. This syndrome can lead to a range of adverse effects, including stress-related health issues (Hebson et al., 2007; Moore et al., 2011), increased teacher turnover (Borman & Dowling, 2008), and a decline in professional efficacy characterized by irritability, negativity, and a weakened sense of identity. Beyond the impact on teachers themselves, emotional burnout can have significant repercussions on students' educational experiences. Arens and Morin (2016) found that teachers' emotional burnout was negatively associated with students' academic performance, as measured by class averages in school grades and standardized test scores, as well as students' overall satisfaction with school and their perceptions of teacher support.

In the context of L2 writing instruction, the risk of emotional burnout may be heightened due to the unique demands of the subject. L2 writing teachers are often required to possess a deep understanding of both the content and pedagogical aspects of L2 writing. They must conduct assessments, provide detailed feedback in both written and oral forms, and support students throughout the complex writing process. These responsibilities can be particularly draining and may contribute to increased levels of emotional burnout among L2 writing teachers. Given the potential for emotional burnout to affect both teacher well-being and student outcomes, it is imperative to investigate the factors that contribute to this phenomenon in the L2 writing context. Understanding these factors can help in developing targeted interventions and support systems to mitigate the risk of burnout and enhance the overall educational environment.

Despite the potential for emotional burnout in teaching, many educators maintain a high level of engagement in their professional roles. This state of being, known as "Work Engagement," is characterized by a positive, fulfilling, and work-related mindset that encompasses vigor, dedication, and absorption (Schaufeli et al., 2009, p. 74). Engaged teachers are energetic, committed, passionate about their work, resilient in the face of challenges, and deeply involved in their teaching activities. Research on language teachers, including those in L2 writing, has often concentrated on the negative aspects of their professional experiences, such as stress, pressure, and burnout (Fathi & Derakhshan, 2019; Gregersen et al., 2020; MacIntyre et al., 2016, 2019). However, there is a dearth of research on how L2 teachers manage their emotions to enhance their work engagement and overall well-being. The burgeoning field of positive psychology offers a new perspective, emphasizing the importance of regulating both positive and negative emotions. For L2 writing teachers, understanding the factors that influence their emotional states and how these emotions impact their work engagement is crucial. This includes examining the role of positive emotions in fostering a sense of satisfaction, professional commitment, and the ability to thrive in their teaching environment. To support L2 writing teachers in their professional development, it is essential to explore strategies that help them manage negative emotions and cultivate positive ones. This can involve professional development opportunities that focus on emotional intelligence, self-care, and the development of coping mechanisms. By doing so, educators can not only mitigate the risks of burnout but also enhance their work engagement, leading to a more fulfilling and effective teaching career.

3.5.2 Consequences of L2 Writing Teacher Emotions on Teacher-Student Relationships

Human emotions play a vital role in shaping social interactions and relationships. Lee (2013) have highlighted that positive emotions are instrumental in initiating, nurturing, and sustaining relationships, while negative emotions can detrimentally impact relationship quality. This principle applies to the teacher-student dynamic within educational settings. Research has shown that teacher emotions significantly influence the nature of relationships in the classroom (Frenzel et al., 2021). When teachers experience positive emotions such as joy and enthusiasm in their teaching, these emotions can foster strong, positive relationships with students, which in turn can enhance teaching effectiveness and student learning. Positive teacher-student relationships are associated with a range of beneficial outcomes, including improved student well-being, increased motivation, and better academic performance. Conversely, when teachers are consumed by negative emotions like anxiety or anger, it can lead to strained relationships with students and a diminished sense of teaching satisfaction. Such emotional states can create a challenging learning environment and may hinder students' ability to thrive academically and emotionally.

In L2 writing classes, teacher emotions can send powerful nonverbal messages that significantly impact the learning environment. Weiner (2000) has noted that teachers' emotional expressions can communicate subtle messages about their expectations and beliefs regarding students' abilities and potential. For example, when a teacher expresses anger in response to a student's writing failure (e.g., "Your writing is full of grammatical mistakes, I am angry about you"), it may imply that the teacher believes the student has the capability to perform better in L2 writing and that the student's effort was insufficient. This reaction can be interpreted as a signal that the student's failure was due to a lack of effort rather than an inability to learn. On the other hand, when a teacher expresses sympathy for a student's struggles (e.g., "Your writing is full of grammatical mistakes, I am sorry for you"), it may suggest that the teacher perceives the student as lacking the necessary prerequisites to succeed in L2 writing. This type of emotional communication can shape the student's own beliefs about their competence and potential in the subject.

As teachers play a crucial role in socializing students into the norms and expectations of L2 writing, the emotionally conveyed messages about competence can profoundly influence students' self-efficacy and motivation. These beliefs can, in turn, affect their approach to learning and their willingness to engage in the writing process. It is, therefore, important for teachers to be aware of the messages their emotions convey and to strive for a supportive and encouraging emotional presence that fosters a positive learning environment and nurtures students' belief in their ability to succeed in L2 writing.

It's important to recognize that the positive impact of teacher anger on student outcomes contradicts the valence-congruent theory, which typically suggests that positive emotions lead to positive outcomes and negative emotions to negative ones. This highlights the crucial role of context in how teacher emotions influence student experiences. For example, in L2 writing classes, a teacher's dissatisfaction with student engagement in writing tasks might lead to more targeted and constructive feedback. However, an overabundance of anger in classroom interactions can be counterproductive, potentially leading to adverse effects on the learning environment and student well-being.

3.5.3 Consequences of L2 Writing Teacher Emotions on Teaching Behaviors

Several studies, including those by Becker et al. (2014) and Saunders (2013), have explored the influence of teacher emotions on pedagogical practices. The consensus from this research suggests that negative emotions experienced by teachers tend to diminish students' likelihood of engaging in deeper cognitive learning strategies (Linnenbrink-Garcia & Pekrun, 2011). Conversely, classrooms where teachers exhibit positive emotions are more conducive to fostering a supportive learning environment that enhances student learning and development (Yan et al., 2011; Zembylas et al., 2014). This underscores the importance of teacher emotional states in shaping the educational experience and outcomes for students.

In the L2 writing context, three broad concepts are widely used to describe teaching practice. The first approach focuses on texts (Hyland, 2009), the text-focused approach views writing as objects, that is, writing is a rule-based structure and is independent of contexts, writers or readers. Therefore, good writers need to be good at grammar. Pedagogically, writing teachers utilize a variety of teaching approaches such as familiarizing students with writing genres, controlled writing activities, guided writing activities (with models), and free writing activities, to improve students' accuracy in writing. One typical example is genre-based writing instruction. Thoreau (2006) states that genre in writing or genre writing is a kind of writing in which it has a typical style, a particular target of readers, and a specific purpose. Hyland implies that the purpose of genre writing is to enable the writer to write and pursue a certain goal. For example, how to retell, how to report, how to describe, how something is done, or how something is carried out. Teachers who follow the genre-based approaches usually make grammatical choices explicit so that students could write effectively. They also raise students' awareness and encourage them to notice, reflect on and produce well-formed texts.

The second approach focuses on writers, this approach emphasizes the writer's cognitive process of idea generation and development. Proponents view writing as a problem-solving activity rather than a communication tool, focusing on the writer's internal processes and the evolution of ideas. These approaches offer different insights into the teaching of L2 writing, each with its own set of pedagogical strategies and goals. Teachers may choose to integrate elements from these approaches to create a comprehensive and effective writing curriculum.

In L2 writing pedagogy, a prevalent instructional model encompasses five distinct stages: (1) Prewriting: This initial stage involves idea generation, where writers ponder questions such as "What do I want to convey? Who is my target audience? And with whom can I discuss my ideas?" (2) Drafting: Here, writers organize their thoughts, considering which ideas to develop and the order in which to present them. (3) Revising: This stage often involves peer feedback and requires writers to refine their work by asking themselves, "Have I clearly expressed my views? Is my argument logically structured?" (4) Editing: Focused on improving writing mechanics, writers assess their use of complete sentences and correct spelling. (5) Publishing: In the final stage, writers consider the best methods for presenting their work, whether digitally or in print.

This writer-focused approach emphasizes students' cognitive processes over linguistic knowledge. In contrast to a genre-based approach, where students are provided with writing structures, this model encourages self-discovery. The writing teacher's role is primarily to offer feedback. The third approach, reader-focused, challenges writers to consider the reader's knowledge and expectations, which can be particularly demanding for L2 writers, such as Chinese EFL learners, who may have limited English writing proficiency and are unfamiliar with Western reader expectations. Some L2 writing teachers note that their students produce "Chinese mindset" language, which, while not inherently incorrect, may differ from culturally accepted norms of logic, engagement, relevance, and organization in English writing.

In the realm of L2 writing instruction, it has been demonstrated that teachers can effectively employ a variety of approaches, even those that may seem contradictory, to teach L2 writing and other language skills (Chen & Brown, 2016; Hyland, 2009). This flexibility in pedagogical strategies reflects the adaptability of L2 writing teachers in responding to diverse educational needs and contexts. Furthermore, EFL teachers in Chinese mainland universities are undergoing a significant shift towards more learner-centered instruction, a change driven by current educational reforms aimed at enhancing students' academic performance. This shift emphasizes the importance of student engagement and active learning, which can lead to more effective language acquisition and writing skills development. The Covid-19 pandemic, which emerged in late 2019, has further transformed the L2 writing teaching landscape. The transition from traditional classroom settings to blended or fully online environments has necessitated fundamental changes in L2 writing instruction (Jiang & Yu, 2021). This transition has presented both challenges and opportunities for L2 writing teachers, who must now navigate the complexities of remote teaching while maintaining the quality and effectiveness of their instruction.

3.5.4 Recursive Effect of Teachers' Well-Being, Teaching Behavior, and Student Outcomes on Teacher Emotions

Frenzel et al. (2014) have posited a model where teachers' emotional responses are shaped by their assessments of classroom dynamics, particularly in relation to student conduct, motivation, discipline, and the nature of their interactions with the teacher. These emotions then have the potential to significantly impact student outcomes. In this framework, teacher emotions are integral to a reciprocal system that is both influenced by and influences teaching practices, student achievements, and the psychological well-being of the teachers themselves. In L2 writing classrooms, the instructional choices and relational interactions of teachers play a significant role in shaping their perceptions of the teaching environment. Effective instructional approaches that are engaging and responsive to student needs are likely to boost L2 writing teachers' satisfaction with their teaching. Such approaches can foster a closer relationship with students and lead to a more positive and enriching educational experience. On the contrary, when L2 writing teachers adopt inflexible or monotonous instructional methods, it may diminish their teaching satisfaction and trigger negative emotions such as boredom in students. This can also widen the relational gap between teachers and students, resulting in less favorable educational outcomes. The quality of instructional approaches, therefore, has a direct impact on the emotional landscape of the classroom, influencing both teacher and student experiences. It is essential for L2 writing teachers to be mindful of the emotional implications of their teaching strategies and strive to create a dynamic and supportive learning environment that promotes positive interactions and outcomes for all involved.

3.5.5 A Conceptual Framework on the Reciprocal Model of Causes and Effects of Teacher Emotions in L2 Writing Context

The present study rests on a reciprocal model of the causes and effects of teacher emotions in the L2 writing context with three interrelated themes (see Fig. 3.3).

This conceptual framework goes beyond earlier work on teacher emotions, which predominantly focused on the antecedents of teacher emotions (Chang, 2009; Frenzel, 2014; Gustavo et al., 2019) and the social, cultural, and political factors relevant to teacher emotions (Fried et al., 2015). In contrast, the present conceptual framework digs deep into the links between the causes and effects of teacher emotions, and integrates across several processes underlying these links, i.e., the

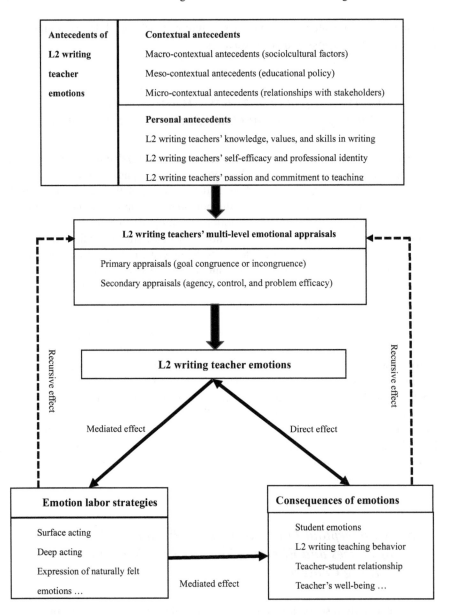

Fig. 3.3 Reciprocal model of causes and effects of L2 writing teacher emotions

antecedents of emotions, appraisals of emotions, and consequences of emotions. As indicated in this conceptual framework, it is proposed that there are (1) direct transmission effects from teacher emotions to student emotions; (2) mediated effects on teaching behaviors, writing assessment practices, and teachers' well-being via emotional labor strategies; and (3) recursive effects back from emotional labor strategies and consequences on teacher emotions, both directly and indirectly, via teachers' multilevel emotion appraisals of their instructional behavior and psychological well-being. Considering the above theoretical framework, the current study is guided by the following main research question: What emotions do teachers experience, and how do they regulate the emotions in the context of Chinese tertiary L2 writing classrooms? The main research question is further operationalized into four specific questions.

This conceptual framework extends previous research on teacher emotions by delving into the intricate relationships between the causes and effects of these emotions, rather than focusing solely on their antecedents (Chang, 2009; Frenzel, 2014; Gustavo et al., 2019) or the broader social, cultural, and political influences (Fried et al., 2015). It incorporates a multifaceted view that includes the antecedents, appraisals, and consequences of teacher emotions, and how these elements interact with each other. The framework posits several key dynamics: (1) Direct transmission effects: teacher emotions directly influence student emotions, shaping the classroom atmosphere and learning experience. (2) Mediated effects: emotional labor strategies affect teaching behaviors, writing assessment practices, and teacher well-being, which in turn can impact both teacher and student emotions. (3) Recursive effects: the outcomes of emotional labor and their consequences feedback into teacher emotions, either directly or indirectly, through teachers' evaluations of their instructional practices and psychological well-being. This comprehensive approach to understanding teacher emotions in the context of Chinese tertiary L2 writing classrooms is guided by a central research question: What emotions do teachers experience, and how do they regulate these emotions in their teaching environment? This overarching question is further broken down into four specific inquiries that aim to explore the nuances of teacher emotional experiences and regulatory strategies:

(1) What discrete emotions do L2 writing teachers encounter in their teaching practice?
(2) How do these emotions arise, and what factors contribute to their emergence?
(3) What strategies do teachers employ to manage and regulate their emotions in the classroom?
(4) How do these emotional experiences and regulatory efforts impact teaching practices, student outcomes, and teacher well-being?

3.6 Summary

This chapter presents a comprehensive review of the theoretical underpinnings and empirical research that inform the current study's exploration of teacher emotions. The literature review has provided a robust foundation for understanding the complexities of teacher emotions by examining various theoretical perspectives, as well as the antecedents, appraisal and regulation processes, and consequences of these emotions. These elements are crucial for developing the conceptual model that guides this study. The exploration of L2 writing teachers' emotional experiences has been enriched by research on teacher emotional intelligence, the concept of emotional labor, the strategies employed to manage emotional labor, and the impact of these factors on teaching behaviors and well-being. This body of research has contributed to a more nuanced understanding of the emotional landscape within the L2 writing context.

By synthesizing this knowledge, the chapter lays the groundwork for the study's conceptual model, which aims to investigate the emotional experiences of L2 writing teachers and how they navigate these emotions in their professional roles. The model will consider the interplay between emotional intelligence, emotional labor strategies, and the outcomes of these strategies on teaching practices and teacher well-being, ultimately aiming to enhance the effectiveness and satisfaction of L2 writing instruction.

References

Acton, R., & Glasgow, P. (2015). Teacher well-being in neoliberal contexts: A review of the literature. *The Australian Journal of Teacher Education, 40*(8), 99–114.

Akin, U., Aydin, I., Erdogan, C., & Demirkasımoğlu, N. (2014). Emotional labor and burnout among Turkish primary school teachers. *Australian Educational Researcher, 41*, 155–169.

Aloe, A. M., Amo, L. C., & Shanahan, M. E. (2014). Classroom management self-efficacy and burnout: A multivariate meta-analysis. *Educational Psychology Review, 26*, 101–126.

Arens, A. K., & Morin, A. J. S. (2016). Relations between teachers' emotional exhaustion and students' educational outcomes. *Journal of Educational Psychology, 108*(6), 800–813.

Ashforth, B. E., & Humphrey, R. H. (1993). Emotional labour in service roles: The influence of identity. *Academy of Management Review, 18*, 88–115.

Bahia, S., Freire, I., Estrela, M., Amaral, A., & Espírito Santo, J. (2017). The Bologna process and the search for excellence: Between rhetoric and reality, the emotional reactions of teachers. *Teaching in Higher Education, 22*(4), 467–482.

Bandura, A. (1989). Regulation of cognitive processes through perceived self-efficacy. *Developmental Psychology, 25*(5), 729–735.

Bandura, A. (1997). *Self-efficacy: The exercise of control.* W.H. Freeman and Company.

Bar-On, R., & Parker, J. D. A. (Eds.). (2000). *The handbook of emotional intelligence: Theory, development, assessment, and application at home, school, and in the workplace.* Jossey-Bass/Wiley.

Basim, H. N., Begenirbaş, M., & Yalçin, R. C. (2013). Effects of teacher personalities on emotional exhaustion: Mediating role of emotional labor. *Educational Consultancy and Research Center, 13*, 1488–1496.

References

Becker, E. S., Goetz, T., Morger, V., & Ranellucci, J. (2014). The importance of teachers' emotions and instructional behavior for their students' emotions—An experience sampling analysis. *Teaching and Teacher Education, 43*, 15–26.

Benesch, S. (2017). *Emotions and English language teaching: Exploring teachers' emotion labor.* Routledge.

Berg, J. K., & Cornell, D. (2016). Authoritative school climate, aggression toward teachers, and teacher distress in middle school. *School Psychology Quarterly, 31*, 122.

Berkovich, I., & Eyal, O. (2018). The effects of principals' communication practices on teachers' emotional distress. *Educational Management Administration & Leadership, 46*(4), 642–658.

Bielak, J., & Mystkowska-Wiertelak, A. (2022). Language teachers' interpersonal learner-directed emotion-regulation strategies. *Language Teaching Research, 26*(6), 1082–1105.

Borman, G. D., & Dowling, N. M. (2008). Teacher attrition and retention: A meta-analytic and narrative review of the research. *Review of Educational Research, 78*, 367–409.

Brown, L., & Roloff, M. (2011). Extra-role time, burnout, and commitment: The power of promises kept. *Business Communication Quarterly, 74*(4), 450–474.

Burić, I., Slišković, A., & Penezić, Z. (2019). Understanding teacher well-being: A cross-lagged analysis of burnout, negative student-related emotions, psychopathological symptoms, and resilience. *Educational Psychology, 39*(9), 1136–1155.

Butt, R. L., & Retallick, J. (2009). Professional well-being and learning: A study of administrator-teacher workplace relationships. *The Journal of Educational Enquiry, 3*, 17.

Cao, D. (2017). "Empirical research on reading teaching of college English from the perspective of metacognitive theory. In *2017 2nd International conference on education & education research (EDUER 2017)*, (Francis Academic Press).

Carson, R. L., & Templin, T. J. (2007). *Emotional regulation and teacher burnout: who says that the management of emotional expression doesn't matter?* Paper presented in the annual meeting of American Educational Research Association Annual Convention, (Chicago, IL).

Chang, M.-L. (2009). An appraisal perspective of teacher burnout: Examining the emotional work of teachers. *Educational Psychology Review, 21*(3), 193–218.

Chen, J. (2019). Exploring the impact of teacher emotions on their approaches to teaching: A structural equation modeling approach. *British Journal of Educational Psychology, 89*(1), 57–74.

Chen, J. (2020). Refining the teacher emotion model: Evidence from a review of literature published between 1985 and 2019. *Cambridge Journal of Education*, 1–31.

Cherkowski, S. (2018). Positive teacher leadership: Building mindsets and capacities to grow well-being. *International Journal of Teacher Leadership, 9*, 63–78.

Chen, J., & Brown, G. T. L. (2016). Tensions between knowledge transmission and student-focused teaching approaches to assessment purposes: Helping students improve through transmission. *Teachers and Teaching,22*(3), 350–367. https://doi.org/10.1080/13540602.2015.1058592

Cheung, F. Y., & Lun, V.M.-C. (2015). Emotional labor and occupational well-being: A latent profile analytic approach. *Journal of Individual Behavior, 36*, 30–37.

Ciarrochi, J., Chan, A. Y. C., & Caputi, P. (2000). A critical evaluation of the emotional intelligence construct. *Personality and Individual Differences, 28*, 539–561.

Collie, R., Shapka, J., & Perry, N. (2012). School climate and social-emotional learning: Predicting teacher stress, job satisfaction, and teaching efficacy. *Journal of Educational Psychology, 104*(4), 1189–1204.

Cowie, N. (2011). Emotions that experienced English as a foreign language (EFL) teachers feel about their students, their colleagues and their work. *Teaching and Teacher Education, 27*(1), 235–242.

Darling-Hammond, L. (1990). Teaching and knowledge: Policy issues posed by alternate certification for teachers. *Peabody Journal of Education, 67*(3), 123–154.

Deborah, C., Lia, P., & Atta, G. (2016). Writing assessment literacy: Surveying second language teachers' knowledge, beliefs, and practices. *Assessing Writing, 28*, 43–56.

den Berg, V., & Sleegers, P. (1996). The innovative capacity of secondary schools: A qualitative study. *International Journal of Qualitative Studies in Education, 9*(2), 201–223.

Devos, G., Hulpia, H., Tuytens, M., & Sinnaeve, I. (2013). Self-other agreement as an alternative perspective of school leadership analysis: An exploratory study. *School Effectiveness and School Improvement, 24*(3), 296–315.

Dewaele, J.-M., Witney, J., Saito, K., & Dewaele, L. (2018). Foreign language enjoyment and anxiety: The effect of teacher and learner variables. *Language Teaching Research, 22*(6), 676–697.

Diener, E. (2009). Subjective well-being. In E. Diener (Eds.), The science of well being (Vol. 37, pp. 11–58). New York. NY: Springer. https://doi.org/10.1007/978-90-481-2350-6_2

Fathi, J., & Derakhshan, A. (2019). Teacher self-efficacy and emotional regulation as predictors of teaching stress: An investigation of Iranian English language teachers. *Teaching English Language, 13*(2), 117–143.

Frenzel, A. C. (2014). Teacher emotions. In R. Pekrun & L. Linnenbrink-Garcia (Eds.), *International handbook of emotions in education* (pp. 494–518). Routledge/Taylor & Francis Group.

Frenzel, A. C., Pekrun, R., Goetz, T., Daniels, L. M., Durksen, T. L., Becker-Kurz, B., & Klassen, R. M. (2016). Measuring Teachers' enjoyment, anger, and anxiety: The Teacher Emotions Scales (TES). *Contemporary Educational Psychology, 46*, 148–163.

Frenzel, A. C., Daniels, L., & Burić, I. (2021). Teacher emotions in the classroom and their implications for students. *Educational Psychologist, 56*(4), 250–264.

Fried, L., Mansfield, C., & Dobozy, E. (2015). Teacher emotion research: Introducing a conceptual model to guide future research. *Issues in Educational Research, 25*(4), 415–441.

Fullan, M. (2006). *Change theory: A force for school improvement* (pp. 1–14). Centre for Strategic Education.

Gallagher, E. N., & Vella-Brodrick, D. A. (2008). Social support and emotional intelligence as predictors of subjective well-being. *Personality and Individual Differences, 44*, 1551–1561.

Gitlin, A. & Margonis (1995). The political aspect of reform: Teacher resistance as good sense. *American Journal of Education, 103*(4), 377–405.

Goddard, R. D., Hoy, W. K., & Hoy, A. W. (2004). Collective efficacy beliefs: Theoretical developments, empirical evidence, and future directions. *Educational Researcher, 33*(3), 3–13.

Grandey, A. A. (2000). Emotional regulation in the workplace: A new way to conceptualize emotional labor. *Journal of Occupational Health Psychology, 5*(1), 95–110.

Gregersen, T., Mercer, S., MacIntyre, P., Talbot, K., & Banga, C. A. (2020). Understanding language teacher wellbeing: An ESM study of daily stressors and uplifts. *Language Teaching Research*, 136216882096589.

Gross, J. J. (1998). Antecedent- and response-focused emotion regulation: Divergent consequences for experience, expression, and physiology. *Journal of Personality and Social Psychology, 74*, 224–237.

Gross, J.J. (2002) Emotion regulation: Affective, cognitive, and social consequences. *Psychophysiology, 39*, 281–291. https://doi.org/10.1017/S0048577201393198

Gross, J., & John, O. (2003). Individual differences in two emotion regulation processes: Implications for affect, relationships, and well-being. *Journal of Personality and Social Psychology, 85*(2), 348–362.

Gustavo, M. S., Yurdia, A. G., Antonia, H. M., & Cristian, N. G. (2019). Daily emotional experiences of a high school mathematics teacher in the classroom: A qualitative experience-sampling method. *International Journal of Science and Mathematics Education, 17*, 591–611.

Hagenauer, G., Hascher, T., & Volet, S. E. (2015). Teacher emotions in the classroom: Associations with students' engagement, classroom discipline and the interpersonal teacher-student relationship. *European Journal of Psychology and Education, 34*, 385–403.

Hargreaves, A. (1998). The emotional practice of teaching. *Teaching and Teacher Education, 14*(8), 835–854.

Hargreaves, A., & Goodson, I. (1996). Teachers' professional lives: Aspirations and actualities. In I. Goodson & A. Hargreaves (Eds.), *Teachers' professional lives* (pp. 1–27). Falmer press.

Hebson, G., Earnshaw, J., & Marchington, L. (2007). Too emotional to be capable? The changing nature of emotion work in definitions of 'capable teaching.' *Journal of Education Policy, 22*(6), 675–694.

Hirvela, A. (2019). Exploring second language writing teacher education: The role of adaptive expertise. In L. Seloni & S. H. Lee (Eds.), *Second language writing instruction in global contexts: English language teacher preparation and development* (pp. 13–30). Multilingual Matters.

Ho, I. T. (2001). Are Chinese teachers authoritarian? In D. A. Watkins & J. B. Biggs (Eds.), *Teaching the Chinese learner: Psychological and pedagogical perspectives* (pp. 99–114). CERC and ACER.

Hochschild, A. R. (1983). *The managed heart: The commercialization of human feeling*. University of California Press.

Hyland, K. (2009). *Teaching and researching writing* (2nd ed.). Routledge.

Jackson, M., & Marks, L.K. (2016). Improving the effectiveness of feedback by use of assessed reflections and withholding of grades. *Assessment & Evaluation in Higher Education, 41*, 532–547.

Jennings, P., & Greenberg, M. (2009). The prosocial classroom: Teacher social and emotional competence in relation to child and classroom outcomes. *Review of Educational Research, 79*(1), 491–525.

John, O. P., & Gross, J. J. (2004). Healthy and unhealthy emotion regulation: Personality processes, individual differences, and life span development. *Journal of Personality, 72*, 1301–1334.

John, O. P., & Gross, J. J. (2007). Individual differences in emotion regulation. In J. J. Gross (Ed.), *Handbook of emotion regulation* (pp. 351–372). Guilford Press.

Karim, J., & Weisz, R. (2011). Emotional labor, burnout and job satisfaction in UK teachers: The role of workplace social support. *Educational Psychology, 31*, 843–856.

Konu, A., Viitanen, E., & Lintonen, T. (2010). Teachers' wellbeing and perceptions of leadership practices. *International Journal of Workplace Health Management, 3*(1), 44–57.

Kyriacou, C., & Kunc, R. (2007). Beginning teachers' expectations of teaching. *Teaching and Teacher Education, 23*(8), 1246–1257. https://doi.org/10.1016/j.tate.2006.06.002

Lassila, E., Timonen, V., Uitto, M., & Estola, E. (2017). Storied emotional distances in the relationships between beginning teachers and school principals. *British Educational Research Journal, 43*(3), 486–504.

Lazarus, R. S., & Folkman, S. (1984). *Stress, appraisal, and coping*. Springer.

Le Cornu, R. (2013). Building early career teacher resilience: The role of relationships. *The Australian Journal of Teacher Education, 38*(4), 1–16.

Lee, I. (2013). Becoming a writing teacher: Using "identity" as an analytic lens to understand EFL writing teachers' development. *Journal of Second Language Writing, 22*(3), 330–345.

Lee, M., & Van, S. V. (2018). Teachers' emotional labour, discrete emotions, and classroom management self-efficacy. *Educational Psychology, 38*(5), 669–686.

Lee, I., & Yuan, R. (2021). Understanding L2 writing teacher expertise. *Journal of Second Language Writing*, 100755.

Linnenbrink-Garcia, L., & Pekrun, R. (2011). Students' emotions and academic engagement: Introduction to the special issue. *Contemporary Educational Psychology, 36*(1), 1–3. https://doi.org/10.1016/j.cedpsych.2010.11.004

Liu, L. H. (2009). *Research on emotional labor of elementary and middle school teachers*. Master's Thesis, Chongqing University, Chongqing.

Locke, E. A., & Latham, G. P. (1990). *A theory of goal setting & task performance*. Prentice-Hall, Inc.

Lopes, P., Nezlek, J., Extremera, N., Hertel, J., Fernández-Berrocal, P., Schütz, A., & Salovey, P. (2011). Emotion regulation and the quality of social interaction: Does the ability to evaluate emotional situations and identify effective responses matter? *Journal of Personality, 79*(2), 429–467.

Macdonald, D. (1999). Teacher attrition: A review of literature. *Teaching and Teacher Education, 15*(8), 835–848.

MacIntyre, P., Gregersen, T., & Mercer, S. (Eds.). (2016). *Positive psychology in SLA* (pp. 147–167). Multilingual Matters.
MacIntyre, P., Ross, J., Talbot, K., Mercer, S., Gregersen, T., & Annbanga, C. (2019). Stressors, personality and well-being among language teachers. *System, 82*, 26–38.
Madrid, S., Baldwin, N., & Belbase, S. (2016). Feeling culture: The emotional experience of six early childhood educators while teaching in a cross-cultural context. *Global Studies of Childhood, 6*(3), 336–351.
Mahoney, K. T., Buboltz, W. C., Jr., Buckner, V. J. E., & Doverspike, D. (2011). Emotional labor in American professors. *Journal of Occupational Health Psychology, 16*, 406–423.
Masoomeh, E., Zahra, B., & Gavin, T. L. (2024). The key competencies and components of teacher assessment literacy in digital environments: A scoping review. *Teaching and Teacher Education, 141*, 104497.
Matsumoto, D., Yoo, S., & Nakagawa, S. (2008). Culture, emotion regulation, and adjustment. *Journal of Personality and Social Psychology, 94*(6), 925–937.
Mayer, J. D., & Salovey, P. (1997). What is emotional intelligence? In P. Salovey & D. J. Sluyter (Eds.), *Emotional development and emotional intelligence: Educational implications* (pp. 3–34). Basic Books.
Moore, S. E., Bledsoe, L. K., Perry, A. R., & Robinson, M. A. (2011). Social work students and self-care: A model assignment for teaching. *Journal of Social Work Education, 47*(3), 545–553.
Noor, N., & Zainuddin, M. (2011). Emotional labor and burnout among female teachers: Work–family conflict as mediator. *Asian Journal of Social Psychology, 14*(4), 283–293.
O'Connor, K. E. (2008). "You choose to care": Teachers, emotions and professional identity. *Teaching and Teacher Education, 24*, 117–126.
Olivier, M. A., & Venter, D. (2003). The extent and causes of stress in teachers in the George region. *South African Journal of Education, 23*, 186–192.
Pianta, R. C., & Hamre, B. K. (2009). Conceptualization, measurement, and improvement of classroom processes: Standardized observation can leverage capacity. *Educational Researcher, 38*(2), 109–119.
Platsidou, M. (2010). Trait emotional intelligence of Greek special education teachers in relation to burnout and job satisfaction. *School Psychology International, 31*, 60–76.
Praetorius, A. K., Klieme, E., Herbert, B., & Pinger, P. (2018). Generic dimensions of teaching quality: The German framework of three basic dimensions. *ZDM, 50*, 407–426.
Rawolle, S. (2013). Emotions in education policy: A social contract analysis of asymmetrical dyads and emotion. In *Emotion and school: Understanding how the hidden curriculum influences relationships, leadership, teaching, and learning* (Vol. 18, pp. 49–60). Emerald Group Publishing Limited.
Reichelt, M. (2009). Chapter 7. A critical evaluation of writing teaching programs in different foreign language settings. In R. Manchón (Ed.), *Writing in foreign language contexts: Learning, teaching, and research* (pp. 183–206). Multilingual Matters.
Russo, J., Bobis, J., Sullivan, P., Downton, A., Livy, S., McCormick, M., & Hughes, S. (2020). Exploring the relationship between teacher enjoyment of mathematics, their attitudes towards student struggle and instructional time amongst early years primary teachers. *Teaching and Teacher Education, 88*, 102983.
Salovey, P., & Mayer, J. D. (1990). Emotional intelligence. *Imagination, Cognition and Personality, 9*(3), 185–211.
Saunders, R. (2013). The role of teacher emotions in change: Experiences, patterns and implications for professional development. *Journal of Educational Change, 14*, 303–333.
Schaufeli, W. B., Leiter, M. P., & Maslach, C. (2009). Burnout: 35 years of research and practice. *Career Development International, 14*(3), 204–220.
Schmidt, J., Klusmann, U., Lüdtke, O., Möller, J., & Kunter, M. (2017). What makes good and bad days for beginning teachers? A diary study on daily uplifts and hassles. *Contemporary Educational Psychology, 48*, 85–97.

Seligman, M. E. P. (2002). Positive psychology, positive prevention, and positive therapy. In C. R. Snyder & S. J. Lopez (Eds.), *Handbook of positive psychology* (pp. 3–9). Oxford University Press.

Seligman, M. E. P. (2011). *Flourish: A visionary new understanding of happiness and well-being*. Free Press.

Soini, T., Pyhältö, K., & Pietarinen, J. (2010). Pedagogical well-being: Reflecting learning and well-being in teachers' work. *Teachers and Teaching, Theory and Practice, 16*(6), 735–751.

Sutton, R. E., & Harper, E. (2009). Teachers' emotion regulation. In L. J. Saha & A. G. Dworkin (Eds.), *International handbook of research on teachers and teaching* (pp. 389–401). Springer.

Sutton, R. E., & Wheatley, K. F. (2003). Teachers' emotions and teaching: A review of the literature and directions for future research. *Educational Psychology Review, 15*(4), 327–358.

Tardy, C., Buck, R., Jacobson, B., LaMance, R., Pawlowski, M., Slinkard, J., & Vogel, S. (2022). "It's complicated and nuanced": Teaching genre awareness in English for general academic purposes. *Journal of English for Academic Purposes, 57*, 101117.

Taxer, J. L., & Frenzel, A. C. (2015). Facets of teachers' emotional lives: A quantitative investigation of teachers' genuine, faked, and hidden emotions. *Teaching and Teacher Education, 49*, 78–88.

Thoreau, M. (2006). *Write on Track*. Pearson Education New Zealand.

Trigwell, K. (2012). Relations between teachers' emotions in teaching and their approaches to teaching in higher education. *Instructional Science, 40*, 607–621.

Wang, H., Hall, N. C., & Taxer, J. L. (2019). Antecedents and consequences of teachers' emotional labor: A systematic review and meta-analytic investigation. *Educational Psychology Review, 31*(3), 663–698.

Watkins, D. A. (2000). Learning and teaching. *School Leadership and Management, 20*, 161–173.

Weiland, A. (2021). Teacher well-being: Voices in the field. *Teaching and Teacher Education, 99*, 103250.

Weiner, B. (2000). Intrapersonal and interpersonal theories of motivation from an attributional perspective. *Educational Psychology Review, 12*, 1–14.

Wilkerson, D. J., Manatt, R. P., Rogers, M. A., & Maughan, R. (2000). Validation of student, principal, and self-ratings in 360° feedback for teacher evaluation. *Journal of Personnel Evaluation in Education, 14*(2), 179–192.

Wrobel, M. (2013). Can empathy lead to emotional exhaustion in teachers? The mediating role of emotional labor. *International Journal of Occupational Medicine and Environmental Health, 26*, 581–592.

Xu, Y., & Brown, G. T. L. (2016). Teacher assessment literacy in practice: A reconceptualization. *Teaching and Teacher Education, 58*, 149–162.

Yao, X. P., Yao, M. L., Zong, X. L., Li, Y. L., Li, X. Y., Guo, F. F., & Cui, G. Y. (2015). How school climate influences teachers' emotional exhaustion: The mediating role of emotional labor. *International Journal of Environmental research and Public Health, 12*, 12505–12517.

Yan, E. M., Evans, I. M., & Harvey, S. T. (2011). Observing emotional interactions between teachers and students in elementary school classrooms. *Journal of Research in Childhood Education, 25*(1), 82–97. https://doi.org/10.1080/02568543.2011.533115

Yilmaz, K., Altinkurt, Y., Guner, M., & Sen, B. (2015). The relationship between teachers' emotional labor and burnout level. *Eurasian Journal of Educational Research, 59*, 75–90.

Yin, H. (2015). The effect of teachers' emotional labour on teaching satisfaction: Moderation of emotional intelligence. *Teachers and Teaching: Theory and Practice, 21*(7), 789–810.

Yin, H. (2016). Knife-like mouth and tofu-like heart: Emotion regulation by Chinese teachers in classroom teaching. *Social Psychology of Education, 19*(1), 1–22.

Yin, H. B., & Lee, J. C. K. (2012). Be passionate, but be rational as well: Emotional rules for Chinese teachers' work. *Teaching and Teacher Education, 28*, 56–65.

Yin, H., Han, J., & Lu, G. (2017). Chinese university teachers' goal orientations for teaching and teaching approaches: the mediation engagement. *Teaching in Higher Education, 22*(7), 766–784.

Yin, H., Lee, J. C. K., Zhang, Z., & Jin, Y. (2013). Exploring the relationship among 410 410 teachers' emotional intelligence, emotional labor strategies and teaching satisfaction. *Teaching and Teacher Education, 35*, 137–145.

Yu, S. (2021). Giving genre-based peer feedback in academic writing: Sources of knowledge and skills, difficulties and challenges. *Assessment and Evaluation in Higher Education, 46*(1), 36–53.

Zembylas, M. (2003). Interrogating "teacher identity": Emotion, resistance, and self formation. *Educational Theory, 53*(1), 107–127.

Zembylas, M. (2005). *Teaching with emotion: A postmodern enactment*. Information Age Publishing.

Zembylas, M. (2011). Teaching and teacher emotions: A post-structural perspective. In C. Day & J. C. K. Lee (Eds.), *New understanding of teacher's work: Professional learning and development in schools and higher education* (pp. 31–43). Springer.

Zembylas, M. (2014). "The place of emotion in teacher reflection: Elias, Foucault and "Critical emotional reflexivity". *Power and Education, 6*(2), 201-222.

Zhang, Q., & Zhu, W. (2008). Exploring emotion in teaching: Emotional labor, burnout, and satisfaction in Chinese higher education. *Communication Education, 57*, 105–122.

Zhang, L., Yu, S., & Jiang, L. (2020). Chinese preschool teachers' emotional labor and regulation strategies. *Teaching and Teacher Education, 92*, 103024.

Suggested Readings

Casanave, C. P. (2017). *Controversies in second language writing: Dilemmas and decisions in research and instruction* (2nd ed.). University of Michigan Press.

Ferris, D. (2014). Responding to student writing: Teachers' philosophies and practices. *Assessing Writing, 19*, 6–23.

Geng, F., Yu, S., & Yuan, R. (2023). Exploring L2 writing teachers' feeling rules, emotional labor and regulation strategies. *System, 119*, 103160.

Lee, I. (2008). Understanding teachers' written feedback practices in Hong Kong secondary classrooms. *Journal of Second Language Writing, 17*(2), 69–85.

Lee, I. (2017). *Classroom assessment and feedback in L2 school contexts*. Springer.

Lee, I. (2020). *Feedback in L2 writing classrooms*. TEFLIN Teacher Development Series, TEFLIN Publication Division.

Webb, M., & Gibson, D. (2015). Technology enhanced assessment in complex collaborative settings. *Education and Information Technologies, 20*, 675–695.

Yu, S. (2021). Feedback-giving practice for L2 writing teachers: Friend or foe? *Journal of Second Language Writing, 52*, 100798.

Yuan, R., & Lee, I. (2016). "I need to be strong and competent": A narrative inquiry of a student teacher's emotions and identities in teaching practicum. *Teachers and Teaching: Theory and Practice, 22*(7), 819–841.

Zhang, C., Yan, X., & Wang, J. (2021). EFL teachers' online assessment practices during the COVID-19 pandemic: Changes and mediating factors. *The Asia-Pacific Education Researcher, 30*(6), 499–507.

Chapter 4
Understanding L2 Writing Teachers' Emotions in Chinese Tertiary Context: A Qualitative Inquiry

This book employs a qualitative research methodology to delve into the multifaceted antecedents—both personal and contextual—that influence the emotions of L2 writing teachers, how these emotions are experienced and expressed, and the mediating role of emotional labor strategies on their teaching practices and overall well-being (Creswell & Miller, 2000; Morrow, 2005). The research questions, which are narrowly tailored to the study's objectives, serve as the guiding force for the design and methodology. In line with the principles outlined by (Onwuegbuzie and Leech, 2005), the research questions dictate the selection of the appropriate methodological design, sampling procedures, and data analysis techniques. This approach ensures that the methodology is aligned with the study's goals and that the research questions are addressed in a systematic and coherent manner.

By adhering to this qualitative approach, the book seeks to provide an in-depth understanding of the complex interplay between teacher emotions, emotional labor, and their implications for L2 writing instruction. The findings from this investigation will contribute to the broader field of educational research by offering insights into the emotional dimensions of teaching and the strategies that can be employed to enhance teacher well-being and teaching effectiveness in the L2 writing context.

4.1 L2 Writing Teachers in Chinese Tertiary Context

Numerous studies have delved into the realm of L2 writing instruction within Chinese university contexts, with a particular emphasis on the pedagogical beliefs and practices of writing educators. Lee's (2009) research highlighted the self-perceived beliefs and instructional approaches of writing teachers, shedding light on their perspectives on the teaching and learning of writing skills. Cumming (2003) furthered this line of inquiry by investigating how writing teachers conceptualize, plan, and execute writing courses, providing insight into the practical application of their beliefs in the classroom. In parallel, studies by Diab (2005) have scrutinized the specific beliefs and practices of L2 writing teachers regarding error feedback. Their findings suggest that a substantial component of these educators' beliefs is centered on the provision of feedback, a critical aspect of the writing instruction process. These collective works contribute to a nuanced understanding of the complexities involved in teaching L2 writing and the diverse approaches adopted by educators in this field.

The second strand of studies concentrated on teacher's knowledge and expertise in teaching L2 writing. For example, Worden (2019) developed a framework of teachers' PCK (pedagogical content knowledge) of genre in writing instruction, which includes their content knowledge of genre, knowledge of learners, pedagogical knowledge, knowledge of curriculum. In a comparable vein, Lee &Yuan (2021) have outlined six essential elements that define the adaptive expertise of L2 writing teachers. These elements include (1) an integrated knowledge base about writing and teaching writing; (2) student-centered pedagogy focusing on learner motivation and confidence building; (3) professional visions, self-agency, and reflectivity; (4) leadership in writing innovations; (5) passion as teachers of writing and as writers; and (6) ongoing teacher learning and progressive problem solving as pivotal to writing teacher expertise. These components together encapsulate the sophisticated expertise required for L2 writing educators to excel in their roles, underscoring the dynamic and evolving nature of teaching writing in a second language.

A third set of research looked into teachers' knowledge, beliefs, and practices regarding writing assessment. Weigle (2007) emphasizes the necessity for these educators to master the creation, administration, and grading of writing tasks, which are integral to their assessment preparation. Crusan (2010) further advocates for L2 writing teachers to become proficient evaluators of student writing. She enumerates several key competencies, such as distinguishing between formative and summative assessments, crafting prompts that yield relevant data, recognizing the significance of clear criteria presentation, and understanding the appropriate and inappropriate applications of writing assessments. Building on this foundation, Crusan et al. (2016) stress the importance of L2 writing teachers' adaptiveness in developing evaluation criteria and scoring rubrics.

Yet another strand of studies has delved into the complex interplay between L2 writing teachers' emotional experiences, their pedagogical beliefs, and their instructional practices. Yu (2021) conducted a study that explored the feedback-giving experiences of Chinese L2 writing teachers, revealing that the majority of these educators find the process of providing feedback to be a learning experience. This finding challenges the prevalent notion that offering feedback is a burdensome and unfulfilling task. Yu's (2021) work also delves into the emotional landscape of teachers as they engage in the act of providing written comments. The study uncovers that the feedback process is emotionally charged, with teachers' emotions being shaped by various factors, including institutional influences, students' levels of engagement with the feedback, and the teachers' own valuation of the feedback's significance. These insights contribute to a more nuanced understanding of the L2 writing classroom, highlighting the importance of considering teachers' emotional responses and beliefs in the development of effective feedback strategies.

The book provides an in-depth examination of the (EFL) context within Mainland Chinese universities, which mirrors the wider EFL landscape in China. It underscores the pivotal role of English language teaching (ELT) at the tertiary level, particularly in higher education settings. In this context, English writing is a critical element of the curriculum for both non-English and English majors, reflecting its significance in the overall educational framework. The book also highlights the inclusion of English writing in several high-stakes assessments that are integral to academic progression. These include the College English Test (CET), which is designed for non-English major university students, and the Test for English Majors (TEM), targeted at English major undergraduates. Additionally, English writing proficiency is evaluated in two key entrance examinations that act as gateways for students seeking to pursue undergraduate and postgraduate studies, further emphasizing its role as a determinant of academic success in the Chinese higher education system.

In the domain of English writing, students are required to master a progression of skills across three proficiency levels. At the foundational level, they should be able to: execute standard writing assignments; narrate personal experiences, insights, emotions, and occurrences; produce essays exceeding 120 words on various topics within 30 min, ensuring their work is comprehensive, lucid, and presented in a fitting and cohesive manner. Intermediate level expectations include the ability to share personal viewpoints on diverse topics; compose a professional thesis; craft essays of at least 160 words within 30 min, maintaining clarity, coherence, and appropriate language use. At the advanced level, students should be capable of authoring research reports and academic essays; fluently articulating personal thoughts and perspectives; writing essays of over 200 words within 30 min, with the same emphasis on thoroughness, clarity, and linguistic suitability.

The qualitative case study approach was selected to investigate the factors leading up to, the process of, and the outcomes following L2 writing teachers' experiences within Chinese mainland university contexts. This methodology was favored for several key reasons, as outlined by Yin (2018). First, a case study is adept at elucidating the "what" and "how" aspects of the research inquiries, providing in-depth insights into the phenomena under study. Second, given the subtle and personal nature of teacher emotions, a case study allows for minimal manipulation or influence over the emotional and behavioral occurrences of L2 writing teachers, ensuring a more authentic exploration of their experiences. Third, by situating participants within their natural environment or a defined system, a case study facilitates a comprehensive understanding of the context in which the teachers operate, capturing the complexity of their interactions and the factors that shape their professional lives. This methodological choice ensures a nuanced and contextually rich investigation, aligning with the intricate nature of studying L2 writing teachers' emotional experiences and practices.

It is important to clarify that the "bounded system" under investigation in this study pertains to the intricate environment within and surrounding L2 writing classrooms where teacher emotions are initiated, managed, and exert influence. The focus of this book is on Chinese university EFL teachers who are engaged in teaching L2 writing courses. These educators bring a diverse array of educational backgrounds and teaching experiences to the table, hailing from institutions of varying prestige and size. Given the inherent variability and unpredictability of emotional and instructional dynamics, the researcher's ability to control or manipulate the teachers' experiences or the involvement of other stakeholders—such as students, colleagues, and educational administrators—is inherently limited. This naturalistic aspect of the teaching context necessitates a research design that can accommodate the complex interplay of factors without imposing artificial constraints. In light of these considerations, a qualitative case study methodology is particularly suited to address the research questions. It allows for a detailed and contextualized exploration of the phenomena, capturing the essence of the teachers' emotional experiences and their impact on the L2 writing classroom environment. This approach ensures that the study remains true to the realities of the educational setting, providing a rich and nuanced understanding of the subject matter.

Against this backdrop, this book approached 20 teachers who were working at the School of Foreign Languages, who were all involved in teaching L2 writing courses to both English and non-English major undergraduates at the time of data collection. These teachers were encouraged to implement curriculum reforms in their L2 writing classes. While they were given a recommended textbook and a set of general guidelines, they had the autonomy to design and structure their teaching activities in alignment with their own teaching goals and strategies. The research ultimately centered on three teachers—Alex, Lina, and Olivia (pseudonyms)—who were chosen for their rich information potential for the main study. The rationale for their selection was multifaceted: (1) They each had over four consecutive semesters of experience teaching L2 writing courses at their institutions and were committed to continuing these pedagogical efforts. This continuity allowed for a longitudinal study, enabling the researcher to deeply engage with the participants' professional teaching journeys. (2) The selected teachers brought a diverse set of personal and professional backgrounds, including demographic characteristics (such as gender, educational background, and academic rank), teaching experience (years dedicated to L2 writing instruction and achievements in this area), and prior accomplishments (research experience and academic publications). This diversity was well-suited to the multi-case approach of the main study. (3) They reported a range of emotions of varying types and intensities in their teaching practices, such as during the provision of teacher feedback, peer review sessions, and collaborative writing activities. This emotional spectrum provided the researcher with opportunities to observe their teaching behaviors at different stages of the semester and to gain insights into their emotional experiences and other teaching-related reflections. By focusing on these three teachers, the study aimed to provide a comprehensive and nuanced understanding of the emotional and instructional dynamics within L2 writing classrooms, contributing valuable insights to the field of EFL education.

4.2 A Qualitative Inquiry

The main case study's data collection and analysis spanned approximately 15 weeks, employing a qualitative approach to gather rich and varied information. Table 4.1 outlines the detailed procedures followed during the data collection phase, while Table 4.2 offers a comprehensive view of the various data sources utilized in the study.

Interviews served as the primary data source, with a comprehensive approach designed to capture the nuanced details of the teacher participants' emotional experiences and reactions to L2 writing instruction. The study involved three rounds of semi-structured interviews with the 20 teacher cases, conducted at strategic points

Table 4.1 Procedures of data collection

Time	Data collection
Week 1–2	Classroom observations Teaching materials and student drafts 1st informal interviews and small talks
Week 3–6	1st formal interviews and small talks 1st formal classroom observations Teaching materials and student draft Assessment of teaching performance Teacher reflection journals
Week 7–10	2nd formal interviews and small talks 2nd formal classroom observations Teaching materials and student draft Assessment of teaching performance Teacher reflection journals
Week 11–15	3rd formal interviews and small talks 3rd formal classroom observations Teaching materials and student draft Assessment of teaching performance Teacher reflection journals

Table 4.2 Summary of data sources of the case study

Data sources	Description
Interviews	Audio-recorded semi-structured interviews, small talks, stimulated recall interviews
Classroom observations	Audio recorded observations and field notes
Teacher reflection journals	Collection of teacher reflection journals
Teaching materials	Coursebook, syllabus, lesson plans, PowerPoint slides, video clips, assignments, etc
Assessment of teaching performance	Collection of assessment and comments on teaching performance
Student drafts	Collection of students' writings and revisions

throughout the semester: beginning, middle, and end. Each round was tailored with a set number of open-ended questions—20 for the first, 14 for the second, and 7 for the third—crafted to align with the study's theoretical framework and research questions (refer to Appendix B). These face-to-face interviews, lasting approximately one hour per participant, aimed to delve deeply into the teachers' perspectives. To further enrich the data, stimulated recall interviews (as described by Gass & Schachter, 2000) and informal conversations were also utilized. These methods were particularly effective in gaining additional insights and explanations of the teachers' instructional practices. All interviews were conducted in Mandarin, the participants' native language, to ensure comfort and clarity of communication. They were audio-recorded and subsequently transcribed manually for detailed analysis. To enhance the reliability and validity of the data, the study employed two additional triangulation methods: conducting open-ended interviews with students from the teachers' classes and observing classroom interactions. Before initiating the first round of interviews, participants were provided with informed consent forms, which outlined the purpose and process of the interviews, the recording procedures, and their right to withdraw at any point. This ensured that the participants were fully aware and comfortable with the research process. During the interviews, the interviewer maintained attentive listening and monitored the teachers' emotional responses to prevent any discomfort or adverse effects on their well-being. Post-interview, the interviewer transcribed the conversations verbatim and sought confirmation from the participants. This process allowed for any necessary corrections or additional contributions from the participants, further solidifying the integrity of the data collected (Simons, 2005).

Classroom observations served as the second key data source, offering a window into the practical aspects of L2 writing instruction. The researcher adopted a non-participant observational approach as described by Cohen et al. (2007). This method allowed for a comprehensive understanding of the teachers' classroom practices, the dynamics of teacher-student interactions during L2 writing lessons, and any post-class teaching-related activities. As an observer, the researcher documented the teaching sessions and took detailed field notes, capturing the essence of the instructional strategies, student engagement, and the overall classroom environment. This approach was non-intrusive, ensuring that the natural flow of the classroom was not disrupted by the researcher's presence. Following the initial interview with each participant, the researcher sought explicit consent for conducting classroom observations. Once the teachers granted permission, the researcher was able to enter their classrooms and observe the writing instruction firsthand. This collaborative approach respected the participants' autonomy and ensured that they were comfortable with the observation process. The classroom observations provided a rich complement to the interview data, offering a more holistic view of the teachers' professional practices and the contextual factors that influence their teaching and emotional experiences. By combining these two data sources—interviews and observations—the study aimed to achieve a multifaceted understanding of the L2 writing teaching landscape.

The classroom observation process was structured into three distinct rounds, each with a specific focus and timing to align with the academic semester and the progression of the study. The initial round of classroom observations occurred following the first interview, marking the beginning of the semester. Over the course of this round, 16 writing classes were observed, with each session lasting approximately one hour. The primary goal was to familiarize the students with the researcher's presence, creating a comfortable environment for subsequent observations. During this phase, the researcher aimed to gather preliminary information about the course, such as the curriculum, teaching plans, overarching objectives, class size, and students' language proficiency levels. The second round of observations was scheduled in the middle of the semester, prior to the second interview. This round involved observing eight writing classes, with each observation extended to about 1.5h. The focus shifted to examining how L2 writing teachers navigated their emotions during actual teaching scenarios. The researcher was tasked with taking detailed field notes or, with the consent of the teacher participants, recording the classes. These observations informed the development of the second-round interview protocols, ensuring that the interviews were grounded in the observed classroom practices. The final round of classroom observations took place at the end of the semester, just before the third interview. Similar to the second round, eight writing classes were observed for approximately 1.5h each. The objective was to track the evolution of the L2 writing teachers' emotional regulation strategies throughout the semester, with a particular emphasis on the implications for L2 writing instruction, student learning outcomes, and teacher well-being. This structured approach to classroom observations allowed for a comprehensive analysis of the teachers' emotional experiences and instructional practices over time, providing a clear picture of the dynamics at play in L2 writing classrooms and the impact of emotional regulation on teaching and learning.

The third data source in this study comprised a variety of teaching materials and student work, which provided additional context and insight into the instructional and learning processes. Specifically, the following documents were collected (1) teaching materials: this included the course textbook, lesson plans, PowerPoint presentations, handouts, and screenshots of classroom activities. These materials were directly related to the teachers' instructional approaches and the content delivered in the classroom. (2) teachers' reflective journals: these journals offered a personal account of the teachers' thoughts, experiences, and reflections on their teaching practices, providing a deeper understanding of their professional development and the emotional aspects of their work. (3) students' writing drafts: the collection of students' work, including initial drafts, feedback received, revisions made, final drafts, and students' own reflection journals. These documents tracked the students' writing development and the impact of the instructional methods employed. (4) teaching performance assessments: this category encompassed any feedback or evaluations of the teaching performance, which could include comments from students, peer reviews, assessments by teaching experts, and evaluations from school administrators. These assessments provided an external perspective on the effectiveness of the teachers' instructional strategies. All these materials were carefully organized and stored in digital format (softcopies) to facilitate easy access and analysis. The comprehensive collection of these documents allowed the researcher to triangulate data from multiple sources, enhancing the reliability and validity of the study's findings. By examining these documents, the researcher could gain a more holistic view of the teaching and learning environment, the effectiveness of the curriculum, and the emotional dimensions of the educational experience for both teachers and students.

Data analysis followed a thematic approach aiming to identify, analyze, and report patterns particular to the current research (Miles et al., 2013). The process was bifurcated into two distinct phases. Initially, the interview transcripts were scrutinized to formulate a preliminary analytical framework. This framework was subsequently refined and substantiated through the systematic coding of classroom observation notes and teaching reflection diaries. The coding task was collaboratively undertaken by the primary researcher and a co-researcher, who is a Ph.D. candidate in education with a background in qualitative research methodology. Regular discussions were held between the two researchers to address any challenges encountered during the coding process, ensuring the rigor and reliability of the analysis.

First, the two coders conducted independent reviews of the three sets of teacher interviews. Prior to the coding process, a preparatory meeting was convened to align the coders' understanding of the theoretical framework, research questions, and the existing literature on teacher emotions, as per Kuckartz (2014). This session was crucial for establishing a shared comprehension of the data among the coders. During the coding, the coders utilized open coding techniques, concentrating on narrative segments that directly related to the research inquiries. These included: specific emotional episodes; the contexts or situations that evoked these emotions; the objectives and standards that informed the teachers' emotional assessments; and the emotional coping strategies employed to manage the emotional challenges of teaching. To enhance the descriptive richness of the data, the coders also quantified the instances of distinct emotions that were precipitated by particular situations for each teacher. This quantification was categorized as "types of emotions" and "triggering situations," providing a more nuanced understanding of the emotional dynamics. Subsequently, the coders adhered to the preliminary coding scheme and utilized Nvivo 12 (https://www.qsrinternational.com/nvivo-qualitative-data-analysis-software) to analyze the interview data, ensuring a systematic and methodical approach to the thematic analysis.

The coders began by independently analyzing the interview transcripts, focusing on the semantic content and the explicit meanings conveyed within the data. This initial coding phase resulted in a comprehensive list of codes, which served to familiarize the coders with the nuances of the data set. Following this, the coders engaged in a continuous comparison of their respective coding efforts, making adjustments to the codes as needed, in accordance with Kuckartz's (2014) methodology. In instances where consensus was not immediately achieved, the coders engaged in collaborative discussions to resolve any discrepancies. This process, known as consensual coding, is a key strategy for enhancing coding reliability. It involves a group of coders working together to reconcile differences in their interpretations of the data, ultimately reaching a shared understanding (Kuckartz, 2014). Building on the coding results that were mutually agreed upon, the coders then synthesized the individual codes and employed an inductive approach to develop five overarching thematic frameworks. These frameworks encapsulated the core themes and patterns that emerged from the data, providing a structured basis for further analysis and interpretation of the research findings.

Following the initial analysis of the interview data, this information was used to guide the subsequent coding of classroom observation and teaching document data. This iterative process allowed the preliminary coding results to be tested, evaluated, and expanded upon with additional data from the participants, as recommended by Miles et al. (2013). The coders adhered to the tentative coding framework, categorizing relevant excerpts from classroom observations and teaching documents into the predefined thematic categories. When new data emerged that did not align with the existing scheme, the coders created new nodes to accommodate these findings. This approach ensured that the coding remained flexible and responsive to the data. To reduce discrepancies in coding, the two coders engaged in regular discussions about their coding results, making adjustments to certain codes when necessary. This collaborative effort led to the integration of codes, particularly the newly created ones, which in turn strengthened and elaborated the initial coding frameworks. The coders' discussions and the subsequent modifications were instrumental in refining the coding process.

Stage 1. Identification of teachers' emotional experiences

To identify teachers' emotional experiences, data coding gave priority to addressing the teacher participant's emotions triggered by macro-, meso-, and micro-contextual issues, coupled with an effort to reveal the differences in the participant's emotional experiences. For the analysis, we only consider excerpts that contain at least one explicit positive or negative emotional appraisal of the triggering situations. The two coders interpreted the positive or negative emotional valence according to the answers reported by the participants in the interview protocols (see Appendix B). Following the emotional appraisal theory, two aspects were considered to identify the types of participants' emotional experiences: (1) explicit phrases that express the triggering situations of the emotions; (2) emotional words, phrases, and other expressions that indicate participants' appraisals of the triggering situations. For example, in the following excerpt:

To accurately capture the emotional experiences of the teachers, the data coding process prioritized the identification of emotions evoked by issues situated at the macro-, meso-, and micro-levels of context. The goal was not only to address these emotional triggers but also to discern the variations in the emotional experiences among the participants. The analysis focused on excerpts that explicitly conveyed a positive or negative emotional evaluation of the situations in question. The coders relied on the participants' own words from the interview protocols (refer to Appendix B for details) to interpret the emotional valence as either positive or negative. This approach ensured that the coding was grounded in the participants' subjective experiences. In line with emotional appraisal theory, two key elements were used to identify the nature of the participants' emotional experiences: (1) Explicit Phrases: The coders looked for phrases that directly described the situations or events that triggered the emotions. These phrases provided a clear indication of the context in which the emotional response occurred. (2) Emotional Lexicon: The use of emotional words, phrases, and other expressions that reflected the participants' evaluations of the triggering situations was also considered. This included any language that conveyed the intensity, quality, and direction of the emotional response. For instance, consider the following excerpt from an interview:

> **Alex**: [The emotions and feelings I experienced in my writing classes were] I am glad to see that my students recited a lot of high-frequency vocabulary used in essay writing *(Satisfaction-Appreciation)*, but they did not know how to use these words and often made mistakes *(Dissatisfaction-Anxiety)*. This makes me think about how to give students precise guidance so that they could activate those "sleeping" words and phrases in the writings. Now, this situation has improved since the *Pigai* system could help my students diagnose and correct their writing errors *(**Happy for-appreciation**)*.

We interpret "students recited a lot of high-frequency vocabulary in essay writing" as a triggering situation (i.e., students take the initiative to improve their writing knowledge) of a satisfaction type of emotion (the teacher is pleased about the prospect of a desirable event). We interpret "students do not know how to use the words and often make mistakes in L2 writing" as a triggering situation (i.e., students encounter difficulties in L2 writing) of a dissatisfaction type of emotion (the teacher is anxious about students' inability to improve L2 writing). In addition, we identified two types of triggering situations and two types of emotions in the same emotional experience. For example, we interpret "the *Pigai* system could help students diagnose and correct their errors in writing" as a triggering situation (students found an effective tool to improve their writing accuracy) of a satisfaction type of emotion and a triggering situation (students learned how to use the words and phrases in their writings more accurately) of an appreciation type of emotion. The second researcher in this book independently identified the triggering situations and types of emotions for each participant. After rounds of discussions, the two researchers reached a consensus on the coding results. Table 4.3 shows one example of these analysis.

In the analysis of the teachers' emotional experiences, the coding process involved a nuanced interpretation of the situations that triggered emotions, as well as the types of emotions that were experienced. Here's a refined explanation of the coding approach. (1) Triggering Situations: These are the specific events or circumstances that initiate an emotional response. For instance, "students reciting a lot of high-frequency vocabulary in essay writing" is interpreted as a proactive action (triggering situation) that leads to a satisfaction type of emotion, as it reflects the teacher's positive reaction to the students' initiative to enhance their writing skills. (2) Types of Emotions: The emotions themselves are categorized based on the nature of the students' actions and the teachers' reactions. The example provided indicates that "students not knowing how to use words and making mistakes in L2 writing" is a source of dissatisfaction, as it triggers the teacher's anxiety regarding the students' struggles to improve their writing abilities. (3) Complex Emotional Experiences: Sometimes, a single event can lead to multiple emotional responses. For example, the "*Pigai* system" being used to help students correct their writing errors is seen as a satisfaction type of emotion because it represents an effective tool for improvement. Simultaneously, it is also a source of appreciation, as it enables students to use words and phrases more accurately in their writing.

4.2 A Qualitative Inquiry

Table 4.3 Types of emotion and triggering situations of Alex

Emotional experience	Types of emotion	Triggering situation
[Positive experience] being happy *because one student revised his writings for nearly 90 times on Pigai, and the writing improved a lot*	Appreciation Satisfaction	The students engaged with the feedback given by Pigai The students exercised great agency in writing
[Positive experience] i learned a lot in course preparation with my colleagues, *because they often gave me practical suggestions and solutions to the problems in my teaching*	Satisfaction Appreciation	I benefited from the course preparation with colleagues Colleagues helped each other in course preparation
[Positive experience] I only gave comprehensive feedback on the selected sample writings (2 to 3 writings in each class), so that *I could focus on the language, genre structure, and other common issues in students' writings. This saved a lot of my labor and was quite effective to students' revisions*	Satisfaction/ appreciation Happy for	The students accepted the feedback on sample writings Students made progress in revisions
[Negative experience] *I could not give comprehensive feedback to every single student; this often made me feel helplessness*	Dissatisfaction	The overwhelming work of giving feedback to students' writings

The second researcher in this study independently assessed the triggering situations and types of emotions for each participant, ensuring that the coding was consistent and reliable. Through iterative discussions, the two researchers achieved consensus on the coding results, which is a critical step in ensuring the validity of the findings. Table 4.3, as mentioned, would provide a concrete example of this analytical process, illustrating how the coders identified and categorized the various elements of the emotional experiences in the context of the study. This table would serve as a reference for understanding the systematic approach taken to analyze the data and the interplay between triggering situations and emotional responses.

Stage 2. Thematic analysis of the triggering situations and the identification of goals and norms

In the second phase of the analysis, a dual approach of thematic and content analysis was utilized to uncover the goals and norms that underpinned the teachers' emotional evaluations of the various triggering situations, as outlined by Bogdan and Biklen (2007). Thematic analysis, as described by Braun and Clarke (2006, p. 82), aims to discern recurring patterns or themes across the data set that align with the research questions. This process involves several steps: (1) data Familiarization: The researchers immerse themselves in the data to gain a comprehensive understanding of its content and context. (2) Data Coding: Segments of data are systematically labeled with codes that represent the themes or concepts being explored. (3) Theme Development: Codes are organized and refined to develop coherent themes that answer the research questions. Informed by the findings from the first research question (RQ1), three primary codes were established to focus on distinct types of emotional triggers: macro-contextual, meso-contextual, and micro-contextual. These codes facilitated a targeted examination of the factors that evoked emotional responses from the teachers. Simultaneously, the study drew upon emotion appraisal theory to identify the goals and norms that influenced the teachers' evaluations of the triggering situations. In this context, goals refer to the objectives that teachers aim to accomplish in their L2 writing classes, which are derived from their teaching philosophy and instructional strategies. Norms refer to the standards or expectations that teachers believe should be upheld in the classroom, often shaped by their professional experiences and educational values.

The analytical procedure in this stage involved pinpointing the triggering situations that aligned with the teachers' stated goals and perceived norms. This information was extracted from various sources, including course design, lesson plan, Instructional Reflections. By integrating thematic and content analysis with insights from emotion appraisal theory, the study was able to provide a detailed understanding of the emotional landscape within the L2 writing classrooms, revealing how teachers' goals and norms shape their emotional experiences and appraisals of classroom events.

The current study finally decided on six types of triggering situations across three participants: (1) achievement of the planned teaching objectives; (2) performance of students' writings; (3) students' participation in writing assessment activities; (4) student engagement with writing feedback; (5) motivation and attitude of students in L2 writing; (6) collaboration with and support from colleagues and administrative leaders. We also identified goals and norms associated with these types of triggering situations. In the following excerpt, for example, it was discovered that the goal "the students understand the evaluation criteria in the writing rubrics" matched the norm that "students could diagnose and make evaluative judgements in peer feedback":

> Lina: I often found some students sneaking off the peer feedback [the planned teaching **goal** is "students conduct peer feedback to improve the writing"]. This demonstrates the difficulties students have in making evaluative judgments [I was nervous and disappointed]. Later, I prepared a feedback rubric and asked the students to conduct peer feedback by referring to the rubrics. To my delight, students show greater interest in peer feedback [**norm**: "students improve their writing by receiving peer feedback"].

Researchers continued to establish relationships between the identified goals and norms in this way to build the appraisal structures. During the construction of teachers' appraisal structures, two important notions were identified: "students' attitude toward L2 writing" and "student engagement with writing feedback." Because the two notions not only support the goals in relation to students' participation in writing activities but also their behaviors (e.g., revisions) and performance norms. In the interviews with teacher participants, they were asked to clarify "students' good attitude toward L2 writing" and "student engagement with writing feedback" in detail. Such clarifications could help the researchers confirm that the two notions support the rest of the goals identified in the data.

In the process of constructing the appraisal structures for the teachers, the researchers meticulously examined the interplay between the identified goals, norms, and the emotional responses they elicited. This involved establishing a comprehensive framework that linked the teachers' educational objectives with the students' attitudes and behaviors in the context of L2 writing. Two pivotal concepts emerged as central to this framework: "students' attitude toward L2 writing" and "student engagement with writing feedback." These notions were critical because they not only underpinned the teachers' goals related to student participation in writing activities but also influenced the students' actions (such as revisions) and the performance standards that the teachers expected.

To validate the significance of these concepts and their alignment with the broader set of goals, the researchers sought detailed clarification from the teacher participants during interviews. By asking the teachers to elaborate on what constitutes a "good attitude toward L2 writing" and how they perceive "student engagement with writing feedback," the researchers were able to confirm the relevance of concepts, validate the appraisal structures, enhance the depth of analysis, and gain a more nuanced understanding of the teachers' perspectives, which could reveal additional layers of meaning and complexity in the data. This methodical approach to establishing relationships and seeking clarification ensured that the appraisal structures were grounded in the actual experiences and perceptions of the teachers. It also allowed the researchers to construct a robust and contextually rich understanding of the factors that shape the emotional landscape of L2 writing instruction.

Stage 3. Identification of teachers' emotional labor strategies and the influence on their instructional behavior and well-being in L2 writing classrooms

In the third stage of the analysis, the focus shifted to understanding how teachers manage the discrepancies and tensions between their genuine emotional responses and the goals and norms they adhere to. This stage was informed by the findings from Research Question 2 (RQ2), which centered on the teachers' appraisal structures. To analyze the emotional labor strategies employed by the teachers, an inductive thematic analysis approach was adopted. This approach is well-suited for identifying, analyzing, and forming patterns that are specific to the research context, as suggested by Braun and Clarke (2006). The process involved several steps: (1) Inductive Coding: teachers' self-reported emotional labor strategies were initially coded using open codes, which are descriptive labels applied to segments of data. This allowed for a detailed and context-specific representation of each strategy. (2) Multiple Coding: For responses that encompassed multiple strategies, the coders applied multiple codes to capture the complexity of the emotional labor being described. (3) Consistent Comparison and Integration: The codes were then analyzed through a process of comparison, modification, and integration. This iterative process led to the development of a preliminary framework that encapsulated the teachers' emotional labor strategies within the context of L2 writing instruction. (4) Deductive Validation: The second coder reviewed the same data set using a deductive approach, which involves applying pre-existing theoretical concepts to the data to test the robustness of the emerging framework. This step ensured that the framework was not only inductive but also grounded in established theory. (5) Finalization of Strategies: The coding results were synthesized into three overarching emotional labor strategies: surface acting, deep acting, and the expression of naturally felt emotions. These strategies represent the various ways in which teachers manage their emotions in the classroom to align with their professional goals and norms. (6) Recursive Effect Analysis: The study also examined the reciprocal impact of emotional labor strategies on the teachers' emotions. This analysis considered how the act of regulating emotions can, in turn, influence the emotional experiences of the teachers, creating a dynamic interplay between emotional regulation and emotional experience. By employing this comprehensive analytical approach, the study provided a nuanced understanding of the emotional labor involved in L2 writing instruction, highlighting the strategies teachers use to navigate the emotional demands of their profession and the implications of these strategies for their overall emotional well-being.

In summary, the data analysis was a systematic and iterative process that integrated multiple data sources, considered the recursive effects of emotional labor on various aspects of teaching, and was guided by the research questions and theoretical insights to provide a comprehensive understanding of the influence of emotional labor on teaching behavior and psychological well-being.

4.3 Research Methodology and Ethical Issues

In qualitative research, establishing trustworthiness is crucial for ensuring the credibility and reliability of the findings from the perspectives of both the participants and the researcher, as emphasized by Merriam and Tisdell (2015). The current study employed a series of strategies to enhance the trustworthiness and quality of the research, drawing on Yin's (2018) case study tactics:

(1) Triangulation. This book collected data from multiple sources, such as interviews, classroom observations, field notes, and teacher reflection journals. This approach allowed for cross-validation of information and increased the richness and depth of the data.
(2) Purposive Sampling: Teacher participants were selected purposefully to represent a wide range of experiences and contexts, which maximized the variability and diversity of the sample. This strategy aimed to enhance the transferability of the findings to other settings.
(3) Causal Relationships: The analysis sought to establish causal links between teacher emotions and various conditions or factors by employing techniques such as pattern matching, explanation building, addressing rival explanations, and logic models. These tactics helped in understanding the complex relationships and provided a more nuanced view of the phenomena.
(4) Member Checking: After interviews or observations, participants were asked to review and provide feedback on the transcripts, ensuring the accuracy of the data and the participants' perspectives were accurately represented.

(5) Peer Debriefing: Another co-researcher was involved in the coding process, and regular discussions with supervisors and colleagues were held to reflect on the identified themes and categories. This process helped to identify and mitigate potential biases or subjective assumptions.
(6) Data Management: A case study database was created, and a chain of evidence was maintained throughout the data collection process. This systematic approach facilitated the repeatability of the research operations and results.
(7) Ethical Considerations: The study adhered to the ethical standards of educational research, including obtaining Institutional Review Board (IRB) approval, informed consent from participants, maintaining research relations, and ensuring freedom to publish.
(8) Data Security and Confidentiality: The researcher was the sole custodian of the data, which were securely managed. Copies or discussions of the data were not shared with the university or any other institutions. The data were to be disposed of or anonymized and archived after five years following the publication of the study.
(9) Informed Consent: Consent forms were developed and provided to both teacher and student participants, ensuring they were fully informed about the study and their rights. The consent forms are detailed in Appendices C and D, respectively.
(10) Ethical Data Collection: During the data collection phase, the researchers ensured the confidentiality, privacy, and anonymity of the participants, addressing ethical concerns and maintaining a professional relationship to avoid conflicts.

By implementing these measures, the study aimed to produce trustworthy and ethically sound research that contributes valuable insights into the field of educational research, particularly in the area of teacher emotions in L2 writing instruction.

4.4 Summary

This chapter delineates the methodological framework of the study, which has been judiciously selected to align seamlessly with the study's defined scope, objectives, research inquiries, and the broader context. The narrative unfolds the research journey, illustrating the methodical progression through the sequential stages of planning, conceptualization, preparation, data collection, analysis, and dissemination, as advocated by Yin (2018).

The chapter further delves into the exposition of the research milieu, the participant demographics, and the comprehensive methodology for data gathering and subsequent analysis that underpins the study's core. A dedicated section is reserved for an exposition of the strategies implemented to fortify the trustworthiness of the research, detailing the multifaceted approaches adopted to satisfy the stringent criteria of case study research. In the concluding segment, the chapter outlines the ethical protocols adhered to throughout the research endeavor, ensuring compliance with the ethical standards intrinsic to educational research. This sets the stage for the subsequent chapter, which will unveil the study's findings, grounded in the methodological rigor and ethical considerations detailed in this chapter.

References

Bogdan, R. C., & Biklen, S. K. (2007). *Qualitative research for education: An introduction to theory and methods* (5th ed.). Allyn & Bacon.

Braun, V., & Clarke, V. (2006). Using thematic analysis in psychology. *Qualitative Research in Psychology, 3*(2), 77–101.

Cohen, L., Manion, L., & Morrison, K. (2007). *Research methods in education* (5th ed.). Routledge Falmer.

Creswell, J. W., & Miller, D. L. (2000). Determining validity in qualitative inquiry. *Theory into Practice, 39*, 124–130.

Crusan, D. (2010). *Assessment in the second language writing Classroom.* University of Michigan Press, Ann Arbor, MI.

Crusan, D., Plakans, L., & Gebril, A. (2016). Writing assessment literacy: surveying second language teachers' knowledge, beliefs, and practices, *Assessing Writing, 28*, 43–56. https://doi.org/10.1016/j.asw.2016.03.001

Cumming, A. (2003). Experienced ESL/EFL writing instructors' conceptualizations of their teaching: Curriculum options and implications. In *Exploring the Dynamics of Second Language Writing,* 71–92. Cambridge University Press.

Diab, R, L. (2005). Teachers' and students' beliefs about responding to ESL writing: a case study, *TESL Canada Journal, 23*(1), 28–43.

Gass, S., & Schachter, J. (2000). *Stimulated recall methodology in second language research.* Lawrence Erlbaum Associates.

Kuckartz, U. (2014). *Qualitative text analysis: A guide to methods, practice & using software.* SAGE Publications Ltd.

Lee, I. (2009). Ten mismatches between teachers' beliefs and written feedback practice. *ELT Journal, 63*, 13–22.

Lee, I., & Yuan, R. (2021). Understanding L2 writing teacher expertise. *Journal of Second Language Writing,* 100755.

Merriam, S. B., & Tisdell, E. J. (2015). *Qualitative research: A guide to design and implementation.* John Wiley & Sons.

Miles, M. B., Huberman, M., & Saldana, J. (2013). *Qualitative data analysis: A methods sourcebook* (3rd ed.). Sage Publication.

Morrow, S. L. (2005). Quality and trustworthiness in qualitative research in counseling psychology. *Journal of Counseling Psychology, 52*, 250–260.

Onwuegbuzie, A., & Leech, N. (2005). Taking the "Q" out of research: Teaching research methodology courses without the divide between quantitative and qualitative paradigms. *Quality and Quantity, 38*, 267–296.

Simons, H. (2005). Ethics of case study in educational research and evaluation. In R. G. Burgess (Ed.), *The ethics of educational research* (pp. 106–130). The Falmer Press.

Yin, R. K. (2018). *Case study research and applications: Design and methods* (6th ed.). London: Sage.

Yu, S. (2021). Giving genre-based peer feedback in academic writing: sources of knowledge and skills, difficulties and challenges. *Assessment and Evaluation in Higher Education, 46*(1), 36–53.

Weigle, S. (2007). Teaching writing teachers about assessment. *Journal of Second Language Writing, 16*(3), 194–209. https://doi.org/10.1016/j.jslw.2007.07.004

Worden, D. (2019). Developing L2 writing teachers' pedagogical content knowledge of genre through the unfamiliar genre project. *Journal of Second Language Writing,* 100667. https://doi.org/10.1016/j.jslw.2019.100667

Suggested readings

Creswell, W. J. (2013). *Research design: Qualitative, quantitative and mixed method approaches.* Sage Publication.

Emma, R. B. (2023). Developing teacher feedback literacy through self-study: Exploring written commentary in a critical language writing curriculum. *Assessing Writing, 56,* 100709.

Hyland, K. (2003). Genre-based pedagogies: A social response to process. *Journal of Second Language Writing, 12*(1), 17–29.

Hyland, K., & Anan, E. (2006). Teachers' perceptions of error: The effects of first language and experience. *System, 34*(4), 509–519.

Junqueira, L., & Payant, C. (2015). "I just want to do it right, but it's so hard": A novice teacher's written feedback beliefs and practices. *Journal of Second Language Writing, 27,* 19–36.

Lee, I., Luo, N., & Mak, P. (2021). Teachers' attempts at focused written corrective feedback in situ. *Journal of SeCond Language Writing, 54,* 100809.

Lee, I., Karaca, M., & Inan, S. (2023). The development and validation of a scale on L2 writing teacher feedback literacy. *Assessing Writing, 57,* 100743.

Wu, P., Yu, S., & Luo, Y. (2023). The development of teacher feedback literacy in situ: EFL writing teachers' endeavor to human-computer-AWE integral feedback innovation. *Assessing Writing, 57,* 100739. https://doi.org/10.1016/j.asw.2023.100739

Yu, S., Xu, H., Jiang, L., & Chan, I. K. I. (2020). Understanding Macau novice secondary teachers' beliefs and practices of EFL writing instruction: A complexity theory perspective. *Journal of Second Language Writing, 48,* 100728.

Yu, S., Zhang, Y., Liu, C., & Lee, I. (2022). From theory to practice: Understanding the long-term impact of an L2 writing education course on writing teachers. *Language Teaching Research*, 13621688221130852.

Chapter 5
Teacher Emotions and Instructional Practices: Evidence from a Genre Based L2 Writing Classroom

Chapters 5 through 7 delve into the nuanced realm of teachers' emotional experiences in the context of L2 writing instruction. These chapters are informed by a qualitative case study featuring three university-based L2 writing educators, with the aim to achieve the following objectives: (1) to uncover the distinct emotional episodes that teachers encounter within the L2 writing classroom; (2) to elucidate the underlying appraisal structures that shape these emotional responses; and (3) to examine how these emotions influence the teachers' instructional behaviors, including their approach to feedback and writing assessments in the L2 writing classroom. These chapters underscore the intricate dynamics between the emotional landscape of the teachers and the broader educational context, such as teacher-student interactions, the provision of feedback, and the assessment of student writing. They provide a window into how emotions play a pivotal role in shaping pedagogical practices and the classroom environment. In this particular chapter, we focus on Alex, one of the case study participants, to present a detailed account of his emotional experiences and the instructional strategies he employs in his L2 writing classes. By examining Alex's perspective, the chapter aims to offer a deeper understanding of the emotional dimensions of teaching L2 writing and the ways in which these emotions intersect with teaching practices.

5.1 Introduction

Alex, an experienced EFL instructor, has been an integral part of an ordinary university in northeast China. Armed with a Master's degree in Linguistics, he embarked on his teaching career in 2009, focusing on College English across Levels I to IV. His curriculum is designed to equip students with foundational knowledge of various writing genres, such as narration, exposition, and argumentation, as well as the methodologies and strategies for essay development and the standard practices for essay evaluation and revision, tailored to meet the requirements of the CET4/6 exams. To enhance their pedagogical expertise, Alex and his peers actively participated in training programs, workshops, and lectures dedicated to L2 writing. These professional development opportunities provided them with a comprehensive understanding of L2 writing pedagogy, technological tools like *Pigai* and *iWrite*, and assessment techniques, including the concept of assessment for learning.

In a forward-thinking move to augment his traditional classroom instruction, Alex ventured into the digital realm in 2018 by creating an official WeChat account, "Teacher Alex's Writing Class." This online platform served as an extension of his classroom, offering supplementary materials, writing models, and targeted feedback to assist students in honing their writing skills for high-stakes English proficiency tests such as IELTS and the Admission Examination for Postgraduate Students. Recognized for his teaching prowess, Alex has been crowned a three-time winner in the National English Teaching Contest, an accolade bestowed by the Ministry of Education. His leadership skills extend beyond his classroom, as he spearheads a community of practice with eight fellow educators. Together, they collaborate on the development of teaching materials, provide constructive writing feedback, and engage in other pedagogical activities, fostering a collaborative environment that enriches their collective teaching practice.

5.2 Alex's Emotional Experiences: A Genre based L2 Writing Pedagogical Approach

This book has uncovered a rich tapestry of emotional experiences within Alex's teaching journey, pinpointing a total of 28 distinct emotional episodes as detailed in Table 5.1.

Most of the emotions reported by Alex are negative (54%), followed by positive emotions (36%), and complex emotions (10%) came at last. This book identified four negative emotional experiences and four positive emotional experiences triggered by macro-contextual issues such as school educational policies. This book identified four positive emotional experiences, two negative emotional experiences, and two complex emotional experiences triggered by meso-contextual issues such as collaboration with colleagues.

In the micro-classroom context, several situations were negatively appraised by Alex, including students' low participation in writing activities, poor engagement with feedback in revisions, and underperformance in writing assessment activities. This is because the goal of "facilitating students' writing performance through classroom writing activities" was not accomplished. Besides, situations appraised positively by Alex included students' commitment to writing and improvement in revisions. This is because the goal of having students write independently was achieved. It should be noted that Alex experienced complex emotions, such as "self-questioning" in his responses to the student's errors. This is because Alex was not sure how to

Table 5.1 Types of emotions and triggering situations in Alex's case

Types of emotion	Triggering situation	Contextual issues
Stress Anxiety	1. School's policy and requirement on EFL teachers' teaching and research performance	Macro-contextual issues
Gratitude	2. School's recognition of EFL teachers' efforts in teaching innovations and achievement	
Disappointment Dissatisfaction	3. Lack of high-quality resources to improve EFL teachers' knowledge and expertise in teaching and doing research on L2 writing	
Satisfaction Inspiration Happy-for	4. Attending lectures and workshops, receiving professional guidance on L2 writing instruction and research	
Happy-for Achievement	5. Cooperating with colleagues in course preparation, teaching contest and other collaborative activities	Meso-contextual issues
Self-questioning Happy-for	6. Receiving comments on L2 writing instruction from colleagues and administrative leaders	
Cautious Encouragement	7. Giving comments to colleagues in course evaluation	
Exhaustion Confusion	8. Dealing with administrative affairs and student affairs	
Stage 1. Modeling a text		
Satisfaction Appreciation	9. Students recite the genre knowledge, and languages frequently used for L2 writing	Students study and practice the writing knowledge and skills
Anxiety Sorry-for	10. Students do not know how to use the genre knowledge or languages in L2 writing	
Satisfaction Happy-for	11. Sharing knowledge and skills of L2 writing with students on *WeChat* account	
Uneasiness Disappointment	12. Students believe they could write well and do not take the writing tasks seriously	
Stage 2. Joint construction of a text		
Sorry-for	13. Students passively participate in the planned writing activities	Students reconstruct the given genre writing
Amusement	14. Students use good languages in L2 writing	
Disappointment Anger	15. Students use template languages from models in L2 writing	
Satisfaction Appreciation	16. Students are committed to revising the writings by referring to the computer-mediated feedback	Student engagement with writing feedback Teacher continuously guides the writing
Sorry-for Anxiety	17. Students could not learn from peer feedback, and they do not know how to give feedback either	
Appreciation Happy-for	18. Students show interests and participate in class activities	Classroom interaction with student

(continued)

Table 5.1 (continued)

Types of emotion	Triggering situation	Contextual issues
Happy-for Satisfaction	19. Students show interests and participate in writing assessment activities	Students' performance in writing assessment
Sorry-for Anxiety	20. Students have difficulties in conducting writing assessment activities	
Anger Disappointment	21. Students have a bad attitude to L2 writing and make numerous errors in language form	Teacher's response to errors in text
Self-questioning	22. Students make mistakes in the genre structure of L2 writing	
Self-questioning	23. Students make mistakes in the content of L2 writing	
Disappointment Reproach	24. Students make mistakes in the mechanics of L2 writing	
Self-questioning Confusion	25. Students are deficient in critical thinking skills and fail to understand the writing task	
Reproach Disappointment	26. Students commit plagiarism in L2 writing	
Stage 3. Student independently construct a text		
Sorry-for	27. Students fail to revise the difficult problems in L2 writing as expected	
Disappointment Anxiety	28. Students refuse to revise the problems in L2 writing in accordance with teacher feedback	

respond to the student's errors concerning the content of the writing and carry on his instruction.

Alex's emotional landscape, as reported, is predominantly shaded by negative emotions, which constitute 54% of his emotional experiences. These are succeeded by positive emotions at 36%, with complex emotions trailing at 10%. The study's findings reveal that macro-contextual factors, such as school educational policies, have instigated four instances of negative emotional experiences and an equal number of positive ones. Similarly, meso-contextual elements, including interactions with colleagues, have led to four positive, two negative, and two complex emotional experiences.

Within the micro-classroom setting, Alex has encountered several scenarios that have elicited negative emotional responses. These include low student participation in writing activities, lackluster engagement with feedback for revisions, and subpar performance in writing assessments. These situations are negatively appraised because they thwart the goal of enhancing students' writing abilities through classroom activities. On the flip side, Alex has also experienced positive emotions when observing students' dedication to writing and their progress in making revisions. These positive appraisals stem from the realization of his goal to foster independent writing skills among his students.

It is important to highlight the complexity of Alex's emotional experiences, such as the "self-questioning" he faces when addressing students' writing errors. This internal conflict arises from his uncertainty regarding the most effective way to respond to students' content-related mistakes while continuing his instructional duties. Such complex emotions underscore the multifaceted nature of teaching and the intricate balance teachers must strike between addressing immediate concerns and maintaining a constructive learning environment.

5.3 Goals and Norms Supporting Alex's Appraisal of Emotional Situations

In general, Alex appraised three overarching triggering situations: "macro-level school policies", "meso-level collaboration with colleagues and administrative leaders", and "micro-level L2 writing instruction" in different ways (see Table 5.2). This book identified seven specific goals and norms in Alex's emotional appraisal of the situations across the L2 writing instruction process.

First, Alex listed "students learn and practice the knowledge and skills of the given genre" as the goal, for he expected to give students sufficient "input" to encourage their writing through "modeling a text." Second, in the stage of "joint construction of a text", Alex proposed various goals across the writing process. For instance, he listed "students' participation in teacher-guided writing activities" as a goal, for he could guide students' writing progressively through collaborative learning activities. He also listed "students engage with teacher feedback" as a goal, for he expected students to improve their writing with the feedback. Furthermore, Alex listed "students' participation and involvement in writing assessment activities" as a goal, for he expected to develop students into assessment-literate writers. Finally, Alex proposed students' independence in writing as a goal in the stage of "independent construction of a text". He expected students to write independently by referring to the knowledge, skills, feedback, and other forms of scaffolding resources obtained in the classroom.

5.4 Influence of Alex's Emotion-Regulation Strategies on L2 Writing Instruction and His Psychological Well-Being

Given the context-specific nature of Alex's emotional experiences, this section presents Alex's emotional experiences, use of emotional regulation strategies, and influences on L2 writing instruction and his psychological well-being in line with the macro-, meso-, and micro-contextual issues that trigger Alex's discursive emotional experiences.

Table 5.2 Goals and norms supporting Alex's appraisal of emotional situations

Type of triggering situation	Evaluated in terms of	
	Goals	Norms
School policies on EFL teaching and research	1. School administration could issue favorable polices on EFL teaching and research	
Collaboration with colleagues and educational administrators	2. EFL teachers could improve teaching effectiveness via collaborations and interactions with colleagues	
Providing counseling service to students	3. Understand students' practical difficulties and needs in learning L2 writing	
Modeling a text	4. Students understand the genre and directions of the writing task	1. Students must understand the patterns of the given writing genre
	5. Students learn and practice the knowledge and skills of the given genres	2. Students must be active in preparing for the writing task
Joint construction of a text	6. Students' participation in teacher-guided writing activities	3. Students must have good attitude and follow teacher's guidance to write the text progressively
	7. Teacher's provision of feedback on student writings	4. Teacher must diagnose the errors in student writings and give useful feedback
	8. Students engage with teacher feedback	5. Students must revise the writings by teacher feedback
	9. Students' participation and involvement in writing assessment activities	6. Students must be cooperative and help each other in writing assessment activities
Student independently construct a text	10. Students develop the abilities and literacy necessary for independence in L2 writing	7. Students must be independent in wring

5.4.1 Alex's Use of Emotion Regulation Strategies and Impact: Macro-Level

At Alex's university, the school administration placed increasing emphasis on EFL teaching effectiveness and innovation. Teachers were encouraged to participate in various teaching and research projects. This policy led to teachers' emotional labor by placing a higher demand on EFL teachers' achievement in teaching and research.

> *"These policies present a challenge for me, as my expertise is rooted in teaching L2 writing rather than conducting research. Having not received formal training in academic publishing, I find myself without the pressure or the ambition for promotion. My focus remains on honing my teaching skills and providing the best possible support for my students in their journey to improve their L2 writing abilities." (1st interview)*

It became evident that the school's educational policies for EFL teaching and teacher development were causing Alex to experience emotional dissonance. Despite this, his wealth of experience in EFL teaching has equipped him with the resilience to adapt to the school's culture, managing his negative emotions through a process known as "emotion compromising." This strategy involves reappraising the events that trigger these emotions, allowing teachers to reconcile themselves with less-than-ideal conditions. Although Alex initially viewed teacher development as a fundamental aspect for university educators, he strategically redirected his focus from L2 writing research to instruction upon encountering the complexities of academic research. Consequently, Alex has successfully navigated his professional environment, finding a balance that enables him to continue his teaching career with a sense of comfort and fulfillment.

5.4.2 Alex's Use of Emotion Regulation Strategies and Impact: Meso-Level

In Alex's department, he was appointed to lead the "L2 writing teaching community" of five members, who signed up for teaching contests hosted by FLTRP (a popular foreign language press in mainland China) each summer. To prepare for the teaching contest, they gathered for course preparation on a regular basis. Despite the different opinions resulting from interacting with colleagues, Alex could manage the emotional labor by releasing positive emotions to create a teaching-friendly environment.

> *"The team was a vibrant hub of diverse ideas and passionate debates. I embraced the multiplicity of perspectives, actively encouraging candid feedback from my colleagues, even when it conflicted with my own views. This open and inclusive atmosphere fostered a culture of creative thinking, which was instrumental in our preparation for the contest. Additionally, our course preparation process was enriched by involving students. We would practice our lessons across various classes and actively seek their feedback, ensuring that our teaching methods were not only effective for the contest but also beneficial for the students' learning experience." (1st interview)*

In the first classroom observation, it was apparent that the team members were forthcoming with their emotions, fostering an environment of open dialogue. In this formal setting, Alex, as the team leader, was focused on enhancing teaching effectiveness for the upcoming teaching contest. His leadership was marked by a strategic approach, including the development of a series of mini lectures for the L2 writing course. These lectures were designed to familiarize students with the functional and structural nuances of various writing genres, proving to be an effective strategy. A distinct theme that emerged was Alex's judicious approach to providing feedback on his colleagues' classes. As the course coordinator, Alex conducted evaluations by observing and commenting on his peers' teaching three times per semester. His comments were highly valued and played a significant role in the course evaluation process, reflecting his commitment to maintaining high standards and supporting professional growth within the team.

> *In my interactions with colleagues, I typically adopted a measured approach to my choice of words and tone. For example, I would phrase my suggestions as questions, such as, "Could you consider incorporating additional exercises to deepen students' understanding of the writing genre's patterns?" or "Is it feasible to provide a demonstration graph for the students?" I also made it a point to offer clear justifications for my suggestions. I believe that employing diplomatic language and a collaborative tone can mitigate potential conflicts and foster a more harmonious professional relationship with my peers. (1st interview)*

Instead of directly expressing his emotions with his colleagues, Alex restrained his negative emotions and kept a positive interpersonal relationship with colleagues who were not in the same teaching community. (1st classroom observation) In this situation, Alex labeled himself primarily as an advisor or observer; thus, he considered it inappropriate to challenge or be critical of the teachers' instruction.

5.4.3 Alex's Use of Emotion Regulation Strategies and Impact: Micro-Level

It is in the micro-context (classroom) that Alex experienced complex emotions, which gave us an insightful look at the relationship between teacher emotions, emotion regulation strategies, and the consequences on instructional practice and his psychological well-being. Reasons that Alex offered for each emotional episode were also presented. Five stages in the teaching procedure were reported by Alex to have experienced the most intensive emotional labor, namely, stage 1: modeling a text; stage 2: co-construction of a text; stage 3: Revising the writings by computer-mediated feedback; stage 4: teacher feedback on sample writings; and stage 5: writing assessment.

Stage 1. Modeling a text

The first salient theme is an indication of Alex's strong willingness and motivation to impart the genre knowledge to students and the high expectations of students to master the genre knowledge. According to Alex, he considered "modeling a text" as the starting stage by instructing students with the knowledge, languages, and strategies that are useful for the construction of the text. In Alex's class, one important step in modeling a text was "teacher and students discuss the text genre". Normally, students were asked to make presentations about the knowledge and patterns of the

5.4 Influence of Alex's Emotion-Regulation Strategies on L2 Writing ...

given genre by referring to model texts. To guarantee the accuracy of the presentation, Alex set up strict guidelines for the evaluations of the students' presentations.

If students made more than three errors, such as spelling or grammatical mistakes, while presenting model texts, I would interrupt their presentation to prevent confusion among the class. This approach was also a way for the presenters to recognize my concern for their performance. (1st interview)

I also observed a trend in some L2 writing classes where teachers seemed to take students' presentations for granted. A common scenario involved assigning topics that were either randomly selected by the students or not aligned with the course objectives. I view this as "fake teaching", a practice where teachers appear to facilitate learning but, in reality, engage in teaching activities that lack effectiveness. (2nd interview)

Alex's commitment to his pedagogical expertise and a deep sense of responsibility for his students' success in L2 writing classrooms motivated him to teach genre knowledge through student presentations of model texts. When he identified errors during these presentations, he conveyed his disappointment and dissatisfaction directly, often stopping the presentation to ensure clarity and accuracy. Furthermore, Alex recognized the value of presentations in enhancing students' understanding of genre structures. This awareness led him to feel regret when he observed presentations in other colleagues' classes that were poorly constructed or misaligned with the writing tasks, as he believed they did not serve the educational purpose effectively.

Alex often found himself disheartened by the enduring influence of his students' previous L2 writing experiences and ingrained habits, which he felt had a profound and lasting impact on their learning. This was especially evident in the writing of argumentative essays, where students tended to misuse or overuse cohesive and coherent devices, a pattern that he believed was deeply entrenched and challenging to alter.

A common issue I've observed is that the majority of students—nine out of ten—employ a formulaic approach to writing argumentative essays. They typically start paragraphs with 'as far as I am concerned..., enumerate arguments with "first, second, third..." and wrap up their essays with "in a nutshell..." This pattern suggests that students have been trained to use these phrases, but they often lack a clear understanding of the structural patterns required for effective argumentative writing. They rely on these stereotypical discourse markers to give the illusion of argumentation. When I identify these issues, I encourage students to explore the actual functions of these markers before incorporating them into their writing. I emphasize to them that while these markers can contribute to the coherence and cohesion of their essays, it is crucial to focus on the substance and organization of their arguments. The goal is to ensure that their writing is not just a collection of phrases, but a well-structured and thoughtfully argued piece. (1st & 2nd interviews)

Classroom observations revealed that Alex adopted a teacher-centered method for imparting genre knowledge. In an effort to address the prevalence of stereotyped language and to inspire students to write in a manner that aligns with the genre structure and writing tasks, Alex openly expressed his disapproval of linguistic clichés and inappropriate language use. He did so directly, aiming to underscore the significance of thoughtful and meaningful content in their writing. This approach was intended to guide students towards a more nuanced and genre-appropriate style of expression. (1st & 2nd classroom observations).

Stage 2. Joint construction of a text

After the instruction of the given writing genre, Alex usually involves students in several writing activities (e.g., group discussion, oral debate, drawing mind maps) to generate more useful information before constructing the texts (2nd classroom observation). In this stage, Alex spent much effort getting students involved in various writing activities.

Some students showed low motivation for participating in the writing activities; they were reluctant to participate in group discussions or refused to brainstorm arguments with their peers. I often asked the students to change their seats and form new groups. Additionally, I would call upon students who appeared to be inattentive or disengaged during group discussions to answer questions. My goal was to actively involve them in the learning process and provide the support they needed to improve their writing skills. (1st & 2nd interviews)

It was observed that Alex took several factors into account in evaluating student writing performance, such as students' contributions to group discussion, the correctness of peer feedback, and improvement in revisions (*2nd classroom observation*). Alex was strict with students because he believed that good students were trained by strict teachers.

I've established clear and specific criteria for assessing students' performance in group writing activities. My policy dictates that if a piece of writing contains more than three errors, the student responsible for the task would be required to redo it. This approach can certainly induce a sense of nervousness and heightened caution among students, as they strive to avoid mistakes. However, my experience has shown that as students become accustomed to this policy, their awareness and attention to linguistic accuracy in writing significantly improve. (2nd interview)

In Alex's approach to teaching writing, there is a strategic preparatory phase aimed at encouraging students to engage in discussions and share their ideas. Alex positions himself as a strict teacher, believing that his methods effectively consolidate students' understanding of genre patterns. However, it's important to recognize that discussions can sometimes exceed students' current cognitive abilities or fail to resonate with their interests. This can result in a significant emotional burden for both the teacher and the students, as they navigate the challenges of sustaining meaningful conversations on assigned topics.

Stage 3. Revise the writings by computer-mediated feedback

As soon as students finished the first draft, Alex asked students to submit the draft to the *Pigai* platform. There, they were tasked with conducting a self-assessment of their writing, guided by the feedback provided through the computer-mediated system.

Previously, providing feedback to students was a time-consuming process, and as a result, the feedback was frequently delayed. With the assistance of the Pigai platform, my role has shifted to focusing solely on the content and organizational aspects of student writings, utilizing the automated feedback generated by Pigai. Additionally, the platform allows me to track the students' efforts, such as the number of revisions and improvements in their scores. The immediate and detailed feedback from Pigai has been instrumental in informing my own decisions regarding the students' work. (3rd interview)

An innovative pedagogical approach is gaining traction, which seeks to optimize the scaffolding benefits of computer-mediated feedback while reducing the emotional toll associated with providing individualized teacher feedback. The *Pigai* platform has significantly lightened Alex's feedback workload, yet it has simultaneously increased the demand for his analytical skills. Alex is now tasked with comparing the automated feedback with his own assessments and making informed evaluative judgments on the factors that hinder the students' writing development.

Alex's perspective on feedback diverges significantly when comparing automated feedback to peer feedback. While he holds a positive view of the former, he expresses a negative stance towards the latter. According to Alex, his past attempts to incorporate peer feedback before revisions were met with mixed results. Classroom observations revealed that many students struggled with the cognitive demands of identifying errors and providing actionable suggestions for improvement. Recognizing the challenges students faced in this process, Alex made a deliberate decision to exclude peer feedback from the writing assessment.

> *I frequently observed that students with advanced language skills did not gain much from peer feedback during L2 writing sessions. This was largely because their peers often lacked the proficiency to critically assess the writing. Some writing mistakes were just too difficult to diagnose in peer feedback. Some errors were too complex for peer diagnosis, leading to situations where students could sense an issue but were unable to pinpoint or address it. This was perplexing, as literature suggests that students can learn from both receiving and providing feedback. However, my classroom experiences did not align with these findings. Additionally, I was concerned about the limited time available to effectively train students in the art of peer feedback. Given these challenges, I harbored doubts about the efficacy of peer feedback in L2 writing and ultimately decided to abandon this approach. (2nd interview)*

It was evident that Alex maintained a skeptical stance on the efficacy of peer feedback for enhancing students' writing. His conviction in the connection between peer feedback and L2 writing was weak, which in turn diminished the role of students as proactive writers in the L2 writing classroom. In essence, Alex preferred to invest his efforts in providing teacher feedback rather than dedicating time to improve peer feedback skills, as he believed the latter would not significantly contribute to writing improvement, according to his reports. This perspective was closely linked to a diminished recognition of the value of peer feedback and a reduced willingness to foster it among his students. Consequently, Alex's approach to feedback in his L2 writing classes became less student-driven, reinforcing a teacher-centered pedagogy in subsequent writing assessment activities.

Stage 4. Teacher feedback on sample writings

Alex continuously guided students' writing by giving teacher feedback at this stage. Instead of giving feedback to each writing, he usually gave teacher feedback on the selected sample writings, that is, the writings diagnosed with typical mistakes in genre structure or common language errors (2nd & 3rd classroom observations). The practice of giving teacher feedback was characterized by complex emotional experiences and intensive emotional labor, and Alex reported frequent disappointment and anger toward linguistic errors in writing.

> I often found myself disheartened by the students whose writing was riddled with linguistic errors. Rather than correcting each mistake myself, I encouraged them to consult grammar books and dictionaries to self-correct their work. I was especially concerned about those who submitted their writings without any form of self-assessment. To address this, I made a point to discuss their work with them individually, ensuring that these conversations took place outside of class. I avoided criticizing them publicly to preserve their confidence in L2 writing, understanding the importance of nurturing a positive attitude towards the language. (1st & 2nd interviews)

Given the emphasis on language input in stages 1 (modeling a text) and 2 (joint construction of a text) of the teaching procedure, it is understandable that Alex chose to express his dissatisfaction and disappointment in front of the students. It seems that Alex was reluctant to give further guidance but asked the students to seek assistance by themselves. However, when it comes to errors in writing structure and content, Alex reported frequent negative emotions such as confusion, anxiety, and self-questioning when he perceived the difficulty in helping students improve the content of their writings. For example, Alex was confused when students failed to construct a "compare and contrast" structure.

> It was easy for students to understand the two basic patterns (i.e., point-by-point and subject-by-subject) in writing a "compare and contrast" essay. However, there were instances where students struggled with the underlying principles of comparison and contrast, sometimes veering off-topic or delving into irrelevant details. To clarify these concepts, I would create additional PowerPoint slides featuring model texts that illustrated the patterns. Subsequently, I would share these instructional materials on our WeChat account to ensure accessibility and reinforce learning. (see Figure 5.1). (2nd interview)

The third salient theme is Alex's responses to students' errors in writing mechanics, which is a common problem for Chinese learners of L2 writing. It was found that in situations where Alex was overwhelmed by this type of error, he usually suppressed his confusion and disappointment by reducing interactions with students and asking them to learn from the models.

> Instead of correcting these errors, I asked students to recite the model texts. Although some students and my colleagues considered recitation a "spoon-feeding" method that should be abandoned, I found this method very effective in pushing students to get familiar with the genre structure, mechanics, and content in a short time.
>
> Rather than directly correcting the errors, I opted to have students recite model texts. While some students and colleagues viewed this approach as "spoon-feeding" and advocated for its discontinuation, I have found recitation to be an effective strategy. It helps students quickly become acquainted with the genre's structure, mechanics, and content, which I believe is particularly beneficial for their learning process. (3rd interview)

From Alex's account, it can be deduced that while he recognizes the significance of writing mechanics, he believes that reacting with frustration to errors is counterproductive. This perspective underpins his decision to have students correct their mistakes through the recitation of model texts. This method not only conserves Alex's emotional energy but also allows him to concentrate on addressing more critical aspects of writing instruction.

The fourth notable theme that emerged pertains to Alex's approach to addressing content-related errors. The interviews revealed a complex emotional landscape, with

5.4 Influence of Alex's Emotion-Regulation Strategies on L2 Writing ...

Alex expressing feelings of confusion, anxiety, and regret when faced with the challenge of enhancing students' essay content. Specifically, Alex admitted to a lack of effective instructional strategies when students struggled to construct compelling arguments or to present evidence in a logical and cohesive format.

> *On the rare occasions when I encountered writings that strayed from the topic, I often found myself puzzled. I struggled to understand why students might misinterpret the writing instructions, and I was at a loss for effective strategies to address this issue. (2nd & 3rd interviews)*

Alex recounted a particularly challenging experience where the quality of writing was compromised due to the students' nascent critical thinking skills. He described the writing as lacking depth, characterized by "hollow" ideas that failed to engage the reader.

> *Initially, I was often frustrated by students' misinterpretation of topics and their disjointed reasoning, which I attributed to their underdeveloped critical thinking skills. These challenges impeded their ability to express ideas accurately and coherently. To foster critical thinking, I implemented a step-by-step argument construction process using pictures as prompts. The process began with students listing their ideas in response to each image. They then engaged in reflective questions such as "What does the picture tell you?", "What is the story behind the picture?", "What message is the picture trying to convey?", and "What solutions could address the issues depicted?". The final step involved articulating their thoughts and connecting them logically. For students who found it challenging to discuss these questions in English, I encouraged brainstorming in Chinese to ease the process. Over time, students reported that this "thinking before writing" approach was instrumental in clarifying their ideas prior to writing. They also expressed feeling more at ease and comfortable when discussing ideas in their native language. (3rd interview)*

Alex recognized the pivotal role of critical thinking in L2 writing, particularly in argumentative tasks that demand students' skills in analyzing, comparing, and synthesizing ideas into coherent written language. Despite facing emotional challenges such as confusion and anxiety, Alex adopted task-related regulatory strategies. He committed to enhancing students' writing performance through targeted instructional activities aimed at remediation.

Stage 5. Writing assessment

Alex conducted a summative assessment of the students' writing performance at this stage. Alex placed much more emphasis on the language accuracy of the writings than on the efforts involved in the revisions (classroom observation). One saline theme in this stage is Alex's disappointment at the students' failure to revise the errors.

> *From the outset, students were clearly informed about the assessment criteria for writing. They were encouraged to leverage automated feedback, teacher comments, and other sources of critique to enhance their writing and achieve a higher score. It was made clear that a refusal to revise identified issues could result in a failed writing assignment. Furthermore, if students only addressed the simpler problems and ignored the more challenging ones, I would view this as a lack of commitment to the revision process. In such cases, I would request that they undertake a more thorough revision of their work. (1st interview)*

Although Alex held high expectations for his students' writing performance, he was equally mindful of the stress that the writing process could induce, particularly for those students grappling with challenges in L2 writing. A prominent theme that emerged during this stage was Alex's empathy for the struggles that some students faced in crafting their written work.

> *Following each writing task, I engaged in one-on-one conversations with my students in the role of a counselor. Despite these efforts, I noticed that some students remained confused. This situation evoked a feeling of helplessness within me, as I grappled with the challenge of fulfilling my responsibilities as a writing instructor, which is to enhance their writing skills. (1st & 2nd interviews)*

In a bid to foster a supportive environment, Alex sought and received positive feedback on his L2 writing instruction after the completion of each writing task. Figure 5.2 illustrates the students' introspections on their writing journey and the progress they made. By openly sharing his own emotions and insights on social media, Alex demonstrated a clear intent to connect with both his students and colleagues in a way that was both encouraging and aimed at bridging the gap between them.

5.5 Summary

From Alex's approach to L2 writing instruction, it can be inferred that his feedback was primarily informational, with a greater emphasis on local aspects such as lexicon and grammar rather than global elements like organization, idea development, and style. This focus is reflected in the noticeable improvements in students' linguistic accuracy, including vocabulary, grammar, and syntax. Alex's strong endorsement of the *Pigai* platform and its instant automated feedback is rooted in its efficacy in enhancing these linguistic skills. Additionally, the use of automated feedback has significantly reduced the emotional labor associated with providing written corrective feedback, leading Alex to be satisfied with his current teaching methods.

However, Alex is also confident and adept at providing both written and oral corrective feedback. As he stated, "I can grade an essay just by reading the first paragraph. If there are more than three mistakes, I categorize it as lower-level and ask the student to self-proofread and correct the errors." In the fourth stage, Alex's provision of teacher feedback on selected sample writings allowed him to concentrate on common errors with less emotional strain.

In essence, despite the considerable workload of providing feedback on student writings across four classes, Alex effectively streamlined his efforts by concentrating on the local elements of their writing. This allowed him to deliver accurate feedback based on his extensive knowledge and experience, as suggested by Lee (2012). However, when addressing more global aspects of writing, such as the structure and content of arguments, the strength of arguments, and other overarching elements, Alex felt less equipped to offer constructive feedback or alternative strategies. Instead, he encouraged students to learn from model texts through recitation.

5.5 Summary

```
┌─────────────────────────────────────┐  ┌─────────────────────────────────────┐
│       Teacher Alex's Writing Class  │  │       Teacher Alex's Writing Class  │
│  Template for writing task 2: Picture Description │  │     Offering suggestions and solutions    │
│                                     │  │                                     │
│     From the simple but compelling  │  │  1. It is suggested that the government should │
│  illustration above we can see ( … ),│  │  make efforts to …                  │
│  which seems to be common around us │  │  Chinese translation: 政府应该做出努力… │
│  but quite thought-provoking. It is │  │  2. In view of the seriousness of this problem, │
│  obvious that this picture is intended│  │  effective measures should be taken before │
│  to draw our attention towards ( … ).│  │  things get worse. (highly recommended │
│  Clearly, this is an important lesson│  │  sentence)                          │
│  of life we should learn.           │  │  Chinese translation: 考虑到问题的严重性，在 │
│     There is no denying that recent │  │  事态进一步恶化之前，必须采取有效的措施。 │
│  years has witnessed a deteriorating│  │  3. To reverse the trend is not a light task, it │
│  phenomenon of ( … ), which has     │  │  requires a good awareness of …     │
│  induced heightened concerns and    │  │  Chinese translation: 要扭转这一趋势并非易 │
│  should call for immediate solutions.│  │  事，需要充分意识到…                │
│  Yo begin with, ( … ) in our life can│  │  4. People are coming to realize the importance │
│  no longer be ignored, because it has│  │  of … They have begun to try their best to … we │
│  already exerted a negative influence│  │  believe that …                     │
│  on people's life. In addition,     │  │  Chinese translation: 人们开始意识到…的重要 │
│  nothing is as destructive to our   │  │  性，正竭力… 我们相信…              │
│  physical and mental health (moral  │  │  5. I suggest the department concerned taking │
│  value) as ( … ). What's more, many │  │  some effective measures to improve the present │
│  countries list it as their primary │  │  situation …                        │
│  apprehensions maintaining harmonious│  │                                     │
│  development. According to a recent │  │                                     │
│  survey, people who can't deal well │  │                                     │
│  with the issue of ( … ) will be    │  │                                     │
│  unlikely to succeed or gain other  │  │                                     │
│  people's respect, which is something …│  │                                     │
└─────────────────────────────────────┘  └─────────────────────────────────────┘
```

Fig. 5.1 An example of WeChat posts of genre patterns in "Alex's writing class"

This approach to feedback helped Alex mitigate emotional stress and conserve his emotional labor, which is crucial for managing classroom emotions and responding to students' emotional needs, as noted by de Costa et al., (2020, p. 213). Despite occasional frustration and skepticism regarding students' writing performance and the effectiveness of certain writing assessment activities, such as peer feedback, Alex's underlying concern for his students' progress and success in L2 writing drove his commitment to an ethical practice of care and guidance.

Wechat Moment

Since March of this year, prior to the release of the postgraduate entrance exam results, students have been proactively reaching out to teachers for assistance in refining their English self-introductions. To date, more than 50 drafts have been revised, each one was crafted to showcase their unique academic journeys and aspirations.

My greatest achievement

Student's reflection

From Alex's English class, what has left a deep impression on your mind? Maybe some efficient English learning strategies, maybe the awful preview tasks or the gentle "see you tomorrow". However, I like the sentence: jump out of your comfort zone.

That afternoon, I revised my speech, and it is a narration of anecdote happened in college. Some feedback is really embarrasing and hit me hard, but some is heartwarming and helpful. Going through the draft brings me back to my first month in college, and I recall a moment when a student raised a question about what college life is all about ...

Fig. 5.2 Alex's reflection on his L2 writing instruction

References

De Costa, P., Li, W., & Rawal, H. (2020). 12. Should i stay or leave? Exploring L2 teachers' profession from an emotionally inflected framework. In C. Gkonou, J. Dewaele & J. King (Ed.), *The emotional rollercoaster of language teaching* (pp. 211–227). Bristol, Blue Ridge Summit: Multilingual Matters.

Lee, I. (2012). Genre-based teaching and assessment in secondary English classrooms. *English Teaching: Practice and Critique, 11*(4), 120.

Suggested readings

Deng, L., Chen, Q., & Zhang, Y. (2014). *Developing Chinese EFL learners' generic competence: A genre-based and process-genre approach.* Springer.

Hyland, K. (2003). Genre-based pedagogies: A social response to process. *Journal of Second Language Writing, 12*, 17–29.

Hyland, K. (2007). Genre pedagogy: Language, literacy and L2 writing instruction. *Journal of Second Language Writing, 16*, 148–164.

Kessler, M. (2021). The longitudinal development of second language writers' metacognitive genre awareness. *Journal of Second Language Writing, 53*, 100832–100815.

Lee, I., & Mak, P. (2018). Metacognition and metacognitive instruction in second language writing classrooms. *TESOL Quarterly, 52*, 1085–1097.

Sun, T., & Wang, C. (2020). College students' writing self-efficacy and writing self-regulated learning strategies in learning English as a foreign language. *System, 90*, 102221.

Swales, J. M. (1990). *Genre analysis: English in academic and research settings.* Cambridge University Press.

Tardy, C. M. (2016). *Beyond convention: Genre innovation in academic writing.* University of Michigan Press.

Zhang, J., & Zhang, L. J. (2022). The effect of feedback on metacognitive strategy use in EFL writing. *Computer Assisted Language Learning*, 1–26.

Zheng, Y., & Yu, S. (2018). Student engagement with teacher written corrective feedback in EFL writing: A case study of Chinese lower-proficiency students. *Assessing Writing, 37*, 13–24.

Chapter 6
Teacher Emotions and Instructional Practices: Evidence from a Process based L2 Writing Classroom

6.1 Introduction

Lina is a seasoned EFL teacher who has been dedicated to enhancing the English writing proficiency of second-year English majors at a reputable university in southeast China. With a Master's in Literature under her belt, she has been instrumental in preparing her students for the TEM-4 exam since 2015. Her course is designed to be both credit-bearing and exam-focused, focusing on genre knowledge, writing skills, and communicative competencies. Lina's teaching materials are a strategic blend of adapted writing textbooks and tasks modeled after the TEM-4, ensuring her students receive a comprehensive and targeted education.

Against this backdrop, Lina initially joined the course as a teaching assistant in 2015, and she helped the course leader (an experienced professor in L2 writing) with course preparation, marking student essays, holding writing conferences, conducting writing evaluations, and other activities pertinent to the instruction of writing for two semesters. From 2020 to 2021, Lina joined an "In-Service EFL Teacher Development" program at BFSU (Beijing Foreign Studies University, a well-known university of foreign language studies and teacher education in Mainland China), in which she not only learned the knowledge, theories, procedure, and methods of designing L2 writing courses, but also observed how the L2 writing courses were delivered at BFSU for one semester. With these experiences, Lina became more confident in curriculum development and course instruction to suit the local conditions of her university.

Lina's career in EFL teaching commenced in 2015 as a teaching assistant, where she collaborated closely with a distinguished professor of L2 writing. Over two semesters, she contributed to course preparation, essay grading, conducting writing workshops, and facilitating evaluations, thereby gaining a solid foundation in writing instruction. Her professional development continued with a dedicated program at BFSU from 2020 to 2021. This "In-Service EFL Teacher Development" initiative allowed Lina to delve into the design of L2 writing courses, encompassing knowledge, theories, and pedagogical strategies. Additionally, she observed the implementation of these courses at BFSU, which provided her with valuable insights. These experiences have significantly bolstered Lina's confidence and capability in tailoring curriculum and instruction to the specific needs of her university's student body.

Since 2016, Lina has been pioneering an innovative approach to her English writing course by merging the traditional genre-based method with the process approach. This integration is aimed at equipping students not only to excel in examinations but also to develop a robust proficiency in English writing. By blending the genre-based method's focus on specific writing conventions with the process approach's emphasis on the iterative nature of writing, Lina's course fosters a comprehensive skill set that enhances students' ability to communicate effectively in English in a variety of settings.

6.2 Lina's Emotional Experiences: A Process based L2 Writing Pedagogical Approach

The current study identified twenty-one different emotional experiences in Lina's case (see Table 6.1).

Lina's emotional experiences as documented in the book are predominantly positive, accounting for 48% of her reported feelings, with negative emotions trailing slightly behind at 43%. Neutral emotions were the least common, making up only 1%. The book delves into various sources of these emotions, highlighting that macro-contextual factors, such as school policy, triggered one instance of positive emotion. Meso-contextual issues, including collaboration with colleagues and communication with L2 writing experts, led to three positive and two negative emotional experiences. The majority of Lina's emotions, however, were influenced by micro-contextual elements within the L2 writing classrooms, with the book identifying six positive, seven negative, and two neutral emotional experiences across the instructional stages. Lina's positive appraisals were typically associated with situations where the goals for a particular instructional stage were met, such as when students understood the writing context and purpose, or when they demonstrated progress in their L2 writing. Conversely, negative appraisals occurred when there was a misalignment between the instructional goals and the actual classroom situation, exemplified by students' lack of engagement or significant avoidable errors in their writing. These instances indicated unfulfilled objectives in teacher-student interaction and writing assessment. It's also worth noting that scenarios requiring minimal teacher-student interaction, such as students' text construction, did not elicit intense emotional responses from Lina. This could be attributed to the reduced involvement of teacher-student interactions in these stages of the writing process.

Table 6.1 Types of emotions and triggering situations in Lina's case

Types of emotion	Triggering situation	Contextual issues
Gratitude	1. School policy on EFL course development and teaching innovation 2. School sponsoring of EFL teacher development program and teaching contest	Macro-contextual issues
Being recognized	3. School administrative leaders gave positive feedback on course evaluation	Meso-contextual issues
Disappointment Confusion	4. Failure to cooperate with some colleagues in course preparation and teaching reform 5. Difficulty in uniting the instructional procedure and assessment practices with some colleagues	
Satisfaction Happy-for	6. Experts' praise and positive feedback on teaching design (read to write) in L2 writing courses	
Stage 1. Pre-class writing activities		
Satisfaction Regret	7. Students are clear of the writing situation and purpose 8. Teacher failed to clarify the writing situation or the writing purpose, which confused students in the subsequent writing activities	1. Teacher identifies the writing situation and purpose
Stage 2. In-class writing activities		
Confidence Boredom	9. Guiding students to study the source reading texts for the writing task 10. Too much teacher instruction reduced students' interactions in classroom writing activities	2. Students read and analyze the source texts
Sorry-for Self-questioning Disappointment Satisfaction	11. Students paid no attention to or drifted away from classroom writing activities 12. Students made mistakes in the genre patterns and structure 13. Students had low motivation in L2 writing 14. Students showed interest and actively engage with the instruction in classroom	3. Teacher-student interaction in classroom writing activities
Peace	15. Students conducted group discussions and drafted the writing outline in classroom	4. Students plan the writing
Peace	16. Students construct the texts independently after class	5. Students construct the writing
Stage 3. Post-class writing activities		

(continued)

Table 6.1 (continued)

Types of emotion	Triggering situation	Contextual issues
Disappointment Self-questioning Happy-for	17. Students made obvious linguistic and mechanical mistakes that could have been avoided 18. Students made mistakes concerning the genre structure and content 19. Students learned new writing skills and gave positive feedback on teacher instruction	6. writing assessment
Happy-for Satisfaction	20. Students fulfilled the writing tasks in high quality 21. Students made progress in L2 writing	8. Students revise and edit the writing

6.3 Types of Triggering Situations of Lina's Emotional Experiences

This book identified five types of triggering situations from the thematic analysis of the data set (see Table 6.2).

Table 6.2 Types of triggering situations of Lina's emotional experiences

Types of triggering situation	Specific triggering situation
School policies on EFL teaching and teacher development	1. Favorable policies on EFL course development and teacher development
Interaction with colleagues and experts	2. Difficulty in collaborating with some colleagues in course preparation and cooperation
	3. Experts' recognition and positive feedback on L2 writing instructional practice
Pre-class writing activities	4. Students are clear/unclear of the writing situation or purpose
In-class writing activities	5. Teacher's instruction and guidance in learning the source text for writing
	6. Teacher-student interactions in classroom writing activities
	7. Students' planning and construction of the writing
Post-class writing activities	8. Teacher-guided writing assessment activities
	9. Students' performance in revising and editing the writing

6.4 Goals and Norms Supporting Lina's Appraisal of Emotional Situations

In general, Lina appraised her emotions in three overarching situations, i.e., interaction with school policies in macro-level context, interaction with colleagues and experts in meso-level context, and interaction with students in micro-level context (see Table 6.3). Like Alex, Lina experienced the most intense emotions across the three stages of L2 writing instruction.

Lina's emotional landscape is characterized by her assessments of interactions across three distinct contextual levels. At the macro-level, she navigates the broader school policies that shape her teaching environment. The meso-level involves her professional interactions with colleagues and experts in the field of L2 writing, which can influence her teaching strategies and perspectives. Finally, the micro-level is where Lina's direct engagement with students takes place, particularly within the L2 writing classrooms, which is the most frequent and often the most emotionally charged context for her.

Similar to Alex, Lina's emotional experiences are particularly intense as they span the three stages of L2 writing instruction. These stages likely include the planning,

Table 6.3 Goals and norms supporting Lina's appraisal of emotional situations

Types of triggering situation	Evaluated in terms of	
	Goals	Norms
School policies on EFL teaching and teacher education	1. School administration supports EFL course development and teacher education	
Interaction with colleagues and experts	2. Colleagues and experts support L2 writing course development	
Pre-class writing activities	3. Students identify the writing situation and purpose	1. Students must understand the writing situation and purpose of the given writing task
In-class writing activities	4. Students understand the language and content of the source reading text	2. Students must understand the language and content of the source reading text
	5. Students participate in teacher-student interactions in classroom writing activities	3. Students have good attitude and participate in the teacher guided interactions
	6. Students plan and construct the writing independently	4. Students must be independent in writing
Post-class writing activities	7. Students get involved in the writing assessment activities	5. Students must develop necessary assessment literacy for writing

execution, and assessment phases, each presenting unique challenges and rewards that can evoke strong emotional responses. Her ability to appraise these situations effectively is crucial for her professional growth and the success of her students in their writing endeavors.

At the pre-class writing stage, Lina viewed "students identify the writing situation and purpose" as a goal because she expects students to understand the background, including the writing context, target readers, and task requirements like genre conventions and language styles. Lina also emphasizes the importance of pre-class activities to stimulate students' interest in the writing assignment.

At the in-class writing stage, Lina outlines specific objectives for each writing process. For instance, Lina's approach to narrative writing instruction is methodical and multifaceted. She has structured her teaching around several key objectives that aim to enhance her students' writing skills in a progressive manner: First, Contextual Understanding: Lina starts by ensuring that students grasp the context of writing. She believes that analyzing source reading texts is crucial as it provides both linguistic and content input necessary for students to understand the genre and style of narrative writing. Second, Active Participation: She emphasizes the importance of students actively engaging in classroom writing activities. These teacher-guided sessions are seen as vital for students to practice and internalize the writing process, which is a fundamental step towards independent writing. Third, Independent Construction: The next goal is for students to independently construct their narratives. Lina expects that by this stage, students will be able to apply the knowledge and skills acquired from previous activities to create their own writing pieces. Fourth, Assessment and Feedback: Finally, Lina incorporates post-class writing assessment activities. She subscribes to the concept of "assessment for learning," which suggests that students can refine their writing through feedback. This stage involves students in the assessment process, allowing them to learn from critiques and improve their final writing product through revision and editing. This approach is designed to scaffold students' learning, providing them with the necessary support at each stage of the writing process, from understanding the context to producing a polished narrative. It's a comprehensive strategy that values both the input from reading and the output from writing, as well as the feedback loop that helps students grow as writers.

6.5 Influences of Lina's Emotion-Regulation Strategies on L2 Writing Instruction and Her Psychological Well-Being

This section delves into the intricate relationship between Lina's emotional landscape and her approach to teaching L2 writing. It examines how various contextual layers impact her emotional experiences and psychological well-being, as well as her teaching methods.

6.5.1 Lina's Use of Emotion-Regulation Strategies and Impact: Macro Level

The first overarching theme is concerned with Lina's emotional experiences triggered by school policies on EFL course development and teacher education. In Lina's university, the school administration placed increasing emphasis on EFL course development and teacher education to improve the university's comprehensive competitiveness and ranking. For instance, the department encouraged Lina and her colleagues to reform and develop English writing courses by developing a "community of teaching practice" and participating in teacher education programs. This policy was in favor of Lina, who has been committed to improving her pedagogical knowledge and skills.

The central theme here revolves around Lina's emotional journey as she interacts with her university's strategic initiatives in English as a Foreign Language (EFL) course development and teacher professional development. The university's administration is actively promoting these initiatives to bolster the institution's competitiveness and reputation. Specifically, the department is encouraging faculty, including Lina, to engage in the following activities: First, Reform and Development of English Writing Courses: Lina and her colleagues are encouraged to innovate and enhance the existing English writing curriculum. This could involve updating course content, incorporating new teaching methodologies, or integrating technology to improve student engagement and learning outcomes. Second, Building a Community of Teaching Practice: The policy encourages the formation of a collaborative network where teachers can share experiences, resources, and best practices. This community fosters a supportive environment for continuous improvement in teaching strategies and course materials. Third, Participation in Teacher Education Programs: The university promotes professional growth by offering programs designed to further the pedagogical knowledge and skills of its teaching staff. These programs may include workshops, seminars, or courses that focus on current trends in EFL education and effective teaching techniques. These policy-driven changes align with Lina's personal dedication to her professional growth and her commitment to enhancing her teaching methods. As a result, she likely experiences positive emotions such as satisfaction, motivation, and a sense of purpose. The support from the administration validates her efforts and provides her with the resources and opportunities to excel in her role as an EFL instructor. This alignment between institutional goals and personal aspirations can lead to a fulfilling professional experience and contribute to Lina's overall well-being.

> *I am grateful to the school's supporting policies on EFL course development, and I benefited a lot. With the project grant, it is possible for us to carry out a series of transformative teaching initiatives. Last year, I was sponsored to join an EFL teacher education project held by BFSU, which enhanced both my content expertise and pedagogical strategies. This professional development has undoubtedly elevated my teaching practice and contributed to my personal and professional growth. (1st interview)*

Nevertheless, Lina's experience with the educational reforms in her department highlights a contrast in teacher engagement. While she found the reforms and the opportunity for professional development to be motivating, not all her colleagues shared the same sentiment. Despite the support and resources provided for educational reforms, there was a spectrum of reactions among the teachers. Lina's proactive approach stood in contrast to the reluctance of some of her peers. Some teachers were daunted by the volume of feedback required for student writings. The workload associated with providing detailed and constructive comments on each student's work seemed overwhelming to them. There was also a perception among some teachers that teaching writing was a monotonous and pedagogically complex task. This view likely stemmed from the challenges of engaging students in the writing process, assessing their work, and finding innovative ways to improve their writing skills.

Some teachers in my department complain that the teaching of L2 writing is difficult, labor-intensive, and unrewarding. Just think about the work of preparing courses, giving feedback, and writing conferences. This explains why some teachers refused to teach writing. In my department, there's a perception among some teachers that teaching L2 writing is a demanding task. They point to the considerable effort required for course preparation, offering feedback on student work, and facilitating writing conferences as particularly burdensome aspects of the job. This workload can lead to a sense of the work being intensive and, from their perspective, not sufficiently rewarding. As a result, this has led to a reluctance among these teachers to take on writing courses. This viewpoint highlights the importance of finding ways to make the teaching of L2 writing more manageable and rewarding, so as to encourage greater participation and enthusiasm among the faculty. (1st interview)

These varying attitudes towards the educational reforms underscore the importance of addressing individual teacher concerns and finding ways to foster a more unified approach to embracing change in the classroom. It suggests that while supportive policies and resources are crucial, they must be accompanied by strategies to address the concerns and motivations of all teachers involved. The school's emphasis on EFL teaching and teacher education played a significant role in fueling Lina's enthusiasm and dedication to L2 writing instruction. These policies were key macro-contextual elements that supported her professional aspirations. However, it was observed that not all EFL teachers who were involved in L2 writing instruction automatically identified themselves as L2 writing specialists. Within Lina's department, she recognized that the implementation of school policies, while beneficial, was not a guarantee for teachers to develop the specific expertise needed for effective L2 writing instruction. This suggests that there might be a gap between policy implementation and the actual professional development of teachers in this specialized area.

6.5.2 Lina's Use of Emotion-Regulation Strategies and Impact: Meso-Level

The second key theme revolves around Lina's emotional journey as she engages with her peers and experts in the field of L2 writing. Recognizing the shortcomings of the existing teaching methods, which lacked adequate pedagogical support and did not align well with students' needs, Lina was inspired to revamp the L2 writing curriculum following her professional development experience at BFSU. However, she faced challenges in convincing her colleagues to embrace these changes, which likely led to a range of emotional responses as she navigated the process of reforming the teaching procedures within her department.

> *I tried to collaborate with a veteran L2 writing instructor, aiming to introduce a more integrated assessment process that would span the various stages of writing. Despite my initiative, my colleague, confident in the effectiveness of her current criteria, was not convinced of the need for such changes. Subsequently, I suggested transitioning from a product-focused approach to one that emphasizes the writing process, by breaking it down into distinct substeps. Unfortunately, this proposal was also met with rejection. Faced with the challenge of altering entrenched teaching practices, I was disappointed and ultimately had to concede and cease my efforts to reform the approach. (1st interview)*

Indeed, Lina faced clear challenges in her efforts to introduce new writing assessment criteria and a process-based approach to L2 writing within her department. These setbacks directly led to her experiencing negative emotions. Despite the difficulties in convincing her colleague and the decision to abandon the idea of collaborative course planning, Lina remained committed to her educational philosophy. She chose not to push her proposals further in a collective setting but continued to apply the process approach in her own L2 writing classes, demonstrating her dedication to improving student learning outcomes even within the constraints she faced.

> *Despite the initial disappointment, I remained persistent in my efforts to improve the teaching process. I recognized that my initial proposal lacked the specificity needed to guide my colleague through the implementation of the new writing assessment activities. Acknowledging this, I took a more detailed and methodical approach by creating rubrics that provided clear, step-by-step guidance for each stage of the teaching procedure. This refinement likely made my proposal more comprehensible and actionable, addressing my colleague's previous confusion and potentially increasing the chances of successful adoption of the new assessment strategy. (1st interview)*

Lina's commitment to enhancing her teaching methods in L2 writing is further demonstrated by her active pursuit of additional knowledge and expertise. By attending lectures and workshops on L2 writing, she sought to broaden her understanding of effective instructional strategies and gain insights into how these courses are conducted at other universities. This proactive engagement with experts in the field not only enriched her own pedagogical knowledge but also provided her with a wider perspective on best practices, which she could then apply or adapt to her own teaching environment. This continuous professional development is a testament to Lina's dedication to staying current with educational trends and her desire to provide her students with the highest quality of instruction.

> *During my visit to Guangdong University of Foreign Studies, I had the opportunity to observe a class that introduced me to the concept of the "reading-writing continuation task", a technique that integrates reading into the L2 writing process. This hands-on experience as an observer not only provided me with a practical approach to teaching but also offered me the opportunity to actively engage with the concept by designing my own teaching plan. The feedback I received from experts, particularly on the integration of reading and writing within a continuation task, was invaluable. It helped me refine my teaching strategies and deepened my understanding of how to effectively combine these two skills in L2 writing instruction. This learning experience has significantly contributed to my professional growth and enhanced my ability to teach L2 writing more effectively. (1st interview)*

Lina's narrative clearly indicates a strong internal drive to enhance her L2 writing instruction. She is deeply dedicated to the continuous improvement of her teaching methods, showcasing a high level of commitment to her professional development. The satisfaction she derives from the feedback of experts is a clear indication of how interactions at the meso-level, such as those with colleagues and experts, significantly shape her identity as an L2 writing instructor. These discourses are integral to her professional narrative. Furthermore, Lina's emotional responses to her colleague's reluctance to change demonstrate her ability to manage disappointment. She transforms the negative emotions stemming from these interactions into a positive outlook. By expressing gratitude for the valuable insights gained from her interactions with experts, she focuses on the constructive aspects of her professional journey. Lina employs a variety of emotional labor strategies to navigate her emotional landscape. Her emotional regulation is influenced not only by the immediate situational context but also by her own professional ethos as a developing L2 writing teacher. This self-regulation is a testament to her resilience and her determination to grow and succeed in her teaching career.

6.5.3 Lina's Use of Emotion-Regulation Strategies and Impact: Micro-Level

Lina's approach to her English Writing course reflects a thoughtful integration of two distinct methodologies: the genre-based and the process-based approaches. Her curriculum development was guided by two main teaching objectives. First, Contextual Knowledge: Lina emphasized understanding the context of writing, which includes recognizing the purpose and audience of the writing task. This aspect aligns with the genre approach, which focuses on the types of texts (genres) that students need to navigate in academic or professional settings. Second, Language Skills: She also prioritized the development of language skills, ensuring that students could effectively use language to express their ideas. This focus on language use is central to the process approach, which encourages students to explore and experiment with language as they write. In her teaching, Lina balanced the provision of reading materials that serve as models or input for students (genre approach) with activities that encourage students to actively engage in writing and develop their linguistic potential (process approach). This dual focus likely led to a range of complex emotions for Lina, as she navigated the challenges of teacher-student interactions and the impact of her teaching methods on both the learning process and her own psychological well-being. Her ability to manage these emotional tensions provides a window into the intricate dynamics of teaching, highlighting the emotional labor involved in crafting a curriculum that resonates with both the structural demands of genre and the creative exploration of the process. Lina's experiences underscore the importance of emotional regulation in the teaching profession and the impact it has on the quality of instruction and the teacher's personal well-being.

Stage 1. Pre-class writing activity

The most salient theme at this stage is Lina's efforts in designing a writing task with appropriate situations and explicit purposes so that students could be motivated in the following writing process. To this end, the teacher must find out what the students know or can do before class. According to Lina, she usually took students' previous writings as important references in deciding the new writing tasks. For instance, if students were familiar with the given genre, she would challenge them by assigning a relatively difficult writing task (e.g., creative writing); if students were still bothered by the genre knowledge, she would reduce the difficulty by selecting the writing task from the textbook and guided students to carry out the elements in a progressive manner (1st classroom observation). In the interview, Lina expressed her uncertainty about designing an appropriate writing task. To motivate student interest in writing, Lina usually decides the writing task and evaluation criteria by referring to students' previous writing performances. At this stage, the most prominent theme is Lina's dedication to crafting writing tasks that are tailored to her students' current abilities and interests, with the aim of enhancing their motivation throughout the writing process. To achieve this, Lina emphasizes the importance of understanding her students' pre-existing knowledge and skills before introducing new material. Here's a refined summary of her approach: First, Assessment of Prior Knowledge: Lina uses her students' previous writings as a critical resource to inform her decisions about new writing tasks. This practice ensures that the tasks are relevant and challenging, yet achievable for the students.

Second, Task Complexity: If students have a good grasp of a particular genre, Lina introduces more complex tasks, such as creative writing, to push them further. Conversely, if students struggle with genre knowledge, she selects tasks from the textbook and guides them through the writing process in a step-by-step manner to scaffold their learning. Third, Designing with Purpose: Lina's goal is to create writing tasks that are not only appropriate for the students' current level but also engaging. She is mindful of the need to balance challenge with support, ensuring that students are motivated and interested in the writing activities. Finally, Uncertainty and Adaptation: Despite her thoughtful approach, Lina acknowledges the uncertainty in designing the perfect writing task. She remains flexible and adaptive, using students' previous writing performances as a guide to determine the writing tasks and evaluation criteria.

Lina's methodical and student-centered approach to task design reflects her commitment to fostering a positive and effective learning environment. Her willingness to adapt her teaching strategies based on student feedback and performance is a key factor in her success as an educator.

> Writing topics that are connected to current economic and scientific events is an effective way to engage students. Take expository writing as an example. I usually provide students with several writing topics on popular economic and scientific events, such as "What causes the rapid transmission of AIDS?", "How to stimulate the potential of human brains?", and "How does the COVID virus spread among people?". These topics are tapping into subjects that are not only informative but also have a direct impact on students' lives. This relevance can significantly enhance their motivation to research, understand, and articulate their findings. (2nd interview)

Lina's perspective on the impact of writing tasks on student motivation is spot on. A well-designed writing task can indeed serve as a powerful motivator, sparking curiosity, encouraging exploration, and fostering a sense of purpose in writing. When students are tasked with writing about topics that are engaging, relevant, and challenging, they are more likely to invest time and effort into their work, which can lead to improved writing skills and a deeper understanding of the subject matter.

> In the past, there were instances where the class failed to meet the set teaching objectives. The student' boredom and disappointment were palpable in their responses to the assigned writing topics, and by the time I recognized this, it was too late to alter the lesson plan. Consequently, the overall writing experience was lackluster. This realization underscores the importance of proactive engagement and adaptability in lesson planning to ensure a dynamic and stimulating learning environment. (2nd interview)

Lina's approach to lesson planning is a testament to her belief in the adage "preparedness ensures success, unpreparedness spells failure." She is acutely aware of the potential for negative emotional responses during the writing process and takes proactive steps to mitigate this. By assigning specific learning tasks and allocating time for pre-class writing activities, Lina sets her students on a structured path. She requires them to submit the background research for their writing assignments and be prepared for classroom discussions, which streamlines the initiation of writing tasks and reduces the emotional toll on her (as observed in the 2nd classroom observation). This method allows Lina to make prompt adjustments to her lesson plans, steering clear of scenarios that could trigger emotions detrimental to the writing process.

Stage 2. In-class writing activities

In Lina's classroom, the commencement of in-class writing activities was often prefaced by an assessment of the students' preparation. For instance, during the narrative writing tasks, Lina would administer a brief quiz. This served two purposes: firstly, it gauged the students' understanding of the narrative context, genre-specific knowledge, and the instructions provided (as observed in the 1st and 2nd classroom sessions). Secondly, the quiz aimed to identify any potential challenges that could impede the students' writing process, allowing Lina to address these issues proactively.

6.5 Influences of Lina's Emotion-Regulation Strategies on L2 Writing ...

> *In narrative writing assignments, the routine was to have students immerse themselves in language input by reading short stories prior to their own writing endeavors. Classic tales penned by authors like O. Henry and Guy de Maupassant were often the chosen texts. These stories were favored for their accessibility and their open-ended nature, which not only facilitated comprehension but also sparked engaging discussions and inspired students to craft their own continuations of the narratives. (2nd interview)*

Lina prioritized the role of teacher-student interaction as a pivotal element in steering students through their reading activities. She actively engaged her students in the "read-to-write" process by providing guidance on how to dissect the language features, genre structure, and rhetorical devices present in the source material. This method of instruction, where she led the "read-to-write" activities, was particularly impactful in evoking her emotional response, highlighting the significance of these interactions in her teaching approach.

> *In my approach to teaching, I focus on guiding students to decipher the genre structure of the reading material, aiming to enhance their comprehension of the narrative techniques employed in the story. To this end, I often pose a rapid succession of questions to the class, with the intention of fostering a deeper understanding of the storytelling methods. However, this strategy sometimes backfires. When students are unable to respond correctly, it can lead to a ripple effect of nervousness and silence, as the classroom energy shifts from engagement to inactivity. If the negative emotions escalate, I find myself compelled to halt the questioning and move on to the next task, acknowledging the need for a more nuanced approach to maintain a positive and interactive learning environment. (2nd interview)*

Lina's narrative suggests that her instructional approach tended to be more teacher-centric, focusing on guiding students through the text with a structured methodology. This approach, however, sometimes led to the emergence of negative emotions during the read-to-write activities, as both the teacher and students experienced anxiety due to the challenging interactions. When the class atmosphere became tense due to the barrage of questions, Lina recognized the need to mitigate these emotions. She did so by engaging more directly in discussions and fostering an environment where ideas could be exchanged freely among students, thus helping to restore a more collaborative and positive dynamic in the classroom.

When faced with students who were struggling to cope with the intensity of questioning, Lina sometimes adopted a more pessimistic outlook, which underscored the emotionally charged nature of L2 writing instruction. This perspective also revealed her tendency to manage her own negative emotions by either discontinuing the questioning or swiftly transitioning to alternative activities, a strategy that could be perceived as "hiding and faking" her feelings. Nevertheless, upon concluding the formal instruction, Lina was open to engaging more authentically with her students. She was willing to step down from her authoritative position and participate in their discussions, fostering a more egalitarian and collaborative learning environment.

> *As with many educators, I embrace the opportunity for students to ask questions, recognizing it as a catalyst for generating valuable ideas for their writing. I often position myself alongside the students, observing their interactions as they engage in cross-questioning and dialogue. Should their discussions veer off-topic or exhibit logical inconsistencies, I gently point out the errors without casting judgment on their creative thoughts. This approach is particularly appealing to me because it allows for authentic conversations with the students,*

where I can share my sincere emotions and perspectives on the subjects under discussion. (2nd interview)

The dialogic nature of the teacher-student interactions in Lina's classroom underscores the positive influence of a nurturing teacher-student relationship and the importance of teachers authentically expressing their emotions during the writing process. This approach aligns with the "process approach" to L2 writing, which Lina embodies through her frequent and profound engagement with students, a dynamic that often evokes strong emotional responses. In the next phase of the writing task, students are encouraged to create a writing outline, a step Lina considers crucial for several reasons. An outline serves as a preliminary framework that reflects the students' comprehension of the source material and their grasp of the genre-specific knowledge necessary for crafting an independent piece of writing. By providing pre-feedback on these outlines, Lina can guide students effectively (as observed in the 1st and 2nd classroom sessions). Lina's role as a writing facilitator is one she finds comfortable, as it allows her to focus on the writing process rather than just the final product. This belief is further reinforced by her view of L2 writing as a socio-cognitive process, which involves not only linguistic skills but also cognitive and social interactions. This perspective necessitates the use of emotional labor strategies to manage classroom dynamics and interactions.

Lina's confidence in this approach is bolstered by her expertise in the interplay between genre and process approaches to writing. Her in-class writing activities typically culminate with the development of writing outlines, with the full text construction taking place outside of class time. This method ensures that students have a structured plan to follow, facilitating a more focused and effective writing process.

Stage 3. Pos-class writing activities

The post-class writing activities in Lina's teaching practice were characterized by a combination of teacher and peer assessments. Lina typically provided feedback on student writing, which she regarded not merely as an evaluative task, but as an opportunity to engage in meaningful dialogue with her students. Her approach to feedback was conversational in nature, aiming to foster a two-way exchange rather than presenting a unilateral judgment.

This method of feedback was designed to be more akin to a series of discussions, where students could reflect on their work and receive guidance in a manner that was less formal and more interactive than a traditional "decision letter." The excerpt below illustrates Lina's preference for a feedback style that is personalized and conducive to ongoing student–teacher communication.

Giving feedback is like having a conversation with students, just embrace it

While providing feedback, I am able to discern the students' thought processes and the degree of effort they have invested in their writing. The content of their work often mirrors their perspectives and stances on the discussed topics; the structure indicates their grasp of genre knowledge; and the language use reflects the time and effort dedicated to writing development. Consequently, I am generally understanding of errors related to the writing's elaboration, organization, and focus, recognizing them as part of the learning process. However, I

6.5 Influences of Lina's Emotion-Regulation Strategies on L2 Writing ...

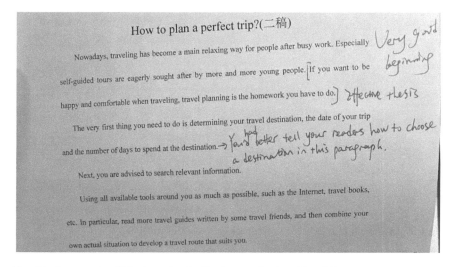

Fig. 6.1 An example of Lina's teacher feedback on student's writing (01)

> *find myself feeling disappointed and somewhat apologetic when I encounter writings riddled with conventional mistakes, such as linguistic and mechanical errors. These issues are more disheartening because they often stem from a lack of foundational understanding or attention to detail, which can be addressed with consistent practice and careful proofreading. My role, then, is to guide students towards a balance between creative expression and adherence to writing conventions, ensuring that their work is both engaging and polished. (1st interview)*

Lina's approach to providing teacher feedback is clearly demonstrated through the following example (Fig. 6.1).

In this example, Lina's interaction with the student was characterized by a conversational approach rather than a straightforward evaluation of the writing's quality. In the initial part of the feedback, Lina acknowledged the student's effective thesis statement, which demonstrated a clear understanding and engagement with the writing task. This positive reinforcement highlighted the student's ability to articulate the purpose and context of their writing. Moving on to the second paragraph, where the student's writing was more of a general description lacking in detail, Lina seized the opportunity to engage in a dialogue. Instead of simply pointing out the lack of depth, she prompted the student to elaborate on their choice of destination, guiding them towards a more detailed and nuanced discussion. This conversational feedback method not only addresses the student's current work but also encourages a deeper level of thinking and writing in future tasks. It fosters a collaborative learning environment where the student feels supported in their development as a writer (Fig. 6.2).

In this teacher feedback example, the underlined sentence in question appeared to be insufficiently detailed, failing to provide clear guidance on the considerations for packing luggage. To address this, Lina initiated a dialogue with the student by posing two targeted questions. These questions served as explicit prompts, aiming to guide

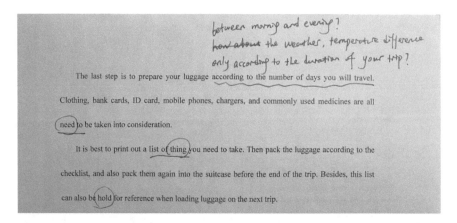

Fig. 6.2 An example of Lina's teacher feedback on student's writing (02)

the student towards a more comprehensive and thoughtful approach to their writing. During the interview, Lina expressed her deep engagement with the feedback process, stating, "I am very absorbed in giving feedback and commenting on student writings so that I can follow the student's train of thought. I usually don't give feedback on every single sentence, but wherever necessary, I will let the student know my feelings and thoughts." This approach is particularly noticeable in her concluding comments, as illustrated in Figs. 6.3 and 6.4, where she provides more substantial feedback to help students understand and improve their writing. Lina's method emphasizes the importance of thoughtful and purposeful feedback, ensuring that students receive the guidance they need without being overwhelmed by critiques on every detail.

In the concluding comments of these two pieces of student writing, Lina conveyed her genuine emotions by providing a balanced critique that included both the strengths and weaknesses of the work, along with clear suggestions for improvement. She deliberately refrained from using harsh language in her feedback, opting instead to underline sentences containing grammatical errors as a more gentle form of correction. Lina's approach was to support the student's development rather than to pass a definitive judgment. She aimed to guide the student by encouraging them to expand on their points with specific details, descriptions, and reactions, thereby scaffolding their writing skills.

Reflecting on her feedback style, Lina expressed satisfaction with this method, as it allowed her to utilize her expertise in providing writing feedback and to connect with students on an emotional level. Additionally, to foster a positive and encouraging atmosphere, Lina incorporated emoticons into her feedback, such as pairing the word "excellent" with a smiling face. This strategy was a deliberate attempt to engage with students in a way that considered their emotional well-being, further enhancing the supportive and motivational nature of her feedback. Peer feedback played a significant role in Lina's writing assessment activities, typically following the teacher's feedback. This approach was rooted in Lina's strong conviction about the mutual benefits of giving and receiving feedback within peer interactions. She

6.5 Influences of Lina's Emotion-Regulation Strategies on L2 Writing …

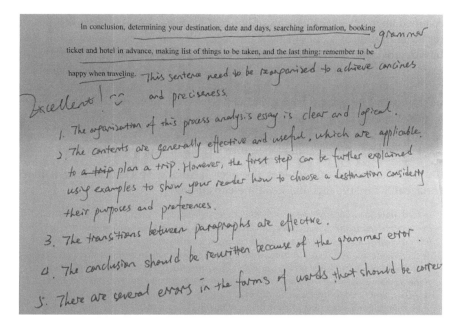

Fig. 6.3 An example of Lina's end comment on student's writing (03)

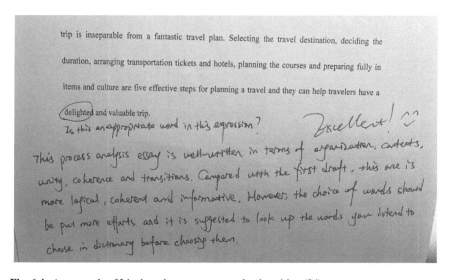

Fig. 6.4 An example of Lina's end comment on student's writing (04)

identified three key characteristics of her peer feedback activities: The first feature was the utilization of rubrics to guide the peer review process (as shown in Fig. 6.3). Rubrics provided a structured framework for students to evaluate their peers' work, ensuring that feedback was focused, objective, and aligned with the learning objectives. By using rubrics, students could offer detailed and constructive comments that were grounded in specific criteria, which helped both the writer and the reviewer to understand the strengths and areas for improvement in the writing. This method not only enhanced the quality of feedback but also taught students how to critically assess writing, a valuable skill in their own writing development (Fig. 6.5).

The use of a rubric streamlines the peer feedback process, making it more manageable for students and less time-consuming

> *Indeed, implementing effective peer feedback can be challenging, and I once felt frustrated by its perceived ineffectiveness. By providing students with a structured rubric, I've given them a clear framework to follow, which can significantly enhance the quality and usefulness of their critiques. Incorporating rubrics into the writing assessment process has likely multiplied the feedback resources available to my students. This method ensures that each student receives a variety of perspectives in a format that is both timely and comprehensive. The structured feedback, delivered in a "packaged" manner, can help students gain a more rounded understanding of their work, allowing them to see their strengths and areas for improvement from multiple viewpoints. This approach not only supports their writing*

Process essay rubric

Category	Excellent (4)	Good (3)	(2)	(0)	Score	
Title	The title applies to the essay and is interesting.	The title applies to the essay but is not interesting.	A title is given but does not relate to the essay.	No title is given.		
Introduction 15	The introduction is states the process and why it is important, gives background information, and includes a thesis.	The introduction states the process and a thesis but lacks background information and/or does not explain the importance of the process.	The introduction does not state the process or its importance, does not give background information, and does not include a thesis.	No introduction is included.	11.	14
Body 20	The body paragraphs include three major supporting details along with at least one minor supporting detail in each paragraph.	The body paragraphs include two major supporting details with at least one minor supporting detail in each paragraph or include three major supporting details with no minor supporting details.	The body paragraphs include one major supporting detail with at least minor supporting detail or less.	No body paragraphs are included.	16.	19
Conclusion 10	The conclusion includes the three major supporting details from the thesis and a new piece of interesting information.	The conclusion includes two major supporting details from the thesis and /or does not include a new piece of interesting information.	The conclusion includes only one major supporting detail from the thesis.	No conclusion is included.	8.	9
Thesis statement 10	The thesis is in the last sentence of the first paragraph and describes the three major supporting details.	The thesis is in the last sentence of the first paragraph and describes two major supporting details.	The thesis is not in the last sentence of the first paragraph and/or only describes one supporting detail.	No thesis is included.	9	10
Unity 10	All sentences support the thesis.	One to three sentences do not support the thesis.	Four or more sentences do not support the thesis.	No sentences support the thesis.	9	10
Coherence 10	All sentences are written in a clear and logical manner. A text structure is clearly used.	Most sentences are written in a logical order. A text structure is used in most of the essay.	A few sentences appear to follow a certain order. A text structure is not clearly seen in most of the essay.	Sentences are written in a confusing manner. There is no order to the placement	8	10

Fig. 6.5 An example of process essay rubric for peer feedback

development but also fosters a collaborative learning environment where students can learn from one another. (3rd interview)

The concept of emergent literacy in the context of designing a constructive feedback environment, as highlighted by Carless & Winstone (2020), is indeed exemplified by the use of rubrics to support peer feedback. This method not only structures the feedback process but also serves as a scaffold for students, helping them to develop their critical thinking and evaluative skills. The post-peer feedback interactions further solidify the effectiveness of this approach. These interactions are crucial as they allow students to engage with the feedback they receive, consider its implications, and apply it to their writing. This reflective process is a natural progression from the initial feedback and is integral to the development of a deeper understanding of writing conventions and strategies.

Lina's commitment to pushing students to reflect on their writing, as indicated in Fig. 6.4, is the second significant feature of her approach. By encouraging reflection, Lina is fostering a learning environment where students are actively involved in their own development. This reflective practice not only enhances their writing abilities but also promotes a growth mindset, where students view their skills as improvable through effort and learning from feedback

Figure 6.6 illustrates the interactive nature of the feedback process between the student reviewer and the writer, with both parties engaging in a dialogue that is informed by the rubric. This virtual space, established by the teacher, serves as a platform for immediate feedback and responses, facilitating a dynamic exchange that goes beyond the initial peer review. The use of the rubric in these post-feedback conversations is particularly beneficial. It not only provides the reviewer with a basis to explain their decisions but also enables the writer to engage in a more informed negotiation. This back-and-forth allows for a deeper exploration of the writing, moving beyond surface-level linguistic issues to delve into the more nuanced aspects of meaning-making. Lina's adoption of this practice, inspired by the Teacher Education Project at BFSU, has been a positive addition to her classroom. She appreciates how it enriches the feedback process, transforming it into a more comprehensive and meaningful experience for her students. The fact that these discussions often continue outside of class hours underscores the impact of this approach, turning writing into a continuous, collaborative, and authentic learning process.

The third notable feature of Lina's approach to peer feedback, which is well-regarded by numerous scholars in the field of L2 writing, involves the teacher's role in evaluating the correctness of the peer feedback provided. This step is crucial as it ensures the quality and reliability of the feedback students receive from their peers. In addition to the interactions between the reviewers and writers, Lina actively participates in the conversation by reassessing the student's writing. She evaluates the correctness of the peer feedback, ensuring that the critiques are valid and constructive. Where appropriate, Lina also contributes additional comments, offering her own insights and guidance to the student writer (as depicted in Fig. 6.7).

Figure 6.7 displays how Lina initiated the conversation with the reviewer by questioning the inconsistency between the positive comment (i.e., the introduction

				of sentences. No text structure is used.		
Sentence structure 10	All sentences have a subject and a predicate.	One to three sentences are missing a subject and/or predicate.	Four or more sentences are missing a subject and/or predicate.	All sentences are missing a subject and/or predicate.	10	9
Transitions 10	Four or more transitions are used.	Two to three transitions are used.	Only one transition is used.	No transitions are used.	10	10
Spelling 5	There are no spelling errors.	The essay contains 1-2 spelling errors.	The essay contains 3 or more spelling errors.	Most words are misspelled	5	5

Total score ~~96~~ 87. 95

Comment and suggestions from the reviewer:

① ~~First~~ mostof, the structure of this essay is very clear. The introduction, the ~~body~~ lastWAS is ... although ~~and~~ conclusion are great, especially the transitions are very excellent! And the languges are clear, ~~howe~~ which should be praised.
② Second, maybe more advanced vocabulary could be used, which can make your essay ~~more~~ better, and maybe the thesis could be ~~clearer~~ and not confus(e) the read(er).
Last ③ Maybe some sentences could be more consise, which can make the stru(cture) more compact(紧凑), maybe some sentences, which is not very important could be deleted.

Feedback from the writer:

① I totally agree with my reviewer. After having the Lesson of "Thesis Statement", I find there are a lot of errors in my artical. Firstly, I think the steps I ~~give~~ gave are not clear I wrote a lot of importance of each step but gav(e) few solutions towards them. The information is weak.
② Secondly, I repeated the same thing during step two and step three. it is confusing.
③ Thirdly, I consider there is scarcely logic in my artical except the first and last paragraphs.
So I will ~~adjusted~~ adjust a lot in my second ~~written~~ passage.

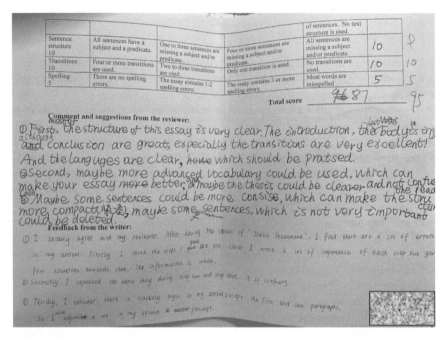

Fig. 6.6 An example of student peer feedback (01)

				of sentences. No text structure is used.		
Sentence structure 10	All sentences have a subject and a predicate.	One to three sentences are missing a subject and/or predicate.	Four or more sentences are missing a subject and/or predicate.	All sentences are missing a subject and/or predicate.	6	9
Transitions 10	Four or more transitions are used.	Two to three transitions are used.	Only one transition is used.	No transitions are used.	8	9
Spelling 5	There are no spelling errors.	The essay contains 1-2 spelling errors.	The essay contains 3 or more spelling errors.	Most words are misspelled	3	5

Total score 69 86

Comment and suggestions from the reviewer:

This favourable content and score seem not ...

Comment: The introduction at the beginning was great, which made people instantly immerse themselves in it. The whole text was written fluently, the thinking was coherent, and the steps to overcome procrastination echo the previous step, which makes people interested to read on.

Suggestion: The general content of this article is how to overcome procrastination, but some parts can be written more detailed, such as the fourth step to overcome procrastination, can write more ways to discuss the hotspot answers, so that readers can be more based

Feedback from the writer:

I do appreciate your comment and suggestion. I add more details on the hotspot answers and make simple examples on ~~How~~ the 2nd draft. And actually I didn't find the spelling errors. Next time I'll pay more attention on writing more details of each step.

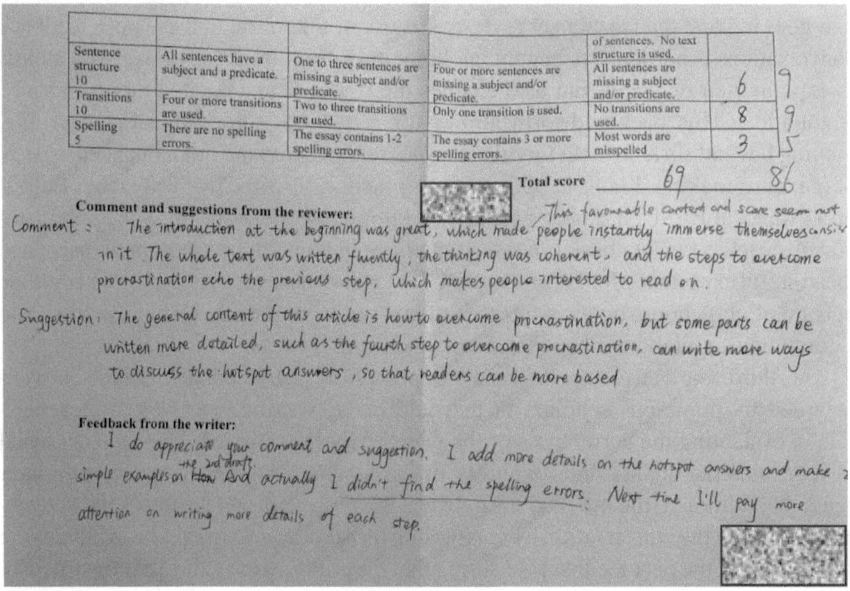

Fig. 6.7 An example of student peer feedback (02)

at the beginning was great, which made people instantly immerse themselves in it) and the relatively low score (total score is 69). Besides, Lina underlined "I didn't find the spelling errors" to ask him to encourage the student reviewer to double-check the misspellings. Lina also joined the peer feedback by adding supplementary suggestions (see Fig. 6.7).

Figure 6.7 illustrates Lina's proactive engagement in the peer review process by addressing a discrepancy between the reviewer's positive comment and the relatively low score given to the student's writing. The introduction's effectiveness, as praised by the reviewer, seems to contrast with the overall score of 69, prompting Lina to question this inconsistency and seek clarification. Additionally, Lina's attention to detail is evident as she underlines the statement "I didn't find the spelling errors," which serves as a prompt for the student reviewer to reexamine the writing for any misspellings. This action not only ensures the accuracy of the feedback but also encourages the reviewer to be more diligent in their assessment. Lina's participation in the peer feedback process extends beyond oversight; she also contributes supplementary suggestions to enhance the student writer's work. By joining the conversation, Lina provides an additional layer of support, ensuring that the feedback is comprehensive and that the student receives a variety of perspectives to consider in their revision process. This approach demonstrates her commitment to fostering a collaborative and constructive learning environment where feedback is used as a tool for growth and improvement.

Figure 6.8 provides a clear example of Lina's meticulous approach to the evaluation process. She not only re-assessed the student's writing, increasing the score from 84 to 96, but also provided feedback on the reviewer's work, commendably marked with "Great in red." This acknowledgment of the reviewer's effort is an important aspect of reinforcing the value of peer feedback. Furthermore, Lina offered additional suggestions in response to the reviewer's recommendation. She focused on enhancing the existing content's clarity and informativeness, as indicated by her comment on the essay's length and the need for specificity in the four steps mentioned. Lina's guidance aimed to refine the writer's existing work rather than suggesting a complete reorganization or the addition of more information, which aligns with the reviewer's original advice to clarify the disease's production process. This approach demonstrates Lina's commitment to guiding the writer towards a more nuanced and detailed elaboration of their content, ensuring that the feedback is constructive and leads to a more polished final piece of writing. By addressing the reviewer's comments in this way, Lina helps the writer to understand the importance of specificity and clarity in their writing, which is a critical skill for effective communication.

In a bid to foster a supportive and inclusive environment, students were given the flexibility to engage in peer feedback in a language they were comfortable with English, Chinese, or a combination of both. Lina's philosophy was that the purpose of peer feedback was to encourage a constructive dialogue between the reviewer and the writer, rather than to create a challenging or intimidating atmosphere. This approach was rooted in the belief that feedback should be a collaborative process aimed at helping students refine their writing skills, rather than a competitive or confrontational one. By allowing students to use their preferred language, Lina ensured that

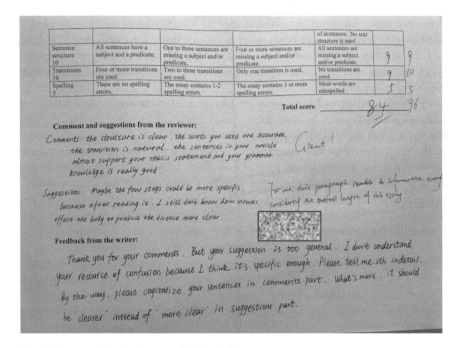

Fig. 6.8 An example of student peer feedback (03)

all students, even those who might be less confident in their English communication skills, felt comfortable participating in the peer feedback sessions (see Fig. 6.9). This inclusive strategy not only promotes a sense of belonging and encourages active participation but also helps students to develop their language skills in a supportive context. It underscores the importance of creating a classroom environment where students are empowered to express their thoughts and provide feedback to their peers, thereby enhancing the overall learning experience.

From Lina's approach to peer feedback, it's clear that she is committed to maintaining student motivation and engagement in the writing process through ongoing dialogue and reflection. Her method of feedback literacy, which involves thoughtful design and active student participation, contributes to a constructive feedback environment. Lina's focus on the writing itself, rather than on the students, creates a positive and constructive atmosphere where both she and the students can express their genuine feelings openly. This contrasts with traditional classroom interactions where immediate responses are often expected, potentially leading to uncertain situations that can trigger unwanted emotional responses from teachers. In Lina's classes, writing assessments are purposefully placed at the end of the writing process, fostering a more dialogic and intimate connection with students. This timing helps to mitigate the emotional labor required from teachers during assessments by breaking down the assessment tasks into manageable parts.

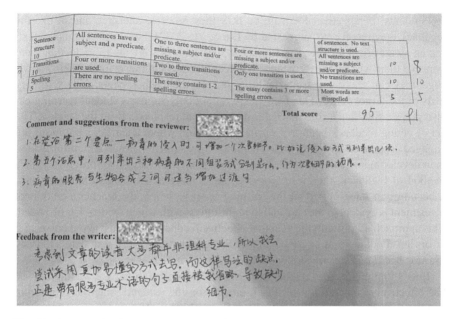

Fig. 6.9 An example of student peer feedback (04)

The use of a rubric streamlines the process, eliminating the need for teachers to spend additional time preparing students for feedback in class. As a result, during teacher feedback, comprehensive comments are not necessary, and during peer feedback, students can focus on specific issues rather than just linguistic aspects of writing. This assessment design not only reduces the emotional intensity for both teachers and students but also creates more opportunities for scaffolding and support, allowing for a more nuanced and effective feedback experience.

6.6 Summary

Taken together, it could be inferred from Lina's instruction of L2 writing that her provision of writing feedback could be viewed as an internal process, for she shifted the focus to the student side, especially how they process, interpret, and use the feedback (Liu & Yu, 2022). On one hand, feedback constitutes the main source of information from which students could make sense of and act upon their writing performance. Hence, when students lack knowledge, they could draw on three sources (i.e., the teacher, other students, and models of the target genre) for input. In this sense, the feedback process constitutes a primary situation triggering the teachers' emotional experiences.

From Lina's instruction in L2 writing, it can be deduced that her approach to providing writing feedback is deeply rooted in an internal process. She prioritizes the students' perspective, focusing on how they process, interpret, and utilize the feedback they receive (as suggested by Liu & Yu, 2022). Feedback, in this context, serves as a critical source of information that enables students to understand and improve their writing performance. When students encounter gaps in their knowledge, they can seek input from multiple sources: the teacher, peers, and exemplary texts of the target genre. This feedback loop not only supports student learning but also plays a significant role in triggering emotional responses from the teacher. The act of giving feedback becomes a primary situation where a teacher's emotions are engaged, as it involves a deep understanding of the students' needs, a commitment to their development, and the satisfaction derived from witnessing their progress. Lina's method of feedback, therefore, goes beyond a mere assessment of student work; it becomes an integral part of the learning process, where the teacher's emotional investment is evident in the care and thoughtfulness with which feedback is provided. This approach aligns with the idea that effective feedback is not just about correcting errors but about facilitating a meaningful dialogue that supports the student's journey towards becoming a more skilled and confident writer.

Lina's implementation of the process genre approach in her L2 writing classes has effectively centered the feedback process on the students' internal processing and application of feedback. This approach emphasizes the importance of students actively acquiring, storing, reproducing, and utilizing information, which is crucial for their development as writers. By observing their peers and the teacher, students can gain direct instruction and access to rich sources of information, which supports their understanding of the writing process and the skills required at each stage. This active engagement with feedback underscores the students' agency and their role as responsive participants in their own learning journey, as highlighted by Boud and Molloy (2013). The feedback process, as an internal one, not only enhances students' abilities to process and interpret evaluative information but also influences the teacher's emotional responses. Teachers may experience emotional reactions based on the comparison between their desired teaching outcomes and the students' current performance. These emotional responses can, in turn, shape and modify the overall writing instruction process, as teachers adjust their strategies to better support student learning. Furthermore, the teacher's emotional appraisal structure is influenced by their knowledge, previous teaching experiences, and the emotional labor strategies they employ in specific situations. In Lina's case, her emotional engagement with the feedback process is evident, and it plays a significant role in how she guides her students through the writing process. This dynamic interplay between teacher and student emotions, knowledge, and strategies is a key factor in creating an effective and supportive learning environment.

In summary, Lina's approach to teaching L2 writing involves a strategic subdivision of the writing task into three distinct phases: pre-class, in-class, and post-class activities. Each phase presents its own set of challenges and emotional labor for the teacher, as there is a constant negotiation between the intended teaching objectives and the students' current level of knowledge and skill. This emotional labor is a response to the perceived gap between what is desired and what is observed, prompting the teacher to consider and employ various emotional labor strategies.

These strategies are aimed at managing the emotional aspects of teaching to ensure that the learning environment remains conducive to student development. Lina's focus on the cognitive aspects of writing, rather than just the textual changes resulting from feedback, reflects her belief in the importance of understanding the underlying thought processes involved in writing. This focus helps her to better guide her students and adapt her teaching methods to support their cognitive development. The case of Lina demonstrates how L2 writing teachers can, through a thoughtful reconstruction of the writing process, continuously adjust their emotional experiences to better facilitate student learning. This adjustment is not only beneficial for the teacher's own emotional well-being but also has a direct impact on the students' writing processes and the quality of their written work. By managing her emotional labor effectively, Lina is able to create a learning environment that fosters growth and improvement in her students' writing abilities.

References

Boud, D., Molloy, E. (2013). Rethinking models of feedback for learning: The challenge of design. *Assessment & Evaluation in Higher Education, 38*(6), 698−712.

Liu, C., & Yu, S. (2022). Reconceptualizing the impact of feedback in second language writing: A multidimensional perspective. *Assessing Writing, 53*, 100630.

Suggested readings

Badger, R., & White, G. (2000). A process genre approach to teaching writing. *ELT Journal, 54*(2), 153–160.

Bitchener, J., & Ferris, D. (2012). *Written corrective feedback in second language acquisition and writing*. Routledge.

Han, Y., & Hyland, F. (2015). Exploring learner engagement with written corrective feedback in a Chinese tertiary EFL classroom. *Journal of Second Language Writing, 30*, 31–44.

Han, Y., & Hyland, F. (2019). Academic emotions in written corrective feedback situations. *Journal of English for Academic Purposes, 38*, 1–13.

Mahfoodh, O. (2017). "I feel disappointed": EFL university students' emotional responses towards teacher written feedback. *Assessing Writing, 31*, 53–72.

Wang, L., & Lee, I. (2021). L2 learners' agentic engagement in an assessment as learning-focused writing classroom. *Assessing Writing, 50*, 100571.

Yang, L., Zhang, J., & Dixon, H. (2023). Understanding the impact of teacher feedback on EFL students' use of self-regulated writing strategies. *Journal of Second Language Writing, 60*, 101015.

Yang, L., & Zhang, J. (2023). Self-regulation and student engagement with feedback: The case of Chinese EFL student writers. *Journal of English for Academic Purposes, 63*, 101226.

Zhang, T. F. (2021). The effect of highly focused versus mid-focused written corrective feedback on EFL learners explicit and implicit knowledge development. *System, 99*, 102493.

Zhang, T., & Mao, Z. (2023). Exploring the development of student feedback literacy in the second language writing classroom. *Assessing Writing, 55*, 100697.

Chapter 7
Teacher Emotions and Instructional Practices: Evidence from a Process-Genre L2 Writing Classroom

7.1 Introduction

Olivia's transition from a prestigious normal university to an engineering university in north China marked the beginning of her career as a novice teacher, tasked with teaching College English. Her professional journey took a significant turn in 2018 when her school embarked on a series of educational reforms aimed at innovating English as a Foreign Language (EFL) courses. This initiative led to Olivia being invited to teach Academic Writing (AW), a course designed for students from diverse disciplines such as Law, Avionics, Air Traffic Management, and Accounting, with the goal of enhancing their disciplinary knowledge through English writing.

The school's commitment to pedagogical innovation was evident in their collaboration with teaching experts from the University of Science and Technology of China and Nanjing University. Olivia and her colleagues were provided with the opportunity to observe AW courses and participate in course preparation sessions, which were instrumental in their professional development. These experiences were followed by reflective discussions and collaborative conferences, allowing the teaching team to consider how to tailor the AW course to the specific needs of their students. From these collaborative efforts, Olivia and her colleagues established two primary teaching objectives: the first was to integrate academic writing knowledge with specific disciplinary content, and the second was to enhance students' disciplinary knowledge through the medium of English writing. To achieve these objectives, they developed a detailed and prescriptive instructional structure for academic writing, setting an expectation for students to complete four small writing tasks each semester. This structured approach to teaching academic writing reflects a comprehensive strategy that aims to equip students with the necessary skills to excel in their respective fields while improving their English writing abilities. It also underscores the importance of aligning teaching methods with the broader educational goals of the institution and the diverse needs of the student body.

Olivia's initial approach to L2 writing instruction was informed by her previous knowledge and experiences, leading her to adopt a genre-centered method that heavily utilized textbooks and teacher-led activities. This method focused on the end product of students' writing rather than the processes involved in creating it. While this approach was successful in enhancing students' performance on academic writing tests, such as the College English Test (CET) Band 4 and 6 writing assessments, Olivia observed a decline in students' motivation to write after they had passed these tests.

Realizing this problem, Olivia and her colleagues found it necessary to reform the course curriculum by including more writing process-related interactions and multiple writing assessment activities in the course. The revised teaching curriculum took effect in the spring semester of 2019, which featured three distinguished characteristics. First, a single writing task was broken into several smaller sub-tasks, students were encouraged to write in a progressive manner. Second, the writing instruction was subdivided into pre-writing, while-writing, and post-writing sessions, which allowed for more interactions and negotiations in the writing process. Third, a wide range of writing assessment activities were integrated into the writing process. The new course curriculum gave Olivia and her colleagues more opportunities to try innovative pedagogical practices (e.g., project-based writing) and conduct research on L2 writing. Acknowledging the need for a more engaging and comprehensive writing curriculum, Olivia and her colleagues undertook a significant reform of the course content. The revised teaching curriculum, implemented in the spring semester of 2019, introduced several key features to enhance the writing experience for students. The first characteristic was the decomposition of a single writing task into several smaller, manageable sub-tasks. This approach encouraged students to write in a step-by-step, progressive manner, which could help them build confidence and develop their writing skills more effectively. The second feature involved the subdivision of writing instruction into distinct phases: pre-writing, while-writing, and post-writing. This structure allowed for increased interaction and negotiation throughout the writing process, providing students with more opportunities for guidance, feedback, and revision. The third characteristic was the integration of a diverse range of writing assessment activities into the curriculum. This not only offered a variety of ways to evaluate students' writing but also encouraged them to engage with different aspects of writing, such as content, organization, and language use.

These changes in the course curriculum provided Olivia and her colleagues with a platform to explore innovative pedagogical practices, such as project-based writing, and to conduct research on L2 writing. The new curriculum was designed to foster a more dynamic and interactive learning environment, where students could develop a deeper understanding of writing and maintain their motivation beyond the scope of standardized tests. By focusing on the writing process and incorporating multiple assessment activities, the curriculum aimed to prepare students for real-world writing challenges and to enhance their overall writing proficiency.

Indeed, Olivia's case illustrates two significant shifts in her teaching philosophy and practice. First, pedagogical transformation: Olivia transitioned from a genre-centered approach, which focused primarily on the end product of writing and was heavily reliant on textbooks and teacher-guided activities, to a genre-process integrated approach. This new approach emphasizes the importance of the writing process itself, encouraging students to engage in pre-writing, drafting, revising, and editing activities. By integrating the process into the curriculum, Olivia aimed to provide a more holistic writing experience that not only improves students' academic writing skills but also fosters a deeper understanding of the writing process and potentially enhances their motivation to write. Second, inclusion of multiple writing assessments, Olivia's efforts to incorporate a variety of writing assessment activities into her teaching process reflect a commitment to evaluating and supporting students' writing development at multiple stages. These assessments are designed to provide feedback on different aspects of writing, such as content, organization, and language use, and to offer students opportunities to reflect on and improve their work. The integration of multiple assessments allows for a more nuanced understanding of each student's progress and needs, enabling Olivia to tailor her teaching strategies accordingly.

7.2 Olivia's Emotional Experiences: A Process-Genre L2 Writing Pedagogical Approach

This book delineated a spectrum of 42 emotional experiences in Olivia's case (see Table 7.1).

In Olivia's case, the study revealed a complex interplay of emotional experiences, with a majority leaning towards the negative side (32 instances, accounting for 56.1%). Positive emotions were also reported, albeit less frequently (23 instances, or 40.4%), while a minimal number (2 instances, 3.5%) were categorized as neutral or without discernible emotional charge.

The analysis further distinguished between macro-contextual and meso-contextual triggers. Macro-contextual issues, primarily related to educational policies from school and faculty administrations, were found to have instigated 7 instances of negative emotional experiences and 2 of positive ones. On the other hand, meso-contextual factors, such as interactions with colleagues and experts in the domain of academic Writing, led to 4 negative and 10 positive emotional occurrences.

The pedagogical approaches employed in *Academic Writing* were noted to elicit a diverse array of emotional responses. Notably, the genre approach yielded a higher number of negative emotional experiences (18 instances) compared to positive ones (2 instances). Table 7.1 indicates that the negative emotions predominantly stemmed from the challenges in achieving instructional objectives, particularly in guiding students to produce literature reviews that adhere to academic writing genres and disciplinary standards. Students frequently encountered difficulties in the writing process, with their work often marked by significant errors in language accuracy and content. Additionally, student interactions in the classroom were reported to be unproductive. These outcomes were likely perceived negatively by the teacher, as

Table 7.1 Types of emotions and triggering situations in Olivia's case

Types of emotion	Triggering situation	Contextual issues
Dissatisfaction anxiety	1. School administration gave insufficient support to Language education (e.g., lack of learning spaces and resources for L2 writing instruction) 2. School administration reduced the teaching hours of *Academic Writing*, leading to difficulties in redesigning the curriculum	Macro-contextual issues
Disappointment	3. The faculty gave less support to *Academic Writing* compared with other parallel courses	
Anxiety disappointment	4. The educational reform to the course *Academic Writing* sustained after the initial success because of the withdrawal of the course leader	
Confusion disappointment	5. The faculty policy of writing test was rigid, which neglected the features and conditions of the course	
Enjoyment	6. Getting involved in course development activities such as curriculum development, course evaluation	

(continued)

7.2 Olivia's Emotional Experiences: A Process-Genre L2 Writing …

Table 7.1 (continued)

Types of emotion	Triggering situation	Contextual issues
Inspiration enjoyment	7. Conducting course preparation with colleagues and learning from the experienced teachers	Meso-contextual issues
Disappointment	8. Being unable to receive constructive suggestions on the teaching of *Academic Writing* from colleagues with doctorate degrees	
Enjoyment gratitude inspiration	9. Sharing sources and ideas in course preparation with colleagues in the team 10. Giving feedback on student writing and reflecting on teaching effectiveness with colleagues in the team	
Disappointment	11. Being rejected by some experienced teachers (e.g., class observation, interviews)	
Enlightenment encouragement	12. Receiving useful information and comments from experts by attending lectures and work shops	
Happiness sense of achievement	13. Students' positive feedback on the course of *Academic Writing* 14. Students made achievement in academic writing	

(continued)

Table 7.1 (continued)

Types of emotion	Triggering situation	Contextual issues
Confusion Sorry-for	15. Disagreement with the findings and pedagogical implications proposed in published research articles 16. Being unable to replicate the research findings in writing classrooms	
Genre approach		
Stage 1. Modeling a text		
No emotion	1. Teaching the writing genre knowledge and skills	
Stage 2. Joint construction of a text		
Sorry for Nervousness	2. Canceling some teaching content due to reduced teaching hours	Instruction of academic writing
	3. Encountering difficulties in revising the lesson plans for the next round of teaching	
Sorry for anger (explicit)	4. Conducting face-to-face writing conferences with the student whose writing was diagnosed with serious mistakes	Teacher-student interactions in writing classrooms
Confusion dissatisfaction	5. Students have difficulties in locating and citing quality sources in academic writing 6. Students do not know when and what to cite or not to cite in writing literature review	
Confusion anxiety	7. Some students resort to copying, near-copying from a text rather than attempting synthesizing of larger chunks	Teacher assessment on student writings
Disappointment	8. Students fail to correct the mistakes in accordance with teacher feedback	
Confusion anxiety	9. Students had difficulties in presenting the discipline-related knowledge in an accurate and logical manner	
Confusion	10. Heavy workload and difficulties in giving feedback on student writings	
Disappointment Sorry-for	11. Students continued to make mistakes in writing literature review after teacher feedback	Students revise and edit the writings
Stage 3. Students independently construct a text		
Sense of achievement	12. Some student made progress in academic (e.g., literature review)	

(continued)

Table 7.1 (continued)

Types of emotion	Triggering situation	Contextual issues
Happy for disappointment unhappiness	13. Some students failed to improve the language accuracy	
Nervousness uneasiness	14. Unfamiliar with students and their writing skills in the first three weeks of teaching 15. Unable to finish all writing tasks by the end of the semester	Teacher reflection on genre-centered approach
Genre-process approach		
Stage 1. Pre-class writing activities		
No emotion enjoyment	16. Teachers gave instructions on the genre knowledge and skills of the planned writing task	Teacher identifies the purpose ad direction of the writing task
Satisfaction	17. Making modifications to textbooks to suit the new teaching objectives	
Stage 2. In-class writing activities		
Satisfaction	18. Implementing genre-process approach in accordance with experts' suggestions	Modeling a text
Happy-for	19. Students conduct more interactions in groups, student–student relationship become closer	Teacher-student, student–student interactions
Sense of achievement satisfaction	20. Teacher places more emphasis on group work and collaborative writing to help students engage in writing process	
Happy-for	21. Students showed higher motivations in discussing the writing plans in groups	Students plan the writing in groups

(continued)

Table 7.1 (continued)

Types of emotion	Triggering situation	Contextual issues
Confusion	22. Students were not motivated in participating in peer assessment	Teacher assessment on student writings
Stage 3. Post-class writing activities		
Happy-for	23. Students made progress in language accuracy, structure, and genre knowledge of academic writing	Students revise and edit the writings
Sense of achievement	24. Students took the initiative to share their writings and writing process	
Sorry-for disappointment	25. Failure to deliver the instruction in strict accordance with the lesson plans 26. The new teaching process led to greater student progress	Teacher reflections on genre-process integrated approach

they did not align with the set instructional goals, leading to a critical evaluation of such educational scenarios.

However, when it comes to the genre-process integrated approach, this book identified more occurrences of positive emotional experiences (n = 8) than those of negative emotional experiences (n = 3). In addition to the development of linguistic and structural-rhetorical aspects of writing, Olivia took the initiative to design process-oriented teaching materials (e.g., pre-writing, while-writing, post-writing activities, and peer feedback forms) and provide customized guidance and encouragement during the writing process. This genre-process integrated approach shifted the focus to the student side and created more instances for the teacher to moderate students' writing processes by employing appropriate pedagogical strategies. Such instances were likely to be appraised positively when the teacher perceived they could match the specific goals set for specific stages of the writing. For instance, the interactions among students in pre-writing activities could help students reflect on their prior experiences and share ideas about the writing tasks at hand, thus making it easier to fulfill the goals set for the pre-writing stage. In addition, the teacher managed to add extra sources (model texts, mini lectures on writing skills) to help students get familiar with the genre knowledge and background information of the writing task. It should be noted that these activities increased student participation by involving them in more writing-related discussions and interactions, which served as important triggers for teacher emotions.

In the realm of the genre-process integrated approach, this study discerned a marked prevalence of positive emotional experiences (8 occurrences) over negative ones (3 occurrences). Olivia proactively crafted process-oriented teaching materials, encompassing pre-writing, in-process, and post-writing activities, as well as peer feedback mechanisms, thereby offering tailored support and motivation throughout the writing journey. This pedagogical shift towards a student-centric model not only fostered linguistic and structural-rhetorical development but also empowered the teacher to actively guide and modulate the writing processes through strategic pedagogical interventions. Such engagements were more likely to be viewed favorably when they aligned with the specific objectives targeted for each phase of the writing process. For example, pre-writing activities facilitated reflective discussions among students, drawing upon their prior experiences and brainstorming ideas for the task ahead. This collaborative environment eased the achievement of pre-writing stage goals. Furthermore, the teacher's introduction of supplementary resources, such as model texts and mini lectures on writing skills, enriched students' genre knowledge and contextual understanding of the writing assignment. It is important to highlight that these activities significantly boosted student engagement by integrating them into writing-related dialogues and interactions. These interactive elements acted as potent catalysts for the teacher's emotions, contributing to the overall positive emotional outcomes observed in the study.

7.3 Goals and Norms Supporting Olivia's Appraisal of Emotional Situations

Overall, Olivia's emotional landscape was shaped by three primary spheres of interaction: at the macro-level, her engagement with school and faculty policies; at the meso-level, her collaborations with colleagues and experts; and at the micro-level, her direct interactions with students within the classroom setting. This multifaceted approach to emotional assessment reflects a nuanced understanding of the various contexts that influence a teacher's professional experiences. Transitioning from a genre-centered to a genre-process integrated pedagogy, Olivia encountered distinct emotional trajectories in her teaching of *Academic Writing*. This evolution in instructional methodology yielded two divergent emotional profiles, as depicted in Table 7.2, showcasing the intricate relationship between teaching practices and the emotional responses they elicit.

Under the genre approach, Olivia meticulously structured the course into three distinct stages, each with its own set of objectives and expectations. Initially, during the modeling phase, her primary aim was for students to acquire a solid grasp of

Table 7.2 Goals and norms supporting Olivia's appraisal of emotional situations

Types of triggering situation		Evaluated in terms of	
		Goals	Norms
School and faculty policies on course development of *Academic writing* and teacher education		Sufficient and consistent policy support for the development of *Academic Writing*, a favorable environment for teacher education	
Interactions with students, colleagues, and teaching experts		Receiving constructive feedback from students, colleagues, and experts in curriculum development, course preparation, and course evaluation	
Genre approach	Modeling a text	1. Students learn the genre knowledge and writing skills of *Academic Writing*	1. Students get familiar with the basic genre knowledge in constructing a particular piece of writing
	Co-construction of a text	2. Students construct the text by synthesizing information from multiple sources	2. Students manage the linguistic and content demand in composing the assigned writing tasks
	Students independently revise and edit a text	3. Students' participation in writing assessment activities	3. Students independently construct the writing by following feedback
Genre-process integrated approach	Pre-class writing activities	Students clearly know the purpose and genre requirement of the writing tasks	Students learn the genre features and subject content knowledge of the writing task

(continued)

Table 7.2 (continued)

Types of triggering situation		Evaluated in terms of	
		Goals	Norms
	In-class writing activities	1. Students participate in group writing activities and construct the writing step by step 2. Students know when and what to cite or not cite 3. Students comprehend and evaluate the writing content	1. Students get involved in classroom writing activities to develop the linguistic and structural-rhetorical knowledge of writing 2. Students improve their subject content knowledge and academic writing skills
	Post-class writing activities	Students construct the writing and present the subject content knowledge	Students improve their skills and motivation in academic writing

the genre knowledge and writing skills essential for academic writing. She anticipated that students would become acquainted with foundational genre elements, such as writing moves, as they crafted specific sections of their work, like an introduction or a literature review. Moving into the second stage, the joint construction of the text, Olivia set a goal for students to synthesize information from various sources, effectively managing the linguistic challenges inherent in composing their assignments. This stage was designed to enhance students' ability to integrate and articulate information coherently within the academic writing framework. Lastly, in the independent revision and editing phase, Olivia emphasized the importance of students' active involvement in writing assessment activities. She believed that engaging with the assessment process would not only improve their writing skills but also foster a sense of autonomy and self-efficacy in their writing endeavors. This comprehensive approach aimed to equip students with the necessary tools to navigate the complexities of academic writing with confidence and competence.

When the course *Academic Writing was* transformed into a genre-process integrated approach, it was broken into pre-class, in-class, and post-class writing activities. At the pre-class stage, Olivia viewed "students clearly knowing the purpose and genre requirements of the writing tasks" as the goal. For this purpose, she rearranged the teaching materials to prepare students with the knowledge necessary for writing. In the writing classrooms, Olivia shifted the focus to the student side by asking students to plan and co-construct the writing in groups. Therefore, she listed "students participate in group writing activities and construct the writing step by step" as the goal for in-class writing activities. She believed that there was more to a genre-process integrated approach than multiple drafting. She then developed a series of teaching materials (e.g., peer feedback forms, writing assessment rubrics) and provided guidance to students before they constructed the text. In addition to the development of linguistic and structural-rhetorical aspects of writing, Olivia puts an emphasis on students' subject knowledge acquisition. Classroom observation indicated that she invited teachers from the school library to guide students to conduct literature research. She also encouraged students to consult with their subject course teacher for further feedback on the content of their writings. Therefore, she listed "students know when and what to cite" and "students comprehend and evaluate the writing content" as another two goals. With the transition to a genre-process integrated approach for the *Academic Writing* course, Olivia restructured the learning experience into three phases: pre-class, in-class, and post-class writing activities, each tailored to enhance the students' writing process.

In the pre-class stage, Olivia aimed to ensure that students had a clear understanding of the writing tasks' purpose and genre requirements. To achieve this, she reorganized the teaching materials to equip students with the prerequisite knowledge for effective writing. During the in-class writing activities, Olivia placed a greater emphasis on student engagement. She encouraged students to plan and collaboratively construct their writing in groups, with the goal of "students participating in group writing activities and constructing the writing step by step." Olivia believed that the genre-process integrated approach encompassed more than just multiple drafts, and thus she developed a suite of teaching resources, including peer feedback forms and writing assessment rubrics, to guide students through the text construction process.

Furthermore, Olivia recognized the importance of subject knowledge in writing and incorporated it into her teaching goals. She facilitated library sessions with teachers from the school library to assist students in conducting literature research and encouraged them to seek additional feedback from their subject course teachers on the content of their writing. This approach aimed to ensure that students would "know when and what to cite" and "comprehend and evaluate the writing content," thereby enriching their academic writing with depth and accuracy.

Upon completion of the initial draft, students were guided to engage in a meticulous revision and editing process, aligning their work with the genre-specific features of academic writing and incorporating feedback received after class. Olivia's ultimate goal for this stage was encapsulated in the phrase "students construct, write, and present the subject knowledge," which underscores the expectation that students would not only articulate their understanding of the subject matter but also do so in a manner that is coherent, well-structured, and adheres to the conventions of academic discourse. This comprehensive approach ensures that students develop a robust command of both the content and the form required for effective academic writing.

7.4 Influence of Olivia's Emotion-Regulation Strategies on L2 Writing Instruction and His Psychological Well-Being

This section delves into Olivia's emotional landscape, examining the spectrum of her emotional encounters, the strategies she employs for emotional regulation, and the impact these emotions have on her second language (L2) writing instruction and overall well-being. The analysis is contextualized within the broader framework of macro-, meso-, and micro-contextual factors that serve as catalysts for her emotional responses.

7.4.1 Olivia's Use of Emotion-Regulation Strategies and Impact: Macro-Level

The initial overarching theme explored in this analysis pertains to the emotional experiences of Olivia, which are significantly influenced by the university's policies regarding course development and teacher education. At Olivia's institution, there exists a uniform course evaluation policy that applies to both English as a Foreign Language (EFL) courses and engineering courses. This standardized approach has led to a sense of confusion and uncertainty for L2 writing instructors like Olivia, as they strive to advance the development of their courses. A notable obstacle within this policy is the "one-size-fits-all" evaluation model, which fails to accommodate the unique pedagogical requirements of academic writing. This mismatch between the policy and the practical needs of teaching academic writing has been a source of frustration for Olivia, as it hinders her ability to effectively implement and refine her teaching methods tailored to the specific demands of L2 writing. The policy's inflexibility not only affects the course development but also has implications for Olivia's professional growth and the overall quality of writing instruction provided to students.

> The latest school policy reduced the course hours for Academic Writing from 54 to 32 h, making it difficult for me to cover all the course content. Even worse, my faculty prescribed that all EFL courses follow the same language assessment policy. Despite my dissatisfaction, I was told to make a compromise to the summative assessment policies (which prescribe that the final examination accounts for 85% of student performance) by cutting down the proportion of formative assessment (which accounts for 15% of student performance) in the course. (1st interview)
>
> The recent policy shift at the school has significantly impacted the structure and delivery of the Academic Writing course, as it has reduced the allocated course hours from 54 to 32. This reduction presents a considerable challenge in ensuring comprehensive coverage of the course material, as there is now less time to delve into the complexities of academic writing. Furthermore, the faculty's directive to adhere to a uniform language assessment policy across all EFL courses adds another layer of difficulty. This policy mandates a heavy reliance on summative assessments, with the final examination contributing 85% to the overall student performance evaluation. Consequently, this approach necessitates a reduction in the weight

of formative assessments, which are relegated to only 15% of the student performance. (1st interview)

Olivia's negative emotional responses to the language assessment policy were also evidenced in her collaboration with other colleagues in joint lesson planning, who complained of the reduced class hours and uncertainties, and two of her colleagues refused to try the process pedagogy in their classes. Olivia's dissatisfaction with the language assessment policy was further reflected in her collaborative efforts with other colleagues during joint lesson planning sessions. The reduced class hours and the resulting uncertainties were a common source of concern among her peers. The policy's implications were not only felt by Olivia but also resonated with her colleagues, leading to a shared sense of frustration and apprehension about the ability to deliver effective instruction within the new constraints.

> Due to the decrease in allocated class time, two of my colleagues have opted to revert to the genre pedagogy, leaving me as the only member of the team who continues to employ process pedagogy. Their decision to step away from the more interactive and gradual process approach is likely driven by the practical challenges of fitting it into the shortened class hours. (1st interview)

Despite facing the challenges posed by the reduced class hours, Olivia successfully adapted her syllabus and lesson plans to incorporate a variety of writing activities. She achieved this by skillfully blending the genre and process approaches within her *Academic Writing* course. Driven by her passion for learning and applying process pedagogy in her writing classes, Olivia remained dedicated to her craft. Her continued practice may also spark a dialogue within the team and the institution about the most effective ways to support student learning within these constraints, potentially paving the way for more nuanced and impactful teaching strategies. She consistently sought out the latest research on merging the genre approach with the process approach and actively experimented with these methods during her classroom sessions, thereby enriching her teaching practice and enhancing the learning experience for her students.

7.4.2 Olivia's Use of Emotion-Regulation Strategies and Impact: Meso-Level

Beyond the classroom, Olivia derived her positive emotional experiences primarily from two key sources: firstly, her enjoyment of engaging with experts through lectures and workshops, which provided her with intellectual stimulation and professional growth; and secondly, the affirmation she received from her colleagues, who recognized the process approach as an effective method for enhancing students' writing skills. Upon joining the team, Olivia observed that her two experienced colleagues, who were well-versed in L2 writing instruction, adhered to a traditional genre-centered teaching methodology. They focused on imparting foundational writing skills to their students, starting with the essentials such as constructing grammatically

7.4 Influence of Olivia's Emotion-Regulation Strategies on L2 Writing ...

correct sentences, mastering punctuation, and utilizing template-based language, all while strictly adhering to the textbook as their guide. This established teaching style contrasted with Olivia's own approach, which sought to integrate the process aspect into the genre-based curriculum.

> I had the pleasure of attending lectures by Rod Ellis in Shanghai in 2019 and workshops organized by FLTRP in Beijing, which were incredibly enriching experiences. These events not only expanded my knowledge and honed my practical teaching skills in L2 writing but also contributed to the development of student literacy in writing. During these interactions, I had the opportunity to connect with numerous educators who were deeply passionate about L2 writing. Among them were accomplished course developers and researchers who generously shared their experiences. They discussed the collaborative efforts in lesson planning with their colleagues and the evolution of their teaching philosophies. It was inspiring to hear about their journey in embracing the process pedagogy in their classrooms. Their stories of gradual change and the positive impact on their teaching practices were a testament to the power of continuous professional development and the willingness to adapt and innovate in the field of language education. (1st interview)

Olivia's enthusiasm and proactive attitude toward the new pedagogical knowledge broadened her mind in L2 writing instruction and curriculum development, which was corroborated by the observational data that showed her active investment in course development and sharing her expertise with other colleagues at the faculty level. To improve the effectiveness of joint course preparation, Olivia and her colleagues followed the "five steps of joint course preparation" (see Table 7.3).

Olivia's eagerness to embrace and integrate new pedagogical insights into her L2 writing instruction and curriculum development was evident and positively noted. Her open-mindedness and initiative were supported by observational data, which highlighted her significant contributions to course development and her willingness to share her expertise with colleagues at the faculty level. In an effort to enhance the collaborative process of course preparation, Olivia and her colleagues adopted a structured approach known as the "five steps of joint course preparation." This methodical framework likely provided a clear pathway for collective planning, ensuring that each stage of the curriculum development was thoughtfully considered and effectively executed. By following these steps, the team could work cohesively, leveraging each

Table 7.3 Five steps of joint course preparation

Steps	Task
1. 1st round of course preparation	Develop the lesson plans and teaching materials
2. Brain storming	Improve the lesson plans via group discussions
3. 2nd round of course preparation	Revise the lesson plans, conduct pilot teaching
4. Demonstration	Demonstrate the teaching process by illustrating the teaching objectives, pedagogical practice, assessment activities
5. Reflection	Reflect on the pros and cons of the lesson plan and teaching practice for further improvement

members strengths and insights to create a comprehensive and effective course that aligns with the educational goals and the needs of the students (see Table 7.3).

> Motivated by the exemplary practices encountered during the workshops, I recognized the importance of establishing a dedicated writing team within my department. Starting from 2019, our team has been dedicated to transforming the course by transitioning from traditional writing tasks to more comprehensive writing projects. This involved breaking down a complex writing assignment into a series of manageable sub-tasks, with students focusing on completing one sub-task at a time. To support this structured approach, we incorporated a variety of writing-related activities, such as brainstorming sessions, group discussions, debates, and video-watching exercises. These activities were designed to assist students in organizing their thoughts and ideas into a coherent writing outline, which then served as a scaffold for their writing process. Additionally, we implemented peer assessment activities to encourage students to engage in critical thinking and constructive feedback, further enhancing their writing skills. This multifaceted strategy not only improved the students' ability to plan and execute their writing but also fostered a more collaborative and dynamic learning environment. (1st interview)

It was evident that Olivia thrived on the collaborative interactions with her colleagues, taking on the role of a "facilitator" to foster an environment that was both innovative and interactive during joint course preparation. She introduced fresh perspectives by involving teachers in cooperative teaching endeavors, with the aim of not only completing assigned writing topics but more importantly, "developing students' writing knowledge, communicative, and critical thinking skills" as she mentioned in her first interview. Reflecting on the initial round of collaborative course preparation, Olivia fondly recalled the mutual benefits that all teachers derived from these activities, particularly in the design of lesson plans and writing projects. However, she also candidly acknowledged areas for improvement that were sources of negative emotions, such as confusion and dissatisfaction. One of the primary challenges she identified was the students' limited or sometimes incorrect understanding of the writing content. This made it challenging to provide targeted feedback on the disciplinary content knowledge within their writings. This issue highlighted the need for a more nuanced approach to feedback and the importance of ensuring that students have a solid grasp of the subject matter before they delve into the writing process. Olivia's observations underscore the complexity of teaching writing in an academic context, where the interplay between content knowledge and writing skills is crucial for student success.

> Navigating the task of providing feedback on students' misconceptions regarding the subject content of their writing proved to be a formidable challenge. A specific example that highlighted this issue was a writing project on global warming, where approximately one-third of the students struggled to accurately identify and explain the primary causes and potential consequences of global warming for humanity and the planet at large. Such content-related inaccuracies not only detracted from the overall quality of the writing but also compounded the complexity of offering constructive teacher feedback. I talked with my colleagues, and it became clear that I was not alone in facing this dilemma. We all shared similar experiences and sentiments, yet we found ourselves at a loss for an effective solution to this problem. The consensus among us was that while we are adept at guiding students in the mechanics and structure of writing, addressing content-related errors requires a different set of strategies that we have yet to fully develop or implement. (2nd interview)

Second, Olivia expressed her uneasiness toward the newly issued school policy of reduced class hours. While Olivia and her colleagues were willing to invite external sources to improve students' subject content knowledge and skills in searching and citing literature, "We want to invite some experienced researchers to give students a workshop on academic writing; we also want to invite a library staff to teach students about searching and citing literature. It may give students and us some fresh ideas and guidance on how to write more effectively" (1st interview). Unfortunately, they had to suspend these plans due to the constraints of class hours.

Secondly, Olivia conveyed her concern regarding the recent school policy that reduced the number of class hours. Despite her and her colleagues' eagerness to enrich the students' subject content knowledge and enhance their research and citation skills by inviting external experts, the policy's restrictions posed a significant obstacle. Olivia had envisioned inviting seasoned researchers to conduct workshops on academic writing and library staff to instruct students on literature searching and citation techniques. She believed that such initiatives could provide both students and teachers with novel insights and guidance on improving their writing effectiveness, as she mentioned in her first interview. However, the limitations imposed by the reduced class hours necessitated the suspension of these valuable plans, leading to a sense of disappointment and frustration over the missed opportunities for professional growth and enhanced student learning.

Olivia's narrative clearly indicates a strong internal drive to innovate and improve the *Academic Writing* course. Proactively, she sought to enhance her pedagogical knowledge, delve into process pedagogy, and absorb best practices from experts in the field. Despite her reservations about the school's policy on EFL course development, Olivia managed to keep her negative emotions in check and convinced herself to adapt to the prevailing conditions. Demonstrating a high degree of self-determination, she successfully transitioned the course from a traditional genre approach to one that integrates both genre and process methodologies. This was achieved through her active participation in workshops and collaborative efforts with her colleagues, whom she regarded as significant others instrumental in her professional development as an L2 writing teacher.

In her interactions with colleagues during joint course preparation, lesson planning, and other collaborative teaching activities, Olivia experienced fewer negative emotions. Through this collaborative practice, she was instrumental in embedding a genre-process approach into the Academic Writing curriculum. However, Olivia was also cognizant of the challenges that remained, such as the difficulty of completing lesson plans within the reduced class hours and the need to enhance students' subject content knowledge by engaging external sources. Faced with feelings of confusion and anxiety, Olivia chose to openly communicate her emotions with her colleagues, prepare for the challenges ahead, and remain committed to making continuous improvements in her teaching practice. Her approach reflects a resilient and proactive stance towards professional growth and student success.

7.4.3 Olivia's Use of Emotion-Regulation Strategies and Impact: Micro-Level

In this section, Olivia's emotional experiences, emotion-regulation strategies, and influences on her instructional practice and psychological well-being are presented. Reasons offered by Olivia for each emotional episode are also presented.

In this section, we delve into the intricate tapestry of Olivia's emotional journey, examining the emotional experiences she encountered, the strategies she employed to regulate these emotions, and the impact they had on her teaching methods and overall mental well-being. We also explore the rationale behind each emotional episode as articulated by Olivia herself. This comprehensive analysis aims to provide a clear picture of how Olivia's emotions interplay with her professional life, shaping her instructional practices and affecting her psychological state.

Before the Course Reform: Genre-Centered Approach

Olivia's tenure with the *Academic Writing* course initially involved a genre-centered pedagogical approach, which led to two distinct emotional profiles associated with her teaching experiences. During this period, the classroom activities were predominantly focused on the modeling of texts and teacher-guided revision and editing processes. These stages consumed a significant portion of the instructional time, and as a result, Olivia experienced a range of intense emotions.

Stage 1. Modeling a Text

In this stage, Olivia spent a lot of effort instructing the features of a specific writing genre by referring to the textbook and modeling texts. She was confident in teaching genre knowledge and writing skills, and she expected students to construct writing with clear genre structure, concise language, and coherent sentence patterns. However, her instruction on genre knowledge and writing skills was not always well accepted by the students (1st classroom observation). She reported that this problem was quite common in the first two to three weeks of a semester when she was not familiar with the students.

During this instructional phase, Olivia dedicated considerable effort to teaching the nuances of specific writing genres. She utilized textbooks and modeled texts as resources to convey the characteristics of each genre. Olivia was self-assured in her ability to impart genre knowledge and writing skills, aiming for her students to produce writing that exhibited a clear genre structure, utilized concise language, and contained coherent sentence patterns. Despite her confidence and preparation, Olivia's attempts to teach genre knowledge and writing skills did not always resonate with her students, as observed during the first classroom observation. She noted that this issue was a recurring challenge, particularly during the initial two to three weeks of a semester. This period often coincided with her getting to know the students, which could imply that the students' receptiveness to her teaching methods was influenced by their own adjustment to the course and their familiarity with her as an instructor. Olivia's experience underscores the importance of establishing rapport and understanding student needs early in the academic term to facilitate a smoother and more effective learning process.

Olivia would often revise her lesson plans and alter her teaching methods to address the underlying issues when she experienced negative emotions

> My goal is to ensure that my students grasp the essential genre features necessary for their writing. However, I frequently encounter challenges during the initial two to three weeks of a new semester, a period I refer to as the "new semester effect." During this time, students often lack motivation for writing and struggle to grasp the intricacies of academic discourse, such as sentence patterns, organizational structures, and other language-related aspects. This is especially true for first-year students who have limited experience with academic writing. These challenges can disrupt my carefully laid-out lesson plans and cause me a great deal of anxiety. Consequently, I find myself having to adapt my teaching approach, which may involve pacing the lessons more slowly, providing more detailed explanations of genre features, and incorporating additional model texts into the classroom to support their understanding. This flexibility is crucial to help students overcome the initial hurdles and build a solid foundation in academic writing. (2nd interview)

> Olivia's focus on imparting genre knowledge, along with her method of demonstrating the writing construction process, led her to realize that her classroom dynamics were predominantly teacher centered. This approach positioned students as passive recipients, akin to an audience, who were more engaged in "listening to" the principles of writing rather than actively "constructing" their own pieces of writing. This realization prompted Olivia to reflect on the need for a more student-centered pedagogy that would encourage active participation and the practical application of writing skills. (2nd interview)

Olivia also encouraged students to observe and recite the genre features of different texts they encountered outside of class. Drawing upon her own writing experiences, Olivia made a collection of 100 model texts and advised students to learn from these models (2nd classroom observation). In this way, she believed "students can develop a deeper understanding of the genre knowledge required for constructing a text."

Olivia sought to expand her students' exposure to genre features beyond the classroom by encouraging them to actively observe and memorize the characteristics of various texts they encountered in their daily lives. Leveraging her personal writing experiences, Olivia curated a diverse collection of 100 model texts, which she recommended to her students as valuable resources for study (as observed during the 2nd classroom observation). By engaging with these models, Olivia aimed to foster a more profound comprehension of the genre knowledge necessary for effective text construction. She believed that through this hands-on learning approach, students would not only acquire a more nuanced understanding of genre conventions but also develop the skills to apply these conventions in their own writing. This strategy was designed to move students from passive recipients of knowledge to active constructors of texts, thereby enhancing their overall writing abilities.

> When I introduce model texts to my students, I consistently draw their attention to the genre features, sentence patterns, and structures employed within these examples. I instruct my students to carefully observe how skilled writers craft their sentences to effectively convey ideas and maintain cohesion, particularly in terms of how they link sentences to present the central argument. However, upon reviewing their initial drafts, I was disheartened to find that the writing knowledge and techniques I had emphasized did not translate into their

compositions as I had hoped. This disconnect between the model texts and the students' application of these principles in their own writing was a source of disappointment and highlighted the need for further exploration of effective teaching strategies to bridge this gap. (2nd interview)

It becomes clear that Olivia placed emphasis on teaching students how to "model a text". She viewed genre knowledge as a prerequisite for students to construct a text. To this end, she offered instructions on genre knowledge both in and outside of the classroom. This labor-intensive work of teaching prioritized the teacher's role while downplaying students' participation in the writing process. Therefore, Olivia might experience negative emotions such as confusion, anxiety, and disappointment when students fail to transform their genre knowledge and skills into writing.

It is evident that Olivia focused on guiding her students through the process of "modeling a text," considering a thorough understanding of genre knowledge as essential for students to effectively construct their own writing. She dedicated herself to providing genre knowledge instruction both during class and as homework, emphasizing the teacher's role in this educational endeavor. This approach, while intensive, tended to minimize the students' active involvement in the writing process itself. As a result, when students did not apply their acquired genre knowledge and skills in their writing as expected, Olivia experienced a range of negative emotions, including confusion, anxiety, and disappointment. These emotions underscore the challenges of teaching writing, where the transition from understanding to application is not always straightforward and can be fraught with obstacles. Olivia's experiences highlight the need for a balanced approach that not only equips students with the necessary knowledge but also encourages their active engagement and practice in the writing process.

Stage 3. Teacher-Guided Revising and Editing the Text

Following the instruction on writing genre knowledge, students were tasked with applying these principles to construct their texts and submit them to *Pigai*, an online writing assessment platform. Utilizing the feedback and scores provided by the system, Olivia reviewed the student submissions, identifying those with the highest and lowest quality. She then meticulously analyzed the selected writings to pinpoint specific errors, as observed during the second classroom observation. During this phase, Olivia grappled with feelings of disappointment and anxiety, particularly in response to the errors she found in the student writings. These errors, which pertained to genre structure and organization, were areas that she had emphasized repeatedly during her instruction. In her view, these mistakes should have been preventable, given the thorough guidance she had provided. This realization led to a deeper concern about the effectiveness of her teaching methods and the students' ability to internalize and apply the genre knowledge they had been taught.

The act of writing assessment served as a means through which olivia's emotions affected the way she gave feedback.

> Usually, I agree with the assessment and feedback offered by Pigai. If a piece of writing is marked with a low score, it is difficult for me to follow what the writer thinks or intends

7.4 Influence of Olivia's Emotion-Regulation Strategies on L2 Writing ...

to convey. Such an unpleasant experience will make me feel that the student did not take the writing seriously or paid no attention to my instruction in previous classes. With such guessing and negative feelings, I often reach out to the writer in person and ask him to brief his writing. (2nd interview)

Typically, I find myself in agreement with the evaluations and feedback provided by Pigai. When a submission receives a low score, I often struggle to understand the writer's thoughts. This challenging experience can lead me to feel that the students may not have approached the writing task with the necessary seriousness or may have disregarded the instructions I provided in earlier classes. Confronted with these assumptions and negative emotions, I usually seek to engage the students directly, inviting them to summarize their writing to gain a clearer understanding of their perspective. (2nd interview)

Reflecting on her students' initial drafts, Olivia described her overall impression as being characterized by "overwhelming grammatical errors and poor expressive abilities in L2 writing." She believed that merely providing written corrective feedback was insufficient to address the students' needs. Consequently, she requested that they engage in face-to-face discussions with her. Olivia recounted a particularly critical incident, which she shared as follows:

When I see her (the student), I point at the score (60, the total score is 100) and ask her (in an angry tone) to explain why she made so many grammatical mistakes and why she neglected the computer-mediated feedback and left the errors unattended. I am sure she felt my anger and dissatisfaction during our talk because she did not look me in the eyes throughout the talk, and I am criticizing her bad attitude toward writing. I used my emotion as a warning to remind her of her mistakes and bad attitudes toward writing. (2nd interview)

When I see her (the student), I pointed to the score (60 out of 100) and, in a tone of anger, questioned her about the numerous grammatical errors and the apparent disregard for the computer-mediated feedback. She expressed her frustration at her lack of attention to the errors. I was certain that she was aware of my anger and dissatisfaction, as she avoided eye contact throughout the conversation. I criticized her poor attitude towards writing and used my emotional response as a form of admonition to highlight her mistakes and the need for a more serious approach to the writing process. (2nd interview)

Olivia recognized that relying solely on written corrective feedback was insufficient to improve the students' writing performance. She observed that some students persistently made the same errors, particularly in crafting topic sentences that failed to present a complete or balanced view, and in structuring paragraphs that lacked coherent reasoning and connections between ideas. Acknowledging the limitations of her current feedback methods, Olivia sought to alter her approach. She aimed to implement new strategies that would more effectively address these recurring issues, thereby helping students to not only identify but also correct their mistakes and enhance their writing skills. This shift in practice reflects her commitment to finding more impactful ways to support her students' academic growth and development.

Acknowledging the limitations of computer-mediated feedback, I resolved to provide more detailed and personalized feedback to my students. After they completed their writing assignments, I invited them to discuss their work with me in my office. These one-on-one conversations allowed me to gain insights into their thought processes, identify the specific challenges they faced in writing, and offer tailored suggestions for improvement. I would then compile a summary of each student's progress and the issues that needed to be addressed in the next class. However, this approach, while beneficial for the students, was demanding on my personal time and energy. Students reported significant benefits from these individual writing conferences, but the reality was that it was not feasible for me to provide this level of attention to every student. Additionally, the curriculum was packed with content that needed to be covered, further complicating the balance between personalized feedback and meeting the broader educational objectives. (2nd interview)

Olivia's emotional journey was closely intertwined with her practices in writing assessment. She rarely incorporated self- and peer evaluation in her classroom, as she observed that students tended to identify only minor errors while failing to recognize more significant ones. Despite implementing various assessment strategies, such as analyzing high and low-scoring writings and holding one-to-one writing conferences, Olivia began to see the limitations in her focus on the end products of students' writing, including genre features, grammatical errors, and scores. She also faced the challenge of managing her time and energy, given the need to attend to each student's progress and encourage their independent thinking and self-regulation. Olivia acknowledged that while the act of writing itself was a central part of her teaching, she had placed less emphasis on the students' autonomous development of their writing skills. Despite finding pleasure in reading her students' work, Olivia found the teaching of *Academic Writing* to be, at times, labor-intensive and emotionally draining. This realization led her to reflect on her teaching methods and consider how she could better support her students in their writing journey while also managing her own well-being.

In her efforts to advance the genre-process integrated approach, Olivia altered her teaching methodology to encourage students to engage with the writing task prior to class. She created opportunities for students to participate in self- and peer-assessment activities, focusing on aspects such as grammar and spelling, to enhance their writing skills. Olivia also paid close attention to the quality of the disciplinary content knowledge that students incorporated into their writing. Following these assessment activities, students were tasked with completing the writing assignment and submitting all related materials, including the writing outline, multiple drafts, and self- and peer evaluations, for a comprehensive final assessment. This approach, observed during the first classroom session, aimed to foster a more interactive and constructive writing process, where students took greater responsibility for their learning and received formative feedback along the way.

7.5 Summary

Taken together, it is evident that Olivia has traversed a complex emotional path as she transitioned her teaching practices from a genre-centered to a genre-process-integrated approach. In pursuit of her teaching goals, Olivia consistently engaged in emotion labor and employed emotion-regulation strategies that she could apply in her professional environment, as suggested by Gkonou and Miller (2021a, 2021b). She demonstrated a strong sense of agency in acquiring both the content knowledge and pedagogical content knowledge of L2 writing, which were essential for curriculum development. The richer her emotional repertoire, the more equipped Olivia was to handle the emotional labor inherent in the teaching process. It is also significant to highlight that Olivia's emotion-regulation strategies were often triggered by the inspiration and joy she derived from learning from experts and sharing her knowledge and practices with colleagues during joint course preparation. Not all teachers share Olivia's inclination to view course development as an opportunity to leverage both external and internal resources to enhance their professional expertise and leadership. However, by setting herself apart from her peers and actively engaging with the challenges presented to her, Olivia's emotional labor in navigating school and institutional demands and expectations can be seen as a positive indicator. It reflects her understanding of the emotional display rules imposed on EFL teachers and her emotional literacy, which are crucial for managing new challenges and obstacles that arise in the classroom.

The research findings on Olivia's emotional experiences in the classroom reveal that both the genre-centered and genre-process-integrated approaches carry emotional implications. Under the genre-centered approach, Olivia prioritized the acquisition of genre knowledge and writing skills by students, viewing teacher instruction and guided writing as pivotal for student writing development. Her classroom teaching experiences, which were detailed and context-specific, suggest that both instruction and feedback were primarily one-directional, occurring subsequent to an external evaluation of student writing performance, as described by Liu and Yu (2022). In this setup, Olivia's focus during instruction and assessment was largely on the quality of feedback and the students' receptiveness to it, considering these elements as crucial for enhancing student writing performance. When students were highly motivated and actively engaged with the teacher's feedback, Olivia tended to experience positive emotions, such as enjoyment and satisfaction. This positive emotional state facilitated the achievement of teaching objectives with less effort in emotion regulation. Conversely, when students showed a lack of interest in the instruction or confusion regarding the feedback, Olivia experienced negative emotions, such as anxiety and dissatisfaction. These emotions made it more challenging to meet teaching objectives and necessitated greater effort in managing her emotional responses. Despite Olivia's determination to enhance teaching effectiveness, the genre-based approach tended to sideline the students' active role and reflected a more teacher-centric paradigm in writing instruction. The course *Academic Writing* was often reduced to a process of information transmission from teacher to student, limiting students' opportunities to exercise autonomy in deciding what and how to write. This approach did not fully leverage the potential for student engagement and the development of independent thinking and self-regulation skills, which are essential components of a more student-centered and process-oriented writing curriculum.

In embracing the genre-process-integrated approach, Olivia endeavored to transform the writing class from a teacher-centered to a learning-centered model by actively involving students in every stage of the academic writing process. She regarded academic writing as a social interaction where students actively participate and engage in various stages of writing. Olivia's emotional experiences throughout the three instructional stages—pre-writing, while-writing, and post-writing—were characterized by her view of students as "meaning-makers" who interact and negotiate meaning with peers, the writing teacher, disciplinary content teachers, library staff, and other stakeholders. To foster collaborative learning, Olivia encouraged group dialogues for writing construction and invited students to engage in discussions with her to interpret and negotiate the meaning of teacher feedback. This dialogic aspect of feedback can be seen as a meaning-making process involving interactive exchanges where interpretations are shared, meanings are negotiated, and expectations are clarified, as suggested by Carless (2016) and Xu and Carless (2017). In this process, students negotiate meaning at three levels: knowledge negotiation, relationship negotiation, and feedback utilization, which can lead to a variety of situations that trigger Olivia's emotions. For example, Olivia might feel positive emotions such as satisfaction and happiness when students demonstrate a proactive learning attitude and achieve their goals, making the fulfillment of teaching objectives easier and reducing the emotional labor required for emotion regulation. On the other hand, she might experience negative emotions like confusion and anxiety when students struggle to overcome challenges, making it harder to meet teaching objectives and necessitating more effort in emotional regulation.

It's important to note that in the genre-process integrated approach, L2 writing acquisition is a negotiation process, with writing mediated through various scaffolding resources within the students' Zone of Proximal Development (ZPD), including teachers, peers, and writing marking systems. In this context, teacher emotional labor can be seen as a mediating tool that initiates teacher-student interactions and promotes self-regulated learning among students. Furthermore, during the text construction process, the use of specific emotion-regulation strategies can prompt collective dialogues between feedback givers and receivers, whether written or oral. These dialogues occur as students discuss their writing during revision rounds and engage in the co-construction of meaning, which can further influence Olivia's emotional experiences and her approach to teaching and feedback.

References

Carless, D. (2016). Feedback as dialogue. In M. A. Peters (Ed.), *Encyclopedia of educational physosophy and theory* (pp. 1–6). Springer.

Gkonou, C., & Miller, E. R. (2021a). An exploration of language teacher reflection, emotion labor, and emotional capital. *TESOL Quarterly, 55*(1), 134–155.

Liu, C., & Yu, S. (2022). Reconceptualizing the impact of feedback in second language writing: A multidimensional perspective. *Assessing Writing, 53*, 100630.

Xu, Y., & Carless, D. (2017). 'Only true friends could be cruelly honest': Cognitive scaffolding and social-affective support in teacher feedback literacy. *Assessment & Evaluation in Higher Education, 42*(7), 1082–1094.

Suggested Readings

Agudo, J. (2018). *Emotions in second language teaching* (1st ed.). Springer International Publishing AG.

Benesch, S. (2012). *Considering emotions in critical English language teaching: Theories and praxis.* Routledge.

Cheng, X., & Liu, Y. (2022). Student engagement with teacher written feedback: Insights from low-proficiency and high-proficiency L2 learners. *System, 109*, 102880.

Dann, R. (2002). *Promoting assessment as learning: Improving the learning process.* Routledge-Falmer.

De Costa, P., Karimpour, S., & Nazari, M. (2023). Developing a taxonomy of teacher emotion labor through metaphor: Personal, interpersonal, and sociocultural angles. *Applied Linguistics Review.*

Gkonou, C., & Miller, E. (2021b). An exploration of language teacher reflection, emotion labor, and emotional capital. *Tesol Quarterly, 55*(1), 134–155.

Han, Y. (2017). Mediating and being mediated: Learner beliefs and learner engagement with written corrective feedback. *System, 69*, 133–142.

Han, J., Jin, L., & Yin, H. (2023). Mapping the research on language teacher emotion: A systematic literature review. *System, 118*, 103138.

Hochschild, A. (1983). *The managed heart: Commercialization of human feeling.* University of California Press.

MacIntyre, P., Gregersen, T., & Mercer, S. (2020). Language teachers' coping strategies during the Covid-19 conversion to online teaching: Correlations with stress, wellbeing and negative emotions. *System (linköping), 94*, 102352.

Chapter 8
Concluding Thoughts

There is an increasing recognition of the importance of emotional labor in the teaching profession. This book targeted university L2 writing teachers, a specific cohort whose emotional experiences, emotional labor, and emotion-regulation strategies are underexplored.

8.1 A Reciprocal Model of L2 Writing Teacher Emotions and Pedagogical Behaviors

This book delves into the complex emotional lives of three L2 writing teachers, examining their emotional responses, how they appraise these emotions, the strategies they use to regulate emotions, and the subsequent effects on their teaching methods and well-being. Echoing previous research about the features and influences of teacher emotions in the L2 context (Chen, 2016; Frenzel et al., 2020; Wang et al., 2019; Zembylas, 2014). The study proposed a reciprocal model concerning the impact of teacher emotions on pedagogical behaviors in the L2 writing classroom context (Fig. 8.1).

The model presented in the book outlines a complex interplay among three key themes, each influencing the other in a cyclical and dynamic manner: (1) Direct Impact: Teachers' emotions directly shape their pedagogical actions in the classroom; (2) Mediating Role: Emotion-regulation strategies serve as a bridge between teachers' emotions and their instructional methods; (3) Recursive Influence: Teaching practices and student interactions feed back into teachers' emotional states and their approaches to managing emotions.

This model emphasizes that teacher emotions can have profound and lasting effects, not only their own well-being but also on students' emotional responses, the rapport between teachers and students, and students' attitudes towards L2 writing. It also suggests that how teachers handle feedback and foster relationships within the

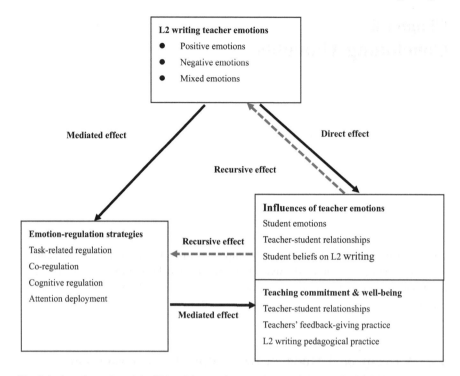

Fig. 8.1 A reciprocal model of L2 writing teacher emotions and pedagogical behaviors

classroom can be significantly influenced by their emotional regulation strategies. Moreover, the model acknowledges that teacher emotions are influenced by a variety of factors related to writing, such as students' proficiency and motivation, teachers' expertise and beliefs, and the demands of the writing tasks. It suggests that positive teacher emotions can inspire successful student writing, reinforcing a positive view of their emotional impact and the effectiveness of their emotion-regulation strategies. Conversely, negative emotions can demotivate students and lead to a critical reassessment of the teachers' emotional management and teaching practices.

8.1.1 Teacher Emotions Could Directly Transmit from Teachers to Students

The idea of emotion transmission entails that if teachers experience and express an emotion in a social context, the same emotion can be induced in their interaction partners (Hatfield et al., 1994). The direct transmission of emotions in the L2 writing classroom, as observed in the study involving three teachers, underscores the powerful influence of emotional exchanges between educators and students. This dynamic is characterized by (1) Expression and Induction: teacher emotions, whether positive or negative, are not only experienced internally but also expressed through non-verbal cues such as facial expressions, tone of voice, and body language. These expressions can induce similar emotions in students, creating a shared emotional experience. (2) Impact on Engagement: when teachers express positive emotions in response to students' achievements, it can inspire students' interest and enjoyment in writing activities. On the other hand, expressions of negative emotions, such as confusion or anxiety regarding students' lack of engagement, can lead to students feeling reluctant and disappointed. (3) Bidirectional Flow: the emotional transmission is not unidirectional; students' emotions can also affect their teachers. Teachers can "catch" the enthusiasm or excitement of students about a writing topic, which can, in turn, influence the teacher's emotional state and teaching approach. (4) Mutual Influence: the findings suggest that the emotional environment in the classroom is a reciprocal system where both teachers and students influence each other's emotions, shaping the overall classroom dynamics and the effectiveness of the learning process.

This bidirectional emotional transmission highlights the importance of emotional intelligence and regulation for both teachers and students. Teachers who are aware of their emotional impact and can manage their emotions effectively are more likely to create a positive learning environment that fosters student engagement and success. Similarly, students who can understand and respond to the emotional cues of their teachers are better positioned to engage in the learning process constructively.

8.1.2 Teacher Emotions Could Shape the Quality of Teacher-Student Relationships

Teacher emotions are critically functional for social relationships with students. In general, positive emotions serve to begin, grow, and successfully maintain relationships, whereas negative emotions can have negative consequences for relationship quality (Wang et al., 2019). Teacher emotions play a vital role in cultivating and sustaining the quality of their relationships with students. Positive emotions typically facilitate the initiation, development, and maintenance of these relationships, while negative emotions may adversely affect their quality (Wang et al., 2019). In this book, the emotions teachers experience and express in the classroom could shape their relationships with students. For instance, Alex encounters frustration, disappointment, and occasionally anger when students make errors in genre structure or language usage. These negative emotions can impact his interactions with students, potentially leading to a less supportive learning environment. Similarly, Lina feels content when students actively engage in writing tasks and adhere to the provided guidance. However, she also experiences anxiety and concern regarding the slow progress of some students and their difficulty in benefiting from feedback, which can strain the teacher-student relationship. Furthermore, Olivia faced challenges in maintaining student enthusiasm and involvement in project-based writing, which is an educational approach that requires students to actively participate in their learning through projects. She experienced anxiety and uncertainty when tasked with providing feedback on the specific subject content within her students' written projects, as this aspect of her role was particularly demanding. The research aligns with established studies indicating that teachers' emotions are crucial in fostering and sustaining teacher-student relationships (Frenzel et al., 2020; Hagenauer et al., 2015). Specifically, the sense of joy in teaching and positive emotional connections with students can enhance the quality of these relationships, leading to a more nurturing and effective instructional environment in L2 writing classes. Conversely, when teachers experience emotional burnout or are frequently overwhelmed by negative emotions, their level of engagement and empathy may diminish, adversely affecting their rapport with students. This highlights the importance of teacher well-being and emotional support in educational settings.

8.1.3 The Use of Emotion-Regulation Strategies Could Mediate L2 Writing Teachers' Commitment and Well-Being

The book's findings reveal that the teachers involved in the study utilized surface acting—a technique where they would put on a display of emotions deemed appropriate for the teaching environment—to manage their emotional expressions. However, this approach did not result in authentic feelings of happiness or contentment with their L2 writing instruction. While the act of feigning emotions was found to be mentally taxing, the strategy of concealing true emotions was effective in preventing teacher-student conflicts and ensuring the continuity of writing activities, especially after disruptions. Additionally, surface acting emerged as a viable tactic for L2 writing teachers to reduce interpersonal tensions and steer clear of awkward situations in broader educational and societal contexts. As such, surface acting, with its mix of negative and positive outcomes, could potentially balance itself out in terms of its overall impact.

The findings also indicate that the teachers used deep acting as a strategy to enhance their dedication and satisfaction with teaching L2 writing. Deep acting involves modifying one's internal emotional state to align with the emotions expected in a given situation. This approach served two main purposes. First, deep acting helped teachers manage the emotional dissonance they experienced and alleviate the emotional toll of teaching L2 writing. By adjusting their internal feelings, they could better cope with the challenges of the classroom. Second, deep acting was also instrumental in creating a positive and collaborative classroom atmosphere, which can inspire students to enhance their writing skills. This, in turn, fosters strong teacher-student relationships and contributes to the teachers' sense of well-being. Moreover, when teachers genuinely expressed positive emotions in response to positive aspects of their work environment, such as supportive colleagues, it reinforced their commitment to teaching L2 writing. This commitment not only improved their well-being but also positively influenced their professional practices. Despite the psychological demands of deep acting, it was shown to be an effective method for upholding professional standards. It encouraged teachers to motivate students in their L2 writing, seek creative pedagogical solutions to address writing errors, and monitor student progress, all of which shaped their emotional experiences and teaching practices in a constructive manner.

This book identified that the natural expression of emotions by the participating teachers positively influenced their commitment and expertise in L2 writing instruction. On one hand, by openly acknowledging and expressing negative emotions, the teachers were able to address specific issues in their teaching. For instance, Alex used his frustration to highlight common mistakes in L2 writing, prompting students to be more attentive to their errors. Lina's dissatisfaction with the existing curriculum led her to revise it for her *Academic Writing* course, aiming to improve its effectiveness. Olivia adjusted her feedback practices to better support her students' writing development. On the other hand, the expression of positive emotions further reinforced the teachers' dedication to their work. For instance, Lina's enthusiasm was evident in her written feedback to students, which likely encouraged them and fostered a positive learning environment. Olivia's satisfaction with her students' writing performances reflected her joy in their progress and her commitment to their success. This natural emotional expression, both positive and negative, not only enhanced the teachers' professional engagement but also contributed to their pedagogical growth and adaptability. It allowed them to respond authentically to the needs of their students and the dynamics of their classrooms, ultimately enriching their teaching practices and the learning experience for their students.

8.1.4 The Use of Emotion-Regulation Strategies Could Mediate L2 Writing Teachers' Feedback-Giving Practice

The research indicates that the three teacher participants employed distinct emotional regulation strategies when providing feedback on their students' written work, and these strategies had a direct impact on their feedback practices.

In Alex's situation, his focus during feedback was predominantly on the micro-level elements of student writing, such as vocabulary and grammar, rather than the macro-level elements like structure, content, and style. The prevalence of language form errors was a significant trigger for his negative emotions. To manage these emotions, which were exacerbated by the demanding nature of providing detailed feedback, Alex adopted surface-acting strategies. These strategies involved suppressing and concealing his negative feelings, which in turn led to notable shifts in his approach to feedback. First, Alex chose to offer less feedback overall, opting instead for more focused and comprehensive written corrections on a subset of student work. Second, to assist students in addressing language form errors, he directed them to use computer-mediated feedback tools, such as *Pigai*, to revise and edit their writing. Third, Recognizing the challenges some students faced with writing, Alex lowered his expectations for these individuals. For example, he suggested that struggling students could memorize model texts as an alternative to passing a writing test. These changes reflect Alex's efforts to balance his emotional well-being with the need to provide effective feedback. By making these adjustments, he aimed to maintain a manageable workload while still supporting student learning, albeit with a different approach to feedback and assessment.

In Lina's approach to writing feedback, she considered it a deeply personal and reflective process, emphasizing the students' reception and application of feedback. Her philosophy as a writing teacher was rooted in the belief that being genuine and emotionally transparent with students could facilitate their gradual improvement in writing. However, she was disheartened by the students' apparent lack of engagement, which was evident in their reactions to her feedback. To manage her emotions, Lina employed a combination of cognitive and co-regulation strategies. First, cognitive regulation: she acknowledged her own authentic emotions, which likely helped her to process and understand her feelings better. Second, co-regulation, she shared her emotions with others, which could provide emotional support and help in moderating her unwanted emotions. Consequently, these strategies influenced her feedback practices in two significant ways. First, Lina provided feedback at various stages of the writing process, encouraging students to engage in discussions with her about the writing tasks. This approach aimed to foster a collaborative understanding of the writing assignment and its requirements. Second, she required multiple drafts for each writing task and offered feedback on each iteration. By comparing drafts, she could assess whether her feedback had been incorporated by the students. When she saw that her feedback was being heeded and students were actively engaged, she experienced a sense of joy in giving feedback, which motivated her to invest more effort into this aspect of her teaching. Lina's methods highlight the importance of a feedback process that is interactive, supportive, and responsive to the students' engagement and progress. Her approach underscores the value of emotional intelligence in teaching and the impact it can have on both the teacher's well-being and the students' learning experience.

In Olivia's teaching journey, she experimented with two distinct pedagogical approaches in her L2 writing classes, each influencing her feedback practices and emotional experiences differently. In implementing the Genre-Centered Approach, Olivia saw feedback as a unidirectional communication, primarily shaped by the students' writing performance and their receptiveness to her guidance. She felt a sense of satisfaction and encouragement when students diligently revised their work based on her feedback, leading her to invest additional time in post-class coaching. Conversely, she experienced negative emotions like confusion, anxiety, and disappointment when students were careless or dismissive of her feedback. To cope, she distracted herself from these negative feelings and sought emotionally neutral situations. In implementing the Genre-Process Integrated Approach, Olivia shifted her focus to a more collaborative and student-centered method. She facilitated group writing, engaging with students throughout the writing process. Instead of evaluating the final product, she allowed students autonomy in content choice and adjusted her oral feedback based on their reactions. This method led to a more diverse emotional experience, and she found it easier to express her genuine emotions. It should be noted that Olivia's use of "dialogic feedback" through conversational interactions with students made the feedback process more engaging and effective. She actively participated in group discussions, especially when students were less active, and used "informal talk" to discuss disciplinary content knowledge. Additionally, she encouraged students to share their writing process with the class, which not only fostered a sense of community but also provided a platform for peer learning. These practices suggest that Olivia's emotional regulation strategy of expressing her authentic emotions was beneficial for the implementation of the genre-process integrated approach. When she observed that her feedback was well-received and students were actively engaged, she found the act of giving feedback to be rewarding, leading her to put more effort into this aspect of her teaching. This approach not only enhanced her emotional well-being but also improved the quality of student engagement and learning outcomes.

Despite the differences among the three teacher participants in terms of their use of emotional regulation strategies, there are some commonalities among them. First, they all believed their feedback practices were valuable and indispensable. Second, they all held positive beliefs about feedback provision, and they considered feedback to be crucial for enhancing students' language proficiency and writing skills. Third, they all experienced negative emotions such as confusion, disappointment, and anger when giving feedback to a large class. Such negative emotions had led to their changing feedback-giving practices. Furthermore, students' bad attitudes, disengagement with feedback, and misconduct (such as plagiarism) in writing are also sources of their feelings of disappointment or anger. Fourth, they all utilized emotional labor strategies to regulate the negative emotions and were able to reap positive emotions such as enjoyment and satisfaction when they observed students' progress from their feedback, although it may not bring direct improvement in students' writing.

Despite their unique approaches to emotional regulation, the three teacher participants shared several common beliefs and experiences regarding feedback in their L2 writing classes. First, All three teachers recognized the importance of feedback as a vital component of the learning process, seeing it as essential for improving students' language and writing abilities. Second, They collectively held the view that providing feedback was a positive and necessary part of their role as educators. Third, they all faced negative emotions such as confusion, disappointment, and anger when providing feedback to large groups, which influenced their approach to feedback. Fourth, the teachers' negative feelings were also triggered by students' poor attitudes towards feedback, lack of engagement, and academic dishonesty, such as plagiarism. Fifth, each teacher employed emotional labor strategies to manage their negative emotions, which helped them maintain a positive demeanor in the classroom. Sixth, Despite the challenges, they were able to derive positive emotions such as enjoyment and satisfaction from their work, particularly when they witnessed student progress as a result of their feedback, even if this progress did not immediately translate into improved writing skills. These commonalities highlight the complex emotional landscape of teaching and the importance of emotional regulation strategies for educators. They also underscore the impact of student behavior on teacher emotions and the need for support systems that help teachers manage these emotions to maintain effective and positive classroom interactions.

8.1.5 The Use of Emotion-Regulation Strategies Could Mediate the L2 Writing Pedagogical Practices

In the present study, the three teacher participants performed various emotional-regulation strategies such as task-related regulation, co-regulation, and attention deployment to soothe the emotions and advance the instruction of L2 writing. It was found that the application of these emotional-regulation strategies played a mediating role in shaping the pedagogical practices of L2 writing. By effectively managing their emotions, the teachers were better able to create a conducive learning environment, provide meaningful feedback, and engage in teaching practices that supported student learning and development. This underscores the significance of emotional intelligence in teaching and the potential benefits of integrating emotional-regulation strategies into teacher training and professional development.

In Alex's scenario, he employed a combination of emotional-regulation strategies that were closely tied to the tasks of teaching and providing feedback. His approach was characterized by the following strategies. First, Task-Related Regulation: Alex addressed writing issues directly by guiding students to analyze and tackle their problems. He also aimed to enhance student performance through methods like reciting model texts, which could help students internalize the structure and style of effective writing. Second, Response Regulation: To manage his negative emotions, particularly those triggered by errors in student writing, Alex practiced suppression. This involved inhibiting his immediate emotional reactions to maintain a calm and focused demeanor in the classroom. Third, Cognitive Regulation: He also engaged in expectation reduction, adjusting his expectations for students who struggled with writing. This strategy likely helped him to avoid frustration and disappointment, allowing him to approach these students with a more supportive attitude.

These strategies underpinned Alex's pedagogical practices, which were teacher-directed and focused on delivering writing genre knowledge and skills. His methods included lecturing, analyzing model texts, and preparing students for exams through writing practice. Alex's approach to feedback was also quite structured, with an emphasis on briefing students on common errors in sample writings. Overall, Alex's teaching style in L2 writing classrooms was centered on the teacher as the primary source of instruction, with a focus on content knowledge, timing, and conditions for providing feedback. This approach suggests that while Alex was dedicated to improving student writing, his methods may have placed less emphasis on student autonomy and the development of critical thinking skills in writing.

Lina's approach to teaching L2 writing was characterized by a focus on cognitive regulation strategies that aimed to maintain a positive and supportive classroom environment. Her methods primarily included (1) Reassurance: Lina reinforced her belief in her ability to guide students through the writing process, helping them to construct their work in a step-by-step manner. This likely fostered a sense of confidence in her teaching approach and in her students' capabilities. (2) Acknowledging Emotions: She accepted and embraced her authentic emotions during interactions with students, which could have created a more genuine and open relationship, allowing for a deeper understanding of student needs. Lina's pedagogical practices were centered around the idea that teacher-student conversation is essential for idea generation and planning in writing. She implemented various innovative strategies to guide student writing, such as (1) Writing by Reading: Using reading as a precursor to writing to help students understand different writing styles and structures; (2) Teacher-Guided Questioning: Posing questions to stimulate critical thinking and guide students through the writing process; (3) Joining Student Discussions: Actively participating in discussions to provide guidance and support; (4) Writing Conferences: Holding one-on-one or small group sessions to discuss writing in more detail.

Additionally, Lina engaged in co-regulation strategies by seeking advice from experts and colleagues, and by sharing her emotions with students, which could have helped in creating a supportive community within the classroom. She viewed feedback as an opportunity for dialogue and negotiation of meaning in students' writing. To facilitate this, she provided tools such as assessment rubrics and a scoring matrix to aid in peer feedback, encouraging students to reflect on the quality of their feedback. This approach suggests that Lina believed in nurturing students' intellectual, emotional, and psychological development as independent individuals in the context of L2 writing. Lina's teaching philosophy and practices were student-centered, emphasizing the importance of dialogue, emotional intelligence, and collaborative learning in the development of writing skills.

8.2 How Does This Book Contribute to Theory, Research and Practice?

This section outlines the study's significant contributions across three main areas: theoretical insights, research advancements, and practical applications. First, this book enriches the theoretical landscape by exploring the emotions experienced by L2 writing teachers and the strategies they employ to regulate these emotions during instruction. It introduces a model that captures the intricate interplay between L2 writing teacher emotions and their pedagogical actions, highlighting the dynamic nature of cause and effect relationships. Second, this book adds to the existing literature by examining the emotional dimensions and regulatory tactics of L2 writing teachers, contributing to a deeper understanding of their professional lives. It provides new perspectives on L2 writing assessments and pedagogy, shedding light on how teacher emotions can shape these critical components of language education. Third, this book prompts L2 writing teachers to consider how their emotions intersect with their instructional practices, fostering a reflective approach to teaching. The findings offer insights for the development of teacher training programs that address emotional intelligence and for the formulation of university policies that support effective L2 writing instruction.

8.2.1 Contribution to Theory

This book stands out as a pioneering effort in exploring the intricate relationship between L2 writing teacher emotions, emotional regulation, and the various factors that precede and follow these emotions within the context of L2 writing instruction. It enriches the theoretical discourse on L2 writing and teacher emotions by examining the interplay among emotional intelligence, emotional labor strategies, and aspects of teaching satisfaction, personal accomplishment, and emotional well-being. The study introduces a reciprocal model that elucidates the causes and effects of L2 writing teacher emotions, offering a comprehensive and positive psychological perspective on the multifaceted and dynamic nature of these emotions within specific educational settings.

This book delves into the emotional appraisal and regulation processes that L2 writing teachers undertake in response to both external factors (such as macro-, meso-, and micro-contextual issues) and internal factors (such as individual differences) that arise from implementing different pedagogical approaches (genre-centered, process-centered, and genre-process-integrated). L2 writing teachers encounter various forms and intensities of emotional labor and employ a range of emotion-regulation strategies tailored to the goals and norms of different instructional stages. This book provides a detailed analysis of the relationships between teacher emotions and their outcomes, considering the categories of emotion-regulation strategies and the direct and indirect impacts of these emotions and strategies on various dimensions, including pedagogical behaviors, teacher-student relationships, feedback practices, teaching satisfaction, and professional well-being.

In summary, this book, informed by positive psychology and ecological perspectives, offers a comprehensive examination of the well-being of L2 writing teachers in Chinese mainland universities. It identifies three key ecological systems that are integral to teacher well-being. First, the macro-context system, which relates to school policy and management, and can have a significant impact on the work environment and the support teachers receive. Second, the meso-context system, which involves relationships with colleagues, and can provide a sense of community and professional support. Third, the micro-context system, which refers to interactions with students within the L2 writing classrooms and are the immediate and daily experiences that shape a teacher's emotional state.

The book details how the three L2 writing teachers navigated various challenges and joys within these systems and encountered additional specific challenges in their classrooms. Despite these challenges, the teachers were able to leverage a range of resources to maintain their well-being, including psychological resources (e.g., self-awareness, expertise, positive thinking, and appreciation for feedback from experts); emotional resources (e.g., effective emotion-regulation strategies); and social and contextual Resources (e.g., support from peers, administrative leaders, and experts provided additional assistance).

The findings align with Fredrickson's broaden-and-build theory of positive emotions, suggesting that individuals with a positive outlook and frequent positive emotions are more likely to experience greater well-being and resilience emotions (e.g., Carver & Scheier, 1998; Scheier & Carver, 1985; Seligman, 2011). The research also resonates with previous studies (e.g., Dodge et al., 2012) indicating that teachers are in a continuous state of dynamic responsiveness, balancing stressors with resources to achieve a sense of well-being. Moreover, the book provides insights for the development and application of targeted strategies to enhance the well-being of L2 writing teachers. These strategies could include preventive measures, interventions, training programs, and remedial actions tailored to the specific needs and contexts of L2 writing educators.

8.2.2 Contribution to Research

This book enriches the academic discourse on L2 writing teacher emotions by uncovering how these emotions directly influence teaching practices and well-being, as well as how emotion-regulation strategies serve as a bridge between the two. It offers an in-depth qualitative analysis of the emotional landscape of L2 writing teachers as they engage with diverse pedagogical approaches. The study delves into the catalysts for teacher emotions, the objectives and standards that inform their emotional evaluations, and the strategies they employ to manage and alleviate emotional stress. It also uncovers how these emotional and regulatory factors impact the execution of L2 writing instruction and the teachers' sense of professional well-being. By providing a nuanced and contextualized view of L2 writing teachers' experiences, the book enables researchers to gain a more authentic understanding of the challenges and realities faced by these educators.

This research enhances the field of L2 writing pedagogy by providing a detailed account of how teachers at three universities in mainland China apply three distinct L2 writing instruction methods to EFL student writers with diverse educational backgrounds and language proficiencies. Over recent decades, there has been a significant shift in the understanding of L2 writing, moving from viewing it as a solitary cognitive task to recognizing it as a socially embedded activity influenced by a myriad of factors involving the writer, the instructor, and the learning environment (Carson & Nelson, 1996; Leki, 1990; Tsui & Ng, 2010; Liu & Yu, 2022). This book presents new empirical data and offers novel perspectives on the influence of teacher emotions and the use of emotion-regulation strategies in the evolution of contemporary L2 writing pedagogy. It highlights the importance of the writing process, teacher-student interactions, formative assessment in writing, student engagement with feedback, collaborative writing endeavors, and the creation of authentic writing contexts. By doing so, it provides a valuable resource for understanding the multifaceted nature of L2 writing instruction and the emotional dimensions that play a critical role in this pedagogical landscape.

The findings significantly contribute to the research on genre-centered L2 writing pedagogy by examining the teaching methods, the practicality of using model texts to teach genre knowledge and writing skills, the role of teacher and computer-mediated feedback, and the influence of teacher emotions in this instructional approach. The focus on the quality of the final writing product often results in teachers' instruction and feedback being primarily informational, as highlighted by Han and Xu (2021) and Liu and Yu (2022). This approach can lead to a discrepancy between teachers' expectations and students' actual writing performance, which frequently triggers negative emotions in teachers, intensifying their emotional labor. Given the emphasis on the "writing product," most of the teachers' emotion regulation strategies are reactive, focusing on managing emotions after they have been aroused, as described by Gross (1998). Additionally, the study reveals that L2 writing teachers often discuss their experiences with negative emotions and strategies for reducing these emotions more frequently than their positive emotional experiences and strategies for enhancing positive emotions. This suggests that if left unaddressed, the persistent negative emotions teachers experience in response to students' writing can lead to emotional burnout and potentially early retirement from the profession, which in turn can have a negative impact on the quality of L2 writing instruction and students' learning outcomes.

Regarding the book's contribution to the research on process-centered L2 writing pedagogy, the insights into process-centered L2 writing pedagogy enrich the research by examining the teaching procedures of this approach, the practicality of engaging students in the sequential stages of writing construction, and the provision of diverse writing assessments and feedback. The focus on the writing process shifts the teacher's role to facilitating an internal process, where the emphasis is on students' comprehension, interpretation, and application of information (Boud & Molloy, 2013; Liu & Yu, 2022). In this pedagogical context, students are expected to evaluate and utilize feedback from external sources, such as writing assessments and various feedback types. However, if students show a lack of engagement or underperform, this can elicit emotional responses from teachers, leading to internal comparisons between the intended teaching outcomes and the students' actual performance. This dynamic shapes the teachers' emotional labor and the strategies they use to regulate their emotions.

Since the focus is on the "writing process," L2 writing teachers often employ antecedent-focused emotion-regulation strategies. These strategies involve managing emotions before and during the emotional experience, allowing teachers to modify the situation or their cognitive interpretation of it (Gross, 1998). The study reveals that L2 writing teachers discuss both their positive and negative emotions, as well

8.2 How Does This Book Contribute to Theory, Research and Practice?

as the strategies they use to enhance positive emotions and reduce negative ones. From the study, it can be inferred that both positive and negative emotions of L2 writing teachers significantly influence the quality of the teacher-student relationship, contributing to a cyclical process in process-centered L2 writing pedagogy. Positive emotions can foster a supportive learning environment, while effective management of negative emotions can prevent burnout and maintain a constructive teaching approach.

Regarding the study's contribution to the research on the genre and process integrated L2 writing pedagogy, this illustration of the difficulties in shifting the instructional fucus from teacher side to student side, coupled with L2 writing teachers' emotional experiences could enrich the L2 writing pedagogical theories by unveiling the underlying mechanism of teacher emotions and the utilization of emotion-regulation strategies in integrating the genre and process pedagogical practices in terms of shaping the teacher-student relationship qualities, sustaining students' positive emotions and motivation in L2 writing, maximizing students' participation and engagement with L2 writing activities, and catering to students' needs in L2 writing (Carless et al., 2011; Lee, 2017; Yang & Carless, 2013). Moreover, in contrast with the language-focused and meaning-focused writing tasks in most of the L2 writing classes, the design of project-based writing of the disciplinary content knowledge is somewhat unique. It is academic writing based on students' disciplinary content knowledge and empirical data to address authentic questions, which requires collaboration with peer classmates, disciplinary content teachers, librarian support, and other stakeholders. For its uniqueness, the current study can offer an alternative perspective for researchers in examining the paths and values of involving students in collaborative writing projects. Lastly, the findings of the study add support to the mediating roles of teacher emotions and emotion-regulation strategies in student collaborative academic writing, a topic frequently raised in theoretical discussion but insufficiently explored in empirical research, particularly in university L2 writing contexts.

Regarding the study's contribution to the research on the genre and process integrated L2 writing pedagogy, the exploration of the challenges in transitioning the instructional focus from the teacher to the student, alongside the emotional experiences of L2 writing teachers, contributes significantly to L2 writing pedagogical theories. It sheds light on the mechanisms through which teacher emotions and emotion-regulation strategies are instrumental in blending genre and process approaches. This integration is crucial for enhancing the quality of teacher-student relationships, maintaining students' positive emotions and motivation in L2 writing, increasing student involvement in writing activities, and addressing students' specific needs in L2 writing contexts (Carless et al., 2011; Lee, 2017; Yang & Carless, 2013). Additionally, the focus on project-based writing, which is distinct from the typical language or meaning-focused tasks in L2 writing classes, provides a unique perspective. This approach involves academic writing that is grounded in students' disciplinary knowledge and empirical data, aiming to tackle real-world questions. It necessitates collaboration among students, content experts, librarians, and other educational partners. The study's findings offer researchers a fresh viewpoint on the benefits and processes of engaging students in collaborative writing projects. Furthermore, the research bolsters the understanding of the mediating role of teacher emotions and emotion-regulation strategies in fostering student collaboration in academic writing. This aspect, though often discussed theoretically, has been under-explored in empirical studies, especially within university L2 writing environments. These insights help fill this gap, providing a more comprehensive view of the emotional dimensions of L2 writing instruction.

8.2.3 Contribution to Practice

The research has the potential to significantly impact university-level L2 writing instruction in two key areas. Firstly, it provides a structured framework for implementing genre-centered, process-centered, and integrated genre-process approaches to teaching. Secondly, it delves into the emotional aspects of L2 writing instruction, highlighting the importance of teacher emotions and emotional regulation strategies. The study offers a detailed account of the teaching methodologies employed by three teacher participants over an entire semester, serving as a practical guide for other educators. It presents valuable teaching materials, such as lesson plans, feedback mechanisms, and mobile learning tools, which are grounded in real classroom experiences. These resources not only illustrate the application of various teaching approaches but also underscore the significance of teacher emotions in the pedagogical process. Furthermore, by examining the emotional dynamics and the strategies used by L2 writing teachers to manage emotional challenges, the study equips educators with insights into the role of emotions in teaching. It encourages teachers to enhance their emotional awareness and employ effective emotional regulation techniques to improve the quality of L2 writing instruction. In essence, the research provides a comprehensive perspective on L2 writing instruction, emphasizing the interplay between pedagogical strategies and teacher emotions, and offers a wealth of practical resources to support educators in their teaching endeavors.

Building on the above contributions, insights from the study could be linked to higher education policies, particularly those concerning L2 writing and English curriculum reform in Chinese mainland universities. Shared views regarding the reform are that developing L2 writing teachers' knowledge and abilities in regulating emotions is important for the development of student-centered L2 writing teaching approaches. Controversies about the reform centered on the function of teacher emotions in implementing the approaches. In this regard, the current study demonstrated three different profiles of L2 writing teacher emotions embedded in the teaching progress, which may serve as references to policy makers at the faculty, institutional, and school levels.

The findings of the study not only enhance the understanding of L2 writing instruction at the classroom level but also have implications for higher education policies, especially in the context of English curriculum reform in Chinese mainland universities. The insights gained can be instrumental in shaping policies that focus on L2 writing and the broader educational landscape. The reform initiatives in

L2 writing education emphasize the need for L2 writing teachers to cultivate their emotional intelligence and regulatory skills. This is seen as a critical component in fostering a student-centered approach to L2 writing, which is aligned with contemporary educational philosophies that prioritize student engagement and personal growth. The study's exploration of the role of teacher emotions in the implementation of pedagogical approaches has sparked debates on the subject. By presenting three distinct profiles of L2 writing teacher emotions and their impact on teaching progress, the research provides a nuanced perspective on this issue. These profiles can serve as a reference for policy-makers at various levels, including faculty, institutional, and school administration, as they consider how to integrate emotional intelligence into teacher training programs and curriculum development. Moreover, the study's findings can help inform policy decisions by highlighting the importance of supporting teachers in managing their emotions effectively. This support can lead to more dynamic and responsive teaching practices, which in turn can enhance the overall quality of L2 writing instruction and contribute to the success of curriculum reform efforts.

8.3 How Does This Book Bridge the Gap Between Research and Practice in L2 Writing?

This section presents the implications for research and practice. Implications for research are listed below in terms of what the findings could imply for theoretical explorations. Implications for L2 writing pedagogical practices, L2 writing teacher training, curriculum development, and university administration.

8.3.1 Implications for Research

The qualitative outcomes of the study delineate the emotional journeys of three L2 writing teachers, capturing the precursors to their emotions, the processes by which they assess these emotions, and the subsequent effects on their pedagogical practices. This comprehensive profile underscores the relevance of teacher emotions and the concept of emotional labor, which extends beyond academic research. It suggests that these concepts are not only valuable for understanding the psychological intricacies of teaching but also have practical applications within the real-world educational sphere. This understanding can lead to the development of strategies that help teachers manage their emotions, thereby improving their instructional practices and student engagement.

The study's findings present a reciprocal model that elucidates the complex interplay of causes and effects of L2 writing teacher emotions, grounded in empirical data. This model offers a framework for future research to explore the emotional dimensions of teaching more deeply. It illustrates how teachers' emotional appraisal mechanisms function in the context of emotional labor and tension regulation across various stages of implementing three distinct L2 writing pedagogical practices, with each stage having its own set of goals and norms. While the generalizability of this model is inherently limited due to the case study approach, it serves as a valuable starting point for subsequent investigations into teacher emotions within L2 writing instruction. Future research could expand upon this model by considering additional factors such as shifts in educational policies, the dynamics of teacher-student and teacher-collegial relationships, and the conditions of students themselves. These factors, along with the roles of administrative leaders and other stakeholders, could be integrated into the model to create more comprehensive conceptual frameworks. Such frameworks would not only enhance our understanding of the emotional landscape of L2 writing instruction but also provide practical insights for educational practitioners seeking to foster supportive and effective teaching environments. By examining these multifaceted elements, researchers can contribute to the development of strategies that address the emotional complexities of teaching and learning, ultimately benefiting both teachers and students in the L2 writing context.

8.3.2 *Implications for Pedagogical Practice*

The findings of this study provide a rich array of pedagogical insights, significantly impacting L2 writing instruction. These insights are actionable across critical educational areas, including curriculum design, course preparation, classroom management, and policy reform. The three L2 writing teachers involved serve as exemplary archetypes, effectively capturing the pedagogical practices and emotional landscapes that define the daily experiences of frontline L2 writing educators.

First, the three L2 writing teachers exhibited a comprehensive understanding of both writing and the pedagogy of teaching writing, a trait that corresponds with the defining characteristics of proficient L2 writing educators as identified in prior research (for instance, Lee & Yuan, 2021; Yigitoglu & Belcher, 2014). This robust knowledge foundation empowered them to engage in ongoing experimentation and critical reflection on their L2 writing instruction methods, thereby nurturing their professional aspirations and clarifying their educational objectives.

Second, the trio of L2 writing teachers recognized the significance of managing their emotional expressions and internal states in the classroom, which is crucial for enhancing teaching methodologies and, by extension, the overall quality of instruction. They were dedicated to fostering a learning environment that nurtured students' interest, motivation, and self-assurance in writing, as well as equipping them with the skills necessary to engage effectively in self-assessment (as supported by Lee & Yuan, 2021). To this end, the teachers were perceptive of the spectrum of emotions, both positive and negative, that writing activities could evoke. They proactively employed a variety of emotion-regulation strategies tailored to the specific needs and conditions of their students within the L2 writing classroom context, thereby enriching the quality of teacher-student interactions.

Third, the three L2 writing teachers exhibited the capacity to introspect on their emotional experiences in conjunction with their teaching practices. The study revealed that these educators possessed a reflective mindset, which allowed them to explore and integrate innovative teaching methods. These methods included providing feedback, brainstorming, creating mind maps, engaging in group work, and facilitating student presentations and project-based writing activities. By embracing these diverse approaches, the teachers not only exercised their professional autonomy but also harmonized their personal beliefs, values, and emotions with their instructional strategies. This alignment contributed to their professional growth and enhanced the effectiveness of their teaching in the L2 writing context.

Fourth, the three L2 writing teachers showcased leadership in driving writing innovations within their educational settings. Despite facing a myriad of challenges such as unfavorable policies, a rigid curriculum, time limitations, resource scarcity, and resistance from colleagues, these educators persevered. The study highlights their strategic maneuvering within these constraints to foster innovative teaching practices, drawing on the work of Sternberg and Horvath (1995). Moreover, their leadership extended beyond their individual classrooms. They actively engaged with the broader teacher community, sharing their experiences and insights. As exemplified by the cases of Alex and Lina, they assumed the role of course leaders, guiding their peers through pedagogical advancements. This collaborative approach not only enriched their own professional development but also contributed to a collective growth within the teaching community, promoting a culture of innovation and continuous improvement in L2 writing instruction.

Despite facing limitations in their pedagogical practices, which stemmed from a lack of comprehensive content and pedagogical content knowledge in L2 writing, as well as encountering various contextual barriers, the three teacher participants have shown remarkable abilities and expertise in managing emotions across different facets of their professional roles as L2 writing teachers. Their diligent approach to identifying and addressing challenges through progressive problem recognition and problem-solving can serve as a model for other L2 writing teachers seeking innovative approaches to pedagogical practices. Their experiences underscore the importance of emotional intelligence in teaching and offer a valuable reference for educators looking to enhance their instructional strategies and navigate the complexities of the classroom environment.

8.3.3 Implications for L2 Writing Teachers

The implications for L2 writing teachers underscore the significance of introspective self-reflection, particularly regarding their emotional experiences, as a cornerstone for professional growth and expertise development (Hayden et al., 2013; Lee & Yuan,

2021; Yu et al., 2021). While professional development encompasses a myriad of aspects, the study emphasizes that L2 writing teachers should critically reflect on their inherent emotional responses rather than suppressing or disregarding negative feelings. This reflection is essential for both personal well-being and professional advancement. To foster this reflection, L2 writing teachers are encouraged to engage in a dialogue with their emotions by posing thoughtful questions: identifying the emotions they experience, understanding the contextual triggers, contemplating appropriate responses, and speculating on potential outcomes. This process involves learning to evaluate and share these insights in a reflexive manner. It is recommended that L2 writing teachers maintain reflection journals and engage in meaningful conversations with students and peers. Such practices can enhance their emotional reflexivity and provide a platform for continuous learning. Moreover, collaborative reflection activities, such as joint writing projects, can be integrated into their professional development. As writing teachers, it is imperative to practice the craft themselves, as suggested by Casanave (2017), which not only improves their own writing skills but also deepens their understanding of the writing process, thereby enriching their teaching capabilities.

Conversely, beyond the cognitive and social facets that contribute to the professional expertise of L2 writing teachers, this study highlights the affective domain as a significant factor in achieving expert-level teaching in L2 writing (Lee & Yuan, 2021; Yu et al., 2021). The challenges faced by the three teacher participants offer valuable insights for other L2 writing teachers, who should be mindful of the multifaceted nature of L2 writing instruction and the expertise required, encompassing cognitive, social, and emotional elements. In light of this, it is advised that L2 writing teachers actively participate in a Community of Practice. Within such a community, they can cultivate shared goals, engage in the exchange of valuable ideas, and collaboratively create suitable teaching materials, writing assignments, and assessment tasks. Additionally, they can develop effective feedback strategies aimed at enhancing students' writing skills (Lee & Yuan, 2021; Yu et al., 2021). By doing so, writing teachers not only foster their own professional growth but also serve as exemplary role models for their students, embodying the principles and practices they aim to instill in their learners. This participatory approach to professional development is instrumental in creating a supportive and dynamic learning environment that benefits both teachers and students alike.

8.3.4 Implications for L2 Writing Teacher Educators

The implications for L2 writing teacher educators are multifaceted, emphasizing the critical role of training that enables teachers to understand and manage their emotions effectively, thereby maintaining their well-being in the context of L2 writing instruction. The training should be comprehensive, covering various aspects, but with a particular focus on (1) pedagogical proficiency: Ensuring that pre-service, novice, and seasoned teachers possess a solid grasp of L2 writing pedagogy. This foundational knowledge is crucial for informed decision-making in the classroom. (2) challenge interpretation: offering teachers diverse experiences and perspectives that allow them to meaningfully interpret and adaptively address the challenges they face in teaching. (3) emotional reflexivity: fostering emotional reflexivity by systematically incorporating reflective practices into the training curriculum. This includes creating an environment that encourages open and supportive discussions about emotions, as highlighted by Song (2021). By integrating these elements into teacher training programs, educators can better prepare L2 writing teachers to navigate the emotional complexities of their profession, ultimately leading to more effective and fulfilling teaching experiences.

Conversely, given that classroom interactions with individual students are pivotal in shaping teacher emotions (Hargreaves, 2000), this study suggests a suite of interventions aimed at enhancing teacher-student dynamics within L2 writing classrooms. The goal is to encourage more authentic emotional expression. Initially, integrating interpersonal skills training into teacher education programs (Zee & Van der Veen, 2013) could empower L2 writing instructors to mitigate the tendency to feign or conceal emotions, particularly among students who exhibit low motivation and engagement with writing. This approach can foster a more genuine connection with learners. Additionally, the Relationship-focused Reflection Program (Bosman et al., 2021; Spilt et al., 2012) stands out as an impactful professional development tool. It is designed to nurture strong, supportive bonds with students by equipping teachers with the skills to navigate complex classroom scenarios and manage their emotional responses effectively. By prompting teachers to reflect on their emotional reactions to specific classroom incidents, this program not only enhances the quality of emotional labor but also contributes to the long-term enhancement of teachers' professional well-being.

8.3.5 *Implications for University Administration*

At the university level, the formulation and execution of top-down educational policies are crucial endeavors that require the concerted efforts of both the university administration and its leadership. To this end, school leaders must embody professionalism, responsibility, and foresight in their decision-making processes. They should be adept at steering educators through effective orientations, oversight, and professional development initiatives that align with the institution's strategic goals. Furthermore, the university administration bears the responsibility of cultivating a supportive academic environment. This environment should be conducive to teachers' endeavors to innovate and enhance their pedagogical approaches. To facilitate this, the administration must ensure that educators have access to the necessary resources and receive encouragement for curriculum development. By doing so, the university not only fosters a culture of continuous improvement but also empowers its faculty to excel in their roles as educators and innovators.

At the faculty level, it is imperative for the administrative body and leadership to equip frontline L2 writing instructors and EFL educators with well-defined directives and ample opportunities for professional growth. This can be achieved by organizing specialized training sessions tailored to their disciplines, facilitating regular pre-service and in-service educational programs, and offering constructive, consistent feedback on teachers' course materials, lesson planning, instructional strategies, and accomplishments. Furthermore, encouraging pedagogical research in partnership with peers from related fields can significantly contribute to their professional advancement. In addition to these initiatives, implementing a faculty mentoring program is highly recommended (Blackwell, 1989; Lechuga, 2014; Zellers et al., 2008). A key benefit of such a program is that both the mentor and the mentee operate within the same educational framework, sharing an intimate understanding of the faculty's regulations, policies, curriculum development practices, teaching resources, classroom dynamics, and student demographics. This shared context fosters a common ground for effective communication and collaboration. Another significant advantage of faculty mentoring is the establishment of an egalitarian relationship between mentor and novice. This level playing field promotes open dialogue, ease of idea exchange, and a supportive environment for seeking guidance in navigating the challenges associated with pedagogical innovation. By leveraging these peer-to-peer interactions, the faculty can cultivate a culture of mutual support and continuous improvement in teaching practices.

8.4 Concluding Remarks

This book stands out as a pioneering effort that embraces a multidimensional framework of teacher emotions, synthesizing insights from appraisal, sociocultural, and positive psychological theories. This comprehensive approach provides a nuanced lens through which to explore the intricate interplay between teachers' emotional experiences, pedagogical approaches, and overall well-being within the unique setting of Chinese university EFL writing classrooms. This book aims to catalyze a shift in research focus towards the emotional landscape of L2 writing educators, with the ultimate goal of enhancing their dedication to teaching and their overall well-being. Such an endeavor is instrumental in bolstering the field of L2 writing research and advancing teacher education. This section endeavors to delineate the study's limitations and offer recommendations that may guide and inspire subsequent scholarly inquiries.

First, it would be beneficial to explore additional theoretical perspectives from the broader field of emotion research to gain a more comprehensive understanding of teacher emotions in L2 writing instruction. While the present study has adeptly utilized the concepts of emotional labor and emotion-regulation strategies to elucidate the emotional journeys of L2 writing teachers during their pedagogical endeavors, there is room to delve deeper. Theories such as Activity Theory could offer a novel

8.4 Concluding Remarks

framework for examining how teachers navigate the complexities of emotional dissonance in their teaching practices and the strategies they employ to address these challenges. The exploration of these coping mechanisms presents a fascinating avenue for future research, potentially unveiling new insights into the emotional dimensions of teaching L2 writing.

Second, it is important to note that the methodologies employed in this book, namely convenience and purposive sampling, were selected due to limitations in resources. As a result, care should be exercised when attempting to extrapolate the study's findings to the broader population of L2 writing teachers within the Chinese university system. To bolster the study's applicability and impact, it is advisable for future research to replicate the investigation with an expanded sample of L2 writing educators. This approach would yield more robust evidence, which could then be leveraged by EFL teachers and administrative leaders to enhance teaching efficacy and inform policy decisions.

Third, while the qualitative findings are primarily drawn from the method of case study, it is desirable to pursue more generalizable results in future research that adopts other methodologies, such as ethnographic research methods and narrative inquiry, to illustrate a whole storyline of the emergence and changes of teacher emotions. In addition, although this book has identified several plausible mechanisms of L2 writing teachers' emotion and emotion-regulation strategies, more questions remain to be answered. For example, what specific guidance and training should be provided to L2 writing teachers, and how could the training for L2 writing teachers make a difference in their pedagogical practice? It is, therefore, possible to explore a range of topics, such as teachers' knowledge of emotional labor and emotion-regulation strategies, experience in managing emotional burden, and expertise in aligning their beliefs, attitudes, and perceptions of L2 writing instruction with the changing educational contexts.

Third, while the qualitative insights presented in this book are richly detailed through the case study approach, future research would benefit from employing a variety of methodologies to achieve more generalizable outcomes. Methods such as ethnographic research and narrative inquiry could be particularly illuminating, offering a comprehensive narrative of the evolution and fluctuations in teacher emotions. Additionally, although this book has shed light on several potential mechanisms underlying L2 writing teachers' emotional experiences and their regulatory strategies, numerous questions persist. For instance, what specific guidance and training modalities should be offered to L2 writing teachers, and how might such training influence their instructional practices? Consequently, there is ample scope for investigation into a spectrum of topics. These include teachers' understanding of emotional labor and regulatory strategies, their experiences in handling emotional demands, and their expertise in reconciling their beliefs, attitudes, and perceptions of L2 writing instruction with the dynamic educational landscape.

In summary, this book lays a solid foundation for further exploration into the nuanced realm of teacher emotions and emotional regulation within L2 writing classrooms. It sets the stage for future research endeavors that can delve deeper into the complexities of these phenomena, ultimately contributing to a more profound understanding of the emotional dynamics that shape the teaching and learning experience.

References

Blackwell, J. E. (1989). Mentoring: An action strategy for increasing minority faculty. *Academe, 75*(5), 8–14. https://doi.org/10.2307/40249734

Bosman, R. J., Zee, M., de Jong, P. F., & Koomen, H. M. Y. (2021). Using relationship-focused reflection to improve teacher–child relationships and teachers' student-specific self-efficacy. *Journal of School Psychology, 87*, 28–47. https://doi.org/10.1016/j.jsp.2021.06.001

Boud, D., & Molloy, E. (2013). Rethinking models of feedback for learning: The challenge of design. *Assessment & Evaluation in Higher Education, 38*(6), 698–712. https://doi.org/10.1080/02602938.2012.691462

Carless, D., Salter, D., Yang, M., & Lam, J. (2011). Developing sustainable feedback practices. *Studies in Higher Education, 36*(4), 395–407. https://doi.org/10.1080/03075071003642449

Carson, J., & Nelson, G. (1996). Chinese Students' Perception of ESL Peer Response Group Interaction. *Journal of Second Language Writing, 5*, 1–19. https://doi.org/10.1016/S1060-3743(96)90012-0

Carver, C.S., & Scheier, M. F. (1998) *On self-regulation and behaviour*. Cambridge University Press. https://doi.org/10.1017/CBO9781139174794

Casanave, C. P. (2017). *Controversies in second language writing: Dilemmas and decisions in research and instructions* (2nd ed.), The University of Michigan Press, Ann Arbor, MI.

Chen, J. (2016). Understanding teacher emotions: The development of a teacher emotion inventory. *Teaching and Teacher Education, 55*, 68–69.

Dodge, R., Daly, A. P., Huyton, J., & Sanders, L. D. (2012). The challenge of defining wellbeing. *International Journal of Wellbeing, 2*(3), 222–235.

Frenzel, A. C., Fiedler, D., Marx, A. K. G., Reck, C., & Pekrun, R. (2020). Who enjoys teaching, and when? Between- and within-person evidence on teachers' appraisal-emotion links. *Frontier in Psychology, 11*, 1092.

Gross, J. J. (1998). Antecedent- and response-focused emotion regulation: Divergent consequences for experience, expression, and physiology. *J. Personal. Soc. Psychol, 74*, 224–237.

Hagenauer, G., Hascher, T., & Volet, S. E. (2015). Teacher emotions in the classroom: Associations with students' engagement, classroom discipline and the interpersonal teacher-student relationship. *European Journal of Psychology and Education, 34*, 385–403.

Han, Y., & Xu, Y. (2021). Student feedback literacy and engagement with feedback: A case study of Chinese undergraduate students. *Teaching in Higher Education, 26*(2), 181–196. https://doi.org/10.1080/13562517.2019.1648410

Hargreaves, A. (2000). Mixed emotions: teachers' perceptions of their interactions with students. *Teaching and Teacher Education, 16*(8), 811–826.

Hatfield, E., Cacioppo, J. T., & Rapson, R. L. (1994). *Emotional contagion*. Cambridge University Press.

Hayden, H. E., Rundell, T. D., & Smyntek-Gworek, S. (2013). Adaptive expertise: A view from the top and the ascent. *Teaching Education, 24*(4), 395–414. https://doi.org/10.1080/10476210.2012.724054

Lechuga, V. M. (2014). A motivation perspective on faculty mentoring: The notion of "non-intrusive" mentoring practices in science and engineering. *Higher Education, 68*(6), 909–926. https://doi.org/10.1007/s10734-014-9751-z

Lee, I., & Yuan, R. (2021). Understanding L2 writing teacher expertise. *Journal of Second Language Writing*, 100755.

Lee, I. (2017). *Classroom Writing Assessment and Feedback in L2 School Contexts*. Springer Singapore.

Leki, I. (1990). Coaching from the margins: Issues in written response. In B. Kroll (Ed.), *Second language writing* (pp. 57–68). N.Y.: Cambridge University Press.

Liu, C., & Yu, S. (2022). Reconceptualizing the impact of feedback in second language writing: A multidimensional perspective. *Assessing Writing, 53*, 100630.

Scheier, M. F., & Carver, C. S. (1985). Optimism, coping, and health: Assessment and implications of generalized outcome expectancies. *Health Psychology, 4*, 219–247. https://doi.org/10.1037/0278-6133.4.3.219

Seligman, M. E. P. (2011). *Flourish: A visionary new understanding of happiness and well-being*. Atria/Simon & Schuster.

Song, J. (2021). Emotional labor and professional development in ELT. *ELT Journal, 75*(4), 482–491. https://doi.org/10.1093/elt/ccab036

Spilt, J. L., Koomen, H. M. Y., Thijs, J. T., & van der Leij, A. (2012). Supporting teachers' relationships with disruptive children: The potential of relationship-focused reflection. *Attachment and Human Development, 14*(3), 305–318.

Sternberg, R. J., & Horvath, J. A. (1995). A prototype view of expert teaching. *Educational Researcher, 24*(6), 9–17. https://doi.org/10.3102/0013189X024006009

Tsui, A. B., & Ng, M. (2010). Cultural contexts and situated possibilities in the teaching of second language writing. *Journal of Teacher Education, 61*(4), 364–375.

Wang, H., Hall, N. C., & Taxer, J. L. (2019). Antecedents and consequences of teachers' emotional labor: A systematic review and meta-analytic investigation. *Educational Psychology Review, 31*(3), 663–698.

Yang, M., & Carless, D. (2013). The feedback triangle and the enhancement of dialogic feedback processes. *Teaching in Higher Education, 18*(3), 285–297.

Yigitoglu, N., & Belcher, D. (2014). Exploring L2 writing teacher cognition from an experiential perspective: The role learning to write may play I professional beliefs and practices. *System, 47*, 116–124. https://doi.org/10.1016/j.system.2014.09.021

Yu, S., Zheng, Y., Jiang, L., Liu, C., & Xu, Y. (2021). "I even feel annoyed and angry": Teacher emotional experiences in giving feedback on student writing. *Assessing Writing, 48*, 100528.

Zee, M., Koomen, H. M. Y., & Van der Veen, I. (2013). Student–teacher relationship quality and academic adjustment in upper elementary school: The role of student personality. *Journal of School Psychology, 51*(4), 517–533. https://doi.org/10.1016/j.jsp.2013.05.003

Zellers, D. F., Howard, V. M., & Barcic, M. A. (2008). Faculty mentoring programs: Reenvisioning rather than reinventing the wheel. *Review of Educational Research, 78*(3), 552–588. https://doi.org/10.3102/0034654308320966

Zembylas, M. (2014). The place of emotion in teacher reflection: Elias, Foucault and "Critical emotional reflexivity." *Power and Education, 6*(2), 201–222.

Suggested Readings

Christenson, S. L., Reschly, A. L., & Wylie, C. (eds.). (2012). *Handbook of research on student engagement*. Springer Science.

Day, C., & Gu, Q. (2010). *The new lives of teachers*. Routledge.

Junqueira, L., & Payant, C. (2015). "I just want to do it right, but it's so hard": A novice teacher's written feedback beliefs and practices. *Journal of Second Language Writing, 27*, 19–36.

Miller, E. R., & Gkonou, C. (2018). Language teacher agency, emotion labor and emotional rewards in tertiary-level English language programs. *System, 79*, 49–59.

Morris, S., & King, J. (2023). University language teachers' contextually dependent uses of instrumental emotion regulation. *System (linköping), 116*, 103080.

Nazari, M., & Molana, K. (2023). "Predators of Emotions": The role of school assessment policies in english language teachers' emotion labor. *TESOL Quarterly, 57*(4), 1226–1255.

Seloni, L., & Lee, H, S. (2019). *Second language writing instruction in global contexts: English language teacher preparation and development.* Bristol, Blue Ridge Summit: Multilingual Matters.

Swain, M. (2013). The inseparability of cognition and emotion in second language learning. *Language Teaching, 46*(2), 195–207.

Tian, L., & Zhou, Y. (2020). Learner engagement with automated feedback, peer feedback and teacher feedback in an online EFL writing context. *System, 91*, 102247.

Yang, S., Shu, D., & Yin, H. (2021). 'Frustration drives me to grow': Unraveling EFL teachers' emotional trajectory interacting with identity development. *Teaching and Teacher Education, 105*, 103420.

Yu, S., & Liu, C. (2021). Improving student feedback literacy in academic writing: An evidence-based framework. *Assessing Writing, 48*, 100525.

Appendix A
Interview Guides for the Main Study

First Round of Interview

A. **General knowledge of L2 writing teacher**

1. How did you learn English writing as a language teacher before? Have your own learning experiences influenced your teaching practice?
2. What theoretical or guiding principles inform your teaching of writing at present? Where do these principles emanate from?
3. Can you generally describe how you teach writing? What do you expect your students to learn?
4. What change, if any, has happened to you as a teacher of writing over the years? How would you account for such a change?
5. What innovations, if any, have you attempted? What challenges did you encounter, and how did you cope with them?
6. What is the relationship between you and your students in writing classes? What kind of teacher do you think you are in front of your students? Give examples.
7. How is your relationship with other teachers at school? How may your colleagues see you and your work? Is there any collaboration between you and other teachers in the teaching of writing?
8. Is there a department policy on the teaching of writing? How do you perceive and respond to the policy?
9. How do you feel about yourself as a writing teacher? What kind of emotions do you usually experience in your work?
10. Looking ahead, how do you want to further improve your teaching practice? What kind of writing teacher would you want to be? What are the possible challenges ahead?

B. **General knowledge of L2 writing teachers' emotional labor**
    1. Tell me about your typical weekly work schedule.
    2. Everyone has good days and bad days at work. Take your time and think back to a really good day you had, and tell me why it was a good day.
    3. Tell me about a time where you felt defeated, e.g., your lesson fell apart, you were unable to meet your principal's timeline goals, your idea was dismissed, etc. How did you work through this experience?
    4. Tell me about a time when you had too much to do but not enough resources (this could include materials, time, and money). How did you handle the pressure?
    5. What processes and techniques have you learned are important for your well-being?
    6. Describe the work environment or culture in which you are most productive and happy.
    7. How do you think your expectations at work affect your well-being?
    8. How do you practice self-care (e.g., training your mind and body well)?
    9. Tell me about yourself in terms of gender, teaching, and research experience.
    10. Is there anything else you would like to share?

Second Round of Interview

1. Can you generally describe the design of the lesson and your intentions?
2. What were the lesson objectives? Why were these objectives important?
3. What roles did you and the students play in the lesson?
4. What L2 teaching approach, if any, informed your teaching design and implementation?
5. Why were these activities/tasks necessary/important?
6. How do you mark student writing?
7. Is your current approach different from what you previously adopted?
8. How do you feel about this lesson in general? What aspects do you think need further improvement?
9. How do you feel about students' performance in class? (Use examples)
10. How do you feel about students' writings? (Use examples)
11. How do you feel about the quality of the feedback? (Use examples)
12. How do you feel about students' evaluations of your teaching?
13. How do you feel about colleagues' or experts' evaluations of your teaching?
14. How do you evaluate your own teaching?

Appendix A: Interview Guides for the Main Study

Third Round of Interview

1. How do you comment on your teaching of L2 writing this semester, and why?
2. Are all teaching objectives fulfilled in your class?
3. Can you describe your feelings towards students' writing improvement, and give examples?
4. To what extent are you engaged with L2 teaching (e.g., affective, cognitive, and behavioral)? give examples.
5. Can you describe your relationships with students, colleagues, teaching experts, and others?
6. To what extent do you find L2 writing teaching meaningful?
7. Can you describe your achievement through the teaching of L2 writing?

Appendix B
Lesson Plan of Alex

1. **Course Information**

Course title	College English (4)
Course category	Courses for non-English major students
Students	Second-year students
Textbook	Unit 2, Book 4, New Horizontal College English (3rd volume)
Teaching task	To improve the teaching efficiency, please conduct a campus survey on students' different learning styles, then write an essay with the title How do male and female students differ in learning styles?
Language points	Comparison/contrast writing structure
Class size	About 50 students (large size)

2. **Teaching Objectives**
   - Understanding the structure of "comparison and contrast"
   - Writing an essay with "subject by subject" or "point to point" pattern
   - Reviewing and revising the writing product

3. **Teaching Method**

Genre-based Pedagogy. Genres can be defined as socially recognized ways of using language to achieve specific communicative goals (Martin, 2009). A genre uses distinctive patterns in terms of vocabulary, grammar, sentence structure, and discourse organization. For instance, the predominance of abstract subject-specific terms, nominalization, and the use of the passive voice are typical features of scientific texts. Indeed, they often possess procedures, procedural retellings, reports, and explanatory texts (Schleppegrell, 2004). According to genre-based pedagogies, academic writing has become increasingly prominent in recent decades (Cargill &

O'Connor, 2013; Cheng, 2018; Li et al., 2020; Swales & Feak, 2012). In a genre-based pedagogy, students are directed by the instructor to examine an example of the target genre in a multilayered manner by asking questions, considering the dimensions of the rhetorical context, the organizational pattern, and the lexical-grammatical features. Likewise, the example is compared with other cases in one's discipline (Cheng, 2018). By asking students to compile a piece of essay and perform different kinds of linguistic and genre analysis, guided by teacher instruction and feedback, we aim to train students' genre knowledge in writing. This kind of discourse analysis will lead to greater awareness and understanding of how academic English is structured, scaffolding students for further gaining specific writing skills. These, in turn, lead to students' texts becoming more readily acceptable to members of their target community.

4. **Teaching content**

The main content of this unit is Text A, *The Confusing Pursuit of Beauty*. To find out why it is difficult for a man to answer when a woman asks him how she looks, the author discusses the differences between men and women. The author organizes the supporting details by using the point-by-point method. The specific "points" or criteria of contrast are how the two sexes perceive their own looks, what factors cause this difference as well as how much care they pay to the details of appearance. The text can be largely divided into three parts.

Part One (Paras. 1–2) is the introduction, It starts by stating a common phenomenon that a man may be asked by a woman to comment on her looks, and hence leads the readers to the topic of the discussion, i.e., beauty (Para. 1). Then it puts forward the author's view, i. e. it is very hard for the man to answer the question correctly (Para. 2).

Part Two (Paras. 3–10) is the body of the essay, in which men and women are contrasted on three points. The first point concerns how the two sexes perceive their own looks (Paras. 3–5), with the attitudes of males discussed first (Paras. 3–4) followed by those of females (Para.S).The second point focuses on the psychological and societal factors that cause the differences in the way men and women view their own appearances (Paras. 6–8).Two factors are discussed, namely childhood experience with toys (Para. 6) and influence of the beauty industry (Paras. 7–8). For each factor, the situation of females is talked about first, followed by that of males. The third point involves the different degrees of attention women and men pay to the extra details of women's appearance (Paras. 9–10).

Part Three (Para. 11) is the conclusion, which restates the author's view that there is no easy way for a man to answer a woman's question of how she looks.

5. **Teaching process**

This class is delivered by following the diagram:

Appendix B: Lesson Plan of Alex

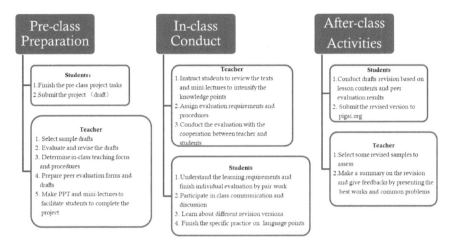

Pre-class activities:

Students watch the mini-lecture on "comparison and contrast" and finish the project assignment before the class.

Students preview Text A and get familiar with new vocabulary before the class.

Teacher selects and evaluates the sample essays, prepare the teaching materials for class discussion and group work.

In-class activities:

Step 1: Teacher checks students' pre-class mini-lecture learning by asking corresponding questions.

Step 2: Teacher asks students to scan for the main points of the text to check the pre-class reading.

Step 3: Teacher focuses on the critical reading of the body paragraphs (paras. 6-8) and presents the "point-by-point" pattern of paragraph 6. Students are required to critically read paras.7−8 to identify the pattern and work within group to draw a mind-map to show their discussion results.

Step 4: Teacher briefly summarizes the structure of the reading materials and uses it to facilitate the teaching on writing.

Step 5: Teacher presents the prepared evaluation of the sample essay to the class and asks students to identify the structure and make evaluation. Then teacher presents the overall feedback and highlight the common problems reflected in students' 1st drafts (e.g.: most of the students choose point-by-point pattern, but fail to state the point clearly) and explains how to improve

Step 6: Students communicate the common findings and reinforce the relevant knowledge points. Teacher makes comments and summary

Post-class activities:

Students improve the writing outcome based on teachers' instruction and feedback

Students submit the final writing outcome online

Teacher summarizes and reports the common problems in the essay, selects and recommends the best essays to the class.

6. **Teaching assessment**

The assessment framework in this lesson includes academic writing knowledge, skills, awareness, and value. Throughout the process of teaching this lesson, we guide students in reading and analyzing the comparison and contrast structure in the text. We assess student writings from four perspectives: (1) Task Response: Students formulate and develop a position to the writing task, ideas should be supported by evidence, 180 words at least. (2) Structure: Students ensure a complete structure of writing, use one of the "Comparison and contrast" structure in the body part.

(3) Coherence and cohesion: Students ensure the overall clarity and fluency of the writing, organize and link information, ideas and language through logical sequence, use appropriate cohesive devices. (4) Mechanism: Students ensure a good writing mechanism, avoid plagiarism, submit on time. We assess students' academic writing knowledge and genre awareness by guiding students in analyzing the structure and generalizing the language resources that instantiate each move in writing a comparison and contrast essay.

Appendix C
Lesson Plan of Lina

1. **Course Information**

Course title	Academic Writing
Course category	Courses for English major students
Students	Second-year students
Textbook	Unit 6, Modern College English (1)

2. **Teaching Objectives**
   - Understand the meaning of multiculturalism.
   - Learn about the context of cultural exchanges in the 1970 and 1990s.
   - Master the basic elements of the composition of the plot: setting, protagonist, plot.
   - Consolidate the application of language and cultural knowledge by writing reflective compositions and completing classroom assignments.

3. **Teaching method**

Based upon the learning-centered principle, this lesson integrated the genre and process approach and designed three teaching stages, namely, pre-class (motivating), in-class (enabling), after-class (assessment). In the teaching process, multiple teaching methods were employed and integrated into a whole, including task-based teaching, translation practice teaching and online teaching.

4. **Teaching content**

The text in this unit is taken from Unit 6, "The Green Banana", on page 128 of *Modern College English* (Intensive Reading 1). The text tells the story of an American who broke down while passing through a Brazilian village, and the local residents helped him solve a leaking water tank with green bananas. This led the author to think deeply: green bananas represent the value and wisdom of various cultures, and we must break through the inner barriers to understand and respect multiple cultures, in order to broaden our horizons and benefit for life. This topic has very profound practical significance in today's increasingly globalized world.

The text can be divided into two parts, the first part is the experience of the author (para. 1–4), and the second part is his reflection (para. 5–8). This lesson is based on "How to write thoughtful, in-depth reflection composition" as the main line, lead students to dig deeper into the topic of the text and deeper understanding of multiculturalism. Through this lesson, students are able to master the composition of writing, consolidate relevant language and cultural knowledge points, exercise writing and critical thinking skills, while realizing that should put aside prejudice and take the initiative to understand and respect ethnic cultures. And as Chinese citizens, students should take the initiative to tell the Chinese story well and let the world know China.

5. **Teaching process**

The teaching process is depicted in the following graph.

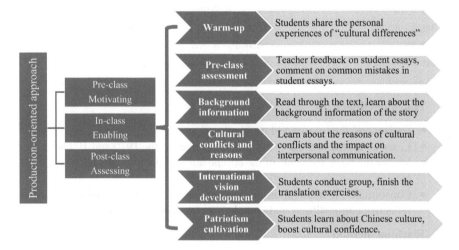

Pre-class activities:

Assign a reflection task: Write a reflective essay of about 200 words (reflection) to express your understanding and reflection on the theme of the film.

In-class activities:

Step 1: Warm-up

- The teacher first guides the students to recall the structure of the text from the previous lesson, and then posts the relevant speaking tasks.

Appendix C: Lesson Plan of Lina 195

Step 2: Language assessment

- Teacher and students identify the shortcomings of the reflective essays written before class through feedback on sample essays.
- Teacher introduces to the students that this lesson will dig deep into the themes of the texts and movies in five parts: story background, cultural conflict, causes of conflict, international perspective, and feelings for family and country.
- Teacher guide students to carry out critical thinking and learn how to improve the reflection essay.

Step 3: Text learning

- Students read text and discuss in groups to refine the background information (including time, place, person, time, etc.) of the film and the story in the text.
- Students share information about the social development in China and the world in the 1970 and 1990s.
- Teacher guides the students to search the text for the cultural conflicts that arise in the development of the story and their consequences and compare them with the films.

Post-class activities:

- Students conduct self-evaluation of the reflective essay, revise and improve the essay according to the knowledge learned in this lesson and submit it again in "i-Write" platform and conduct peer evaluation.

6. Teaching assessment

The comprehensive teaching assessment strategy outlined for the course is designed to provide a well-rounded evaluation of student performance and learning. Here's a detailed look at each component of the assessment:

Real-time Assessment: This is an ongoing process that occurs during class activities. The teacher evaluates students' language use and critical thinking skills during group discussions, which helps to provide immediate feedback and encourages active engagement.

Delayed Assessment: This involves tasks that students complete outside of class time. Before class, students watch a movie and write a reflection essay, which they post on the "i-Write" platform. The teacher reviews these essays before the next class, providing a more thoughtful and detailed feedback.

Self-Assessment: After the class session, students reflect on what they have learned and engage in self-evaluation. They revise their reflective essays based on their own insights and understanding, which promotes self-awareness and independent learning.

Peer Assessment: Although not explicitly mentioned in your description, peer assessment could be another component where students review and provide feedback on each other's work. This can help students learn from different perspectives and develop their critical evaluation skills.

Teacher Assessment: The teacher plays a crucial role in evaluating students' work, both during and after class. They provide guidance on how to improve the language, form, and content of the students' texts, and they also assess the ideological and political elements of the students' work to ensure that the teaching goals of morality and value shaping are being met.

By combining these different forms of assessment, the course aims to foster a deeper understanding of the material, encourage active participation, and promote the development of critical thinking and self-improvement skills. This holistic approach can lead to more effective learning outcomes for the students.

Appendix D
Lesson Plan of Olivia

1. **Course Information**

Course title	General Academic English
Course category	Courses for English major students
Students	Second-year students
Textbook	Unit 6, Contemporary English (1)

2. **Teaching Objectives**

   (1) Help students identify rhetorical moves and use language resources to perform these moves in English when writing abstracts for research articles, conferences, and theses.
   (2) Train students' academic skills in data searching, corpus building, and data analysis.
   (3) Raise genre awareness among students.
   (4) Build students' academic self-confidence in English.
   (5) Make students realize the importance and functions of a well-written English abstract to disseminate Chinese research in an age of information explosion.

3. **Teaching Method**

   Based upon the learning-centered principle, this lesson integrated the genre and process approach and designed three teaching stages, namely, pre-class (motivating), in-class (enabling), after-class (assessment). In the teaching process, multiple teaching methods were employed and integrated into a whole, including task-based teaching, translation practice teaching and online teaching.

4. **Teaching content**

   The main content of this unit is Unit 6 Text A *The Green Banana*, which is planned to be completed in 6 periods. The author recounts his experiences in Brazil in the

Table A.1 Differences between thesis abstracts (TA) and research article abstracts (RA)

	TA	RA
Word length		
Audience		
Completeness of the five moves		
Tense in each move		
Length of each move		
Number of nominalizations		

first person, exploring the attitudes of people in different cultural contexts around the world through green bananas and a rock that is seen as the center of the world. The text can be divided into two parts, the first part is the symbolic meaning of the green banana (Para. 1–4), the second part is a review of cultural exchanges in the 1970 and 1990s and the impact elicited by the implementation of Reform and Opening-up policy and multiculturalism in the global context (para. 5–8). This lesson intends to lead students to dig deeper into the topic of the text and deeper understanding of multiculturalism. Through this lesson, students are able to master the composition of writing, consolidate relevant language and cultural knowledge points, exercise writing and critical thinking skills, while realizing that should put aside prejudice and take the initiative to understand and respect ethnic cultures.

5. **Teaching process**

This unit involves writing English abstracts of research articles, of conferences, and of theses. The core teaching content includes abstracts of research articles and theses. The course is taught in two phases (four periods) and the tasks are both online and offline.

Pre-class activity:

Ask students to compare the structural and linguistic features between English thesis abstracts written by Chinese students and top research article abstracts according to the information in the following table (Table A.1).

During the Class:

(1) Discuss the importance and the functions of thesis abstracts.

- They function as stand-alone mini texts, giving students a short summary of a study's topic, methodology and main findings.
- They function as 'decision-making' tools, helping readers decide whether they wish to read the whole article or not.
- They function as 'knowledge dissemination' tools, helping Chinese scholars disseminate home country's voice, knowledge and research.

(2) Discuss functional, structural, and linguistic differences and similarities between thesis abstracts and research article abstracts.

Appendix D: Lesson Plan of Olivia

Table A.2 '5-Move' model (Swales & Feak, 2012)

Move	Typical labels	Implied questions
Move 1: instruction(I)	Background/ introduction/ situation	What do we know about the topic? Why is the topic important?
Move 2: introduction (II)	Present research/ purpose	What is this study about? What is the purpose of the study?
Move 3: methods	Participants and setting, Data collection and analysis	How was it done?
Move 4: results	Results/ findings	What was discovered?
Move 5: discussion	Conclusion/implications/ recommendations/limitations	What do the findings mean?

Table A.3 Peer review checklist

Items	Points (1–5)	Comments
1. My draft falls within the required word limit		
2. The number of sentences is appropriate		
3. The draft has the expected number of moves		
4. I have made sure that the methods move is not too long		
5. I have reviewed the main tense options of present (for Move 1, 2 and 5) and past (Move 3 and 4)		
6. The main findings are significantly highlighted		
7. As for conclusions, I have followed typical practice in my subfield		
8. Since my research is unusual, I have considered whether I need to justify the topic and/ or the approach in the opening two moves		
9. Throughout I have checked whether any acronyms or abbreviations will be understood		

(3) Give a presentation of some common mistakes in Chinese students' thesis abstracts.
(4) Present, analyze the generic features of research article abstracts (Table A.2).

After-class activity:

Write an abstract based on an English research article and evaluate with each other according to the table (Table A.3):

6. **Teaching Assessment**

Based on our definition of academic writing competence, the elements we will assess in this lesson include academic writing knowledge, skills, awareness, and value. Throughout the process of teaching this lesson, we guide students in reading and analyzing English abstracts of research articles in the corpora. We assess their literature reading and data analysis skills. We assess their academic data searching and analysis skills by asking students to compose and analyze the corpora before the lesson using the instructor's guidelines. We assess students' academic writing knowledge and genre awareness by guiding students in analyzing the rhetorical moves and generalizing the language resources that instantiate each move in English abstracts of research articles. Finally, we assess students' scientific reasoning through reflections on Swales & Feak's (2004) model, and we assess their academic self-confidence and motivation through discussions of the functions of English abstracts of research articles.

References

Cargill, M. & O'Connor, P. (2013). *Writing scientific research articles: strategy and steps* (2nd Ed.). Oxford: Wiley-Blackwell.
Cheng, A. (2018), Genre and graduate-level research writing. University of Michigan Press, Ann Arbor, MI.
Li, Y., Cargill, M., Gao, X., Wang, X., & O'Connor, P. (2020). A scientist in interdisciplinary team-teaching in an English for Research Publication Purposes classroom: Beyond a "cameo role". *Journal of English for Academic Purposes, 40*, 129–140.
Martin, J. R. (2009). Genre and language learning: A social semiotic perspective. *Linguistics and Education, 20*(1), 10–21. https://doi.org/10.1016/j.linged.2009.01.003
Schleppegrell, M. (2004). *The language of schooling: A functional linguistics perspective.* New York: Routledge.
Swales, J. M. & Feak, C. B. (2012). *Academic writing for graduate students: Essential tasks and skills* (3rd ed.). University of Michigan Press, Ann Arbor, MI.